JAME

HOW TO
PREPARE
PROFESSIONAL
DESIGN BROCHURES

HOW TO PREPARE PROFESSIONAL DESIGN BROCHURES

GERRE JONES

MCGRAW-HILL BOOK COMPANY

New York   St. Louis   San Francisco   Auckland   Bogotá
Düsseldorf   Johannesburg   London   Madrid   Mexico
Montreal   New Delhi   Panama   Paris   São Paulo
Singapore   Sydney   Tokyo   Toronto

Library of Congress Cataloging in Publication Data

Jones, Gerre, date.
    How to prepare professional design brochures.

    Bibliography: p.
    Includes index.
    1. Printing, Practical—Make-up.   2. Architectural
services marketing.   3. Engineering services marketing.
I. Title.
Z253.J75   808'.025   75-40383
ISBN 0-07-032801-3

    34567890   VHVH   785432109

The editors for this book were Jeremy Robinson and Tobia L. Worth,
the designer was Richard A. Roth, and the production supervisor
was Frank P. Bellantoni. It was set by University Graphics, Inc.
The body type is Memphis Light; the chapter openers, heads, and
legends are Helvetica; the stock is 50-pound McGraw-Hill matte.

Printed and bound by Von Hoffmann Press, Inc.

CONTENTS

PREFACE

Countless man-hours and untold dollars are wasted every day because there has been no single authoritative source of information about the many facets of brochure planning, layout, writing, and production.

Some idea of the magnitude of the problem facing a person who seeks assistance and guidance on the subject may be illustrated by the fact that the Library of Congress lists more than 22,000 books about layout, typography, photography and the photomechanical process, printing production, and the art and history of writing. The Library has 11 index drawers, representing approximately 10,000 entries, on printing and printing production alone! And not a single entry, up to now, for "how to produce a brochure."

In addition to the thousands of books in the Library of Congress, printing houses and suppliers of fine printing papers publish perhaps 200 related pamphlets and booklets. Assuming that one has the time, facilities, and interest to locate and obtain the industry publications, most of them could be helpful in varying degrees to someone assigned the task of getting out a new brochure for his business, civic, church, or political organization.

This book was written as one answer to the question of where does one begin. Readers who want to delve more deeply into specific aspects of design, illustration, writing, and production will find a number of references throughout the text, plus a bibliography at the end of the book. If time and eyestrain are of no concern, I can recommend taking up semi-permanent residence in the Library of Congress and working your way through that institution's embarrassment of riches on the subject. Since that is hardly a practical solution for most of us, it is my earnest hope that this book will suffice for most cases.

While the book's contents might appear to be somewhat weighted toward the preparation of brochures for design professionals (architects, engineers, and planners), as Gertrude Stein might have said, "A brochure is a brochure is a brochure." Many of the illustrations and examples are of architects' and engineers' general capability brochures, since that is the field of marketing and promotion in which I specialize. However, as must be evident, the principles of scheduling, layout, writing, and production apply across the board, whether the brochure in question is for a local YMCA, a medium-sized university, a design firm, or a corporate annual report for the Xerox Corporation.

Readers not directly involved with the design profession may want to skip the first several pages of Chapter 2, which contain a rather detailed discussion of the restrictions imposed upon members of such professional organizations as the American Institute of Architects, the National Society of Professional Engineers, and the American Institute of Planners. Except for those few pages, all of the material should be useful to anyone not familiar with all of the steps and processes required to produce a pleasing, readable, and effective brochure—on whatever subject and for whatever audience.

This book, then, represents a distillation of well over two decades of personal involvement in brochure design and production, plus the best thinking of perhaps 100 other experts and consultants in the field.

GERRE JONES

HOW TO
PREPARE
PROFESSIONAL
DESIGN BROCHURES

Chapter 1

INTRODUCTION

ASK A PRINCIPAL OF ANY architectural, engineering, or planning firm which single recurring design problem causes the most internal strife and lost time in his office—as evidenced by heated arguments among the principals and the project designer; time-consuming debate about the limits and nuances of professional ethics; wasted time, materials, and work force; and procrastination in taking positive action to arrive at a satisfactory solution and a plan of action—and chances are the answer will have to do with the annual or biannual production of the firm's brochure.

That this unfortunate and unnecessary situation exists in all too many offices has been verified over and over in marketing workshops with which I've been involved in recent years. Several hundred design firms, of widely varying size, experience, and geographic location, have been represented in the sessions, which always include a laboratory on brochure design and production.

In addition to that continuing exposure to the problem, our consulting firm has worked with a number of design offices—small to large—on the preparation of brochures. This book, then, came into being from a knowledge of the real need for understandable, practical information about the subject, as well as from a desire to be of assistance to firms who prefer to go it alone in preparing brochures.

Why must otherwise acute, sensitive, and businesslike design professionals periodically subject themselves to the brochure hair shirt? Are there definable reasons for one marketing consultant to have observed that design professionals' brochures, by and large, are poorly done? Is it accurate to say that probably not more than 10 percent of all such brochures are truly effective? And what goes into an effective brochure?

Marketing and graphic arts consultants can give many reasons why the office brochure *should* be the most important sales tool for the design professional. Whether a brochure fulfills its rightful role as a productive item, or is the least effective tool in the professional's kit of promotion aids, depends upon many factors—practically all of them controllable.

In setting out to design a brochure the designer must first answer a couple of basic questions:

Whom are we talking to? (Audience)

What are we trying to sell? (Image and purpose)

Another way of stating it is that a designer must plan the brochure in terms of the firm's markets and then make certain the contents are organized and presented to provide the information the potential client seeks.

Brochures are a service—a type of reference service for clients, as it were—rather than advertisements. Among other things, a brochure should explain the inner workings of a firm—the overall process by which the firm conceives and designs a study or a building or performs its consulting function—and it should do so in language and with illustrations that are understandable to any lay person who might read the booklet.

Architects, engineers, and planners must always remember that they are in the peculiar position of having to sell themselves, their firms, and their services to clients long before the clients need them—or even know they need them, in many cases. For these reasons, many design professionals overlook, forget, or ignore the need to sell, and the importance of the brochure as a selling tool.

One brochure consultant suggests seven ways in which a brochure may help the overall marketing efforts of a firm:

1. By building prestige
2. By reinforcing the sales story
3. By simplifying oral presentations
4. By building confidence
5. By saving a prospect's time
6. By reaching absent or distant prospects
7. By serving as a handy, continuing reference and as a reminder to the prospect

Yet none of the above mentions a brochure's importance in nonmarketing areas, such as staff recruitment and internal information applications.

In an earlier book I pointed out that a brochure may serve as a calling card, a sales piece, or a catalog—but seldom, if ever, as all three. As a personalized calling card, the brochure acts either as an attention getter or a reminder, depending on whether the prospect receives it before or following a visit.[1]

A brochure is never a substitute for a personal visit, nor is its purpose to get a client. Its raison d'être is to get your firm into the running—and to arouse enough interest in prospective clients to cause them to call your firm in for a meeting. To my knowledge, no firm has ever received a commission just from sending a brochure to a prospect.

Since it basically is an introduction to a firm (the important first introduction, by which individuals—and design firms—are often judged), a brochure should always project quality rather than quantity. Long-winded, many-paged brochures usually are counterproductive.

Brochures should have a theme and contain a message for their readers. Ideally, the primary message will come through from scanning the page headlines. The text (body copy), subheads, photographs, charts, and drawings then reinforce the theme.

According to one marketing consultant, a big league brochure has seven main elements:

1. *Meaningful or provocative front cover.* Based on good graphics and design, may or may not use photographs.
2. *Well-designed format.* Imaginative use of paper, ink, and contemporary design techniques; use of modular units and maintenance of a family relationship between spreads; body copy no smaller than 10/12;* use of two columns rather than a typeline over 75 characters long; use of white space.
3. *Comprehensive graphics.* Titling with active headlines; effective use of charts, maps, and graphs.
4. *Unstilted photographs and artwork.* Nontombstone action pictures of principals and staff at work.
5. *Comprehensive text.* Highlighted with informative headlines and subheads; lively photo captions.
6. *Tasteful merchandising.* Use of the brochure to sell services, but always in a professional, tasteful, and balanced way.
7. *Stylish printing.* Creation of the sought-after firm image in print.

As we work our way through the next nineteen chapters, the detailed processes of planning, scheduling, layout, writing, and production, as they relate to brochures for design professionals, will become increasingly clear. A generous use of examples and sample pages, leading up to the step-by-step layout of a prototype brochure for a fictitious design firm, should enable even a neophyte to do a creditable job with his or her next office brochure project.

REFERENCE

[1]Gerre L. Jones, *How to Market Professional Design Services*, McGraw-Hill Book Company, New York, 1973, p. 91.

*Ten-point type on a twelve-point base, to give spacing (leading) between lines of type of two points. Twelve points equal one pica; a pica is one-sixth of an inch.

Chapter 2
ETHICAL AND PRACTICAL CONSIDERATIONS

TWO OF THE PUBLICATIONS OF the American Institute of Architects (AIA) may be helpful in your early research on brochures. *You and Your Architect*, by David R. Dibner, AIA, and *How to Find, Evaluate, Select, Negotiate with an Architect*.

On page 5 of *You and Your Architect*, we find the following:

> If the [architectural] firm [is interested in doing your work], ask for some literature describing the firm's qualifications and experience. . . . The response to your request will usually be in the form of brochures, possibly containing photographs and biographical data on key personnel. The brochure will almost certainly contain photos and descriptive data on a number of the firm's projects. To evaluate this material, you will have to look beyond the style of the presentation, to analyze the basic design quality of the firm's work. Do you feel good about their design approach? Their experience? One caution. Don't look for projects of identical type and scope to the one you are planning, but rather judge the material on its merits and note your reactions to the work.

Much of the material on pages 4 and 5 of *You and Your Architect* could be adapted as a section in a general capability brochure devoted to explaining how a design firm works with its clients.

SAMPLE BROCHURE INTRODUCTION

On page 3 of *How to Find, Evaluate, Select, Negotiate with an Architect* is a passage that, with little or no rewriting, could be used as the introduction to a general capability brochure for almost any architectural or A-E firm:

4

When you embark on a major construction program, you are in fact committing your organization to what may be a multi-million dollar investment in an unknown quantity. While it is possible to define the proposed facility in terms of size, function, and certain other requirements, which together make up the "functional program" for the project, there are many imponderables.

How well and how long will the facility serve its intended purpose? Will it be responsive to the needs of its users and the community? What will it say about your image?

The architect you select to design the facility will be a major determinant in answering these questions. Investing in a construction project is unlike purchasing a commodity. Only a known need and a few ideas exist at the outset to define the scope of the project. These ideas and requirements become the basis for the architectural program, the conceptual design, and ultimately, the working drawings and specifications from which the facility will be constructed.

The individual primarily responsible for this process is the architect. The architect will determine the functional, esthetic, and financial success of the project. During the process of design and construction, he or she serves as advisor, coordinator, and synthesizer, as well as creative artist. For a period of months or years your architect effectively becomes a partner in your organization.

Obviously, selecting the right architect is not and cannot be a casual or offhand process.

Other ideas for expressing the role and responsibilities of an architect, as well as the client, will be found on pages 118–122 of *How to Market Professional Design Services* (see References, Chapter 1). More information on brochures is in the *Architect's Handbook of Professional Practice:* Chapter 8, "The Architect and Public Relations."

BROCHURE DOS AND DON'TS

And, finally, a few pertinent DOs and DON'Ts from the *Architect's Handbook* section "Ethical Considerations."

An AIA member MAY ethically have his building featured in advertisements, technical bulletins or brochures prepared or paid for by others so long as no endorsement of the sponsor's products or service is made or implied. The Architect's photograph may not be used without the approval of the Secretary of the Institute. Exaggerated or self-laudatory statements about the Architect's professional services are prohibited.

The AIA member MAY prepare a brochure for distribution to prospective clients indicating in a factual way the services his firm provides, but distribution of such material may be made only to those with whom the Architect has had previous personal or professional contact.

The AIA member MAY employ a public relations counsel, on his staff, or retained externally, to assist him with media contacts, presentations, publications, and public relations efforts.

The AIA member MAY NOT indiscriminately distribute through mass mailings his firm's brochure, or other items promoting the firm.

The AIA member MAY NOT have testimonials from others used in his brochure, slide presentation, or other public relations material.[1]

ADVICE TO CLIENTS

In the AIA brochure mentioned in the first paragraph of this chapter, *How to Find, Evaluate, Select, Negotiate with an Architect*, the prospective client is advised to learn the following about all architectural firms under consideration:

1. Name, address, and telephone number of the firm
2. Year in which the firm was established
3. Names of the principals and the states in which they are registered to practice
4. Names of other key personnel, with experience résumés
5. Types of facilities the firm is particularly well qualified to design
6. Firm's current and projected workload
7. Number and type of support personnel
8. Names of previous clients
9. List of awards won

The AIA suggests that clients also obtain a copy of the firm's U.S. Government Architect–Engineer Questionnaire—Standard Form 251. The above list essentially duplicates the information called for in the old Standard Form (SF) 251, now replaced by Standard Forms 254 and 255.

Unexplained, and therefore unclear, in the AIA limitations on distribution of brochures by its members "to those persons with whom the Architect has had previous or personal contact," are situations where government agencies are involved—particularly on the federal level. As any professional knows, office brochures and the SF 254 are widely and routinely distributed to persons within government bureaus and agencies with whom the consultant has had not the slightest previous "professional or personal contact." Since there are enough other problems involved in preparing and distributing brochures, we will pass over this seeming ethical anomaly as less than germane to the primary subject.

NATIONAL SOCIETY OF PROFESSIONAL ENGINEERS ON BROCHURES

Members of the National Society of Professional Engineers (NSPE) are governed in the production and distribution of their brochures by Section 3a(3) of the NSPE Code of Ethics:

> [The Engineer may use] brochures, business cards, letterheads and other factual representations of experience, facilities, personnel, and capacity to render service, providing the same are not misleading relative to participation in the projects cited, and provided the same are not indiscriminately distributed.

The NSPE Code of Ethics has superseded the society's Rules of Professional Conduct, but several of the old rules are worth a brief review. Rule 5 covered advertising by engineers and said, in part:

> . . . Only those media shall be used as are necessary to reach directly an interested and potential client or employer, and such media shall in them-

selves be dignified, reputable and characteristically free of any factor or circumstance that would bring disrepute to the profession. The substance of such advertising shall be limited to fact and shall contain no statement or offer intended to discredit or displace another engineer, either specifically or by implication.

The first paragraph of Rule 50 reads:

It shall be considered ethical for an engineer to solicit an engineering assignment, either verbally or written. Such solicitation may be in the form of a letter or brochure setting forth factual information concerning the engineer's qualifications by training and experience and reference to past accomplishments and clients.

AMERICAN SOCIETY OF CIVIL ENGINEERS ON BROCHURES

Article 6 of the Code of Ethics of the American Society of Civil Engineers (ASCE) prohibits ASCE members from "advertising engineering services in self-laudatory language, or in any other manner derogatory to the dignity of the profession."

Permitted under Article 6 are "brochures which factually describe experience, facilities, personnel and capacity to render service, providing they are not misleading with respect to the engineer's participation in projects described."

AMERICAN INSTITUTE OF PLANNERS ON BROCHURES

The American Institute of Planners (AIP) is somewhat less specific about what its members may publish in the way of brochures. In the AIP's Code of Professional Responsibility and Rules of Procedure, under Section 1.2 (b), is the sole reference: "A planner shall not seek personal publicity, nor shall he advertise in self-laudatory language calculated to attract clients, or in any other manner derogatory to the dignity of the planning profession."

AMERICAN CONSULTING ENGINEERS COUNCIL ON BROCHURES

The Consulting Engineers Council (now the American Consulting Engineers Council [ACEC]) has been perhaps the most active among all the professional societies and associations in advising its members on the preparation of brochures. In an undated pamphlet, "Public Relations Guide for Member Firms," issued under the ACEC's former name of Consulting Engineers Council, we find the following:

The "Brochure"—Its Evolution, Use

A brochure is a fundamental SALES tool of the consulting engineering firm. This particular tool is so important that everything possible should be done to make it effective.

The brochure will reflect a firm's judgement, experience, competence and general "image"—a job best done with the assistance of professionals.

This does not mean the consulting engineer calls in his own PR man, his outside consultant, a graphic arts expert or a printer and merely requests a brochure. It's NOT that easy.

In fact, the preparation and publication of a brochure is not easy at all. It takes TIME and MONEY. But even more important—it takes INFORMATION. Whoever handles the production of your brochure must have continual guidance and direction.

A major consideration—pictures—is a good starting point. Make certain you have photographs—preferably 8 x 10 black and white glossies—of important jobs undertaken by your firm.

Make it a MUST for pictures to be taken! Take a few colored pictures, too. Perhaps you will want to spend the extra money for their inclusion in a brochure.

Next, make certain you have pictures of your offices, your personnel, your equipment. Also make this a MUST.

Maintain a photo library.

Call in your professional and start brainstorming what sort of a brochure you need to do an effective job of communications for you.

And get it clearly understood at the start: A brochure is a sales tool. It is not a monument to the firm. It must be written, designed and printed with one purpose in mind—to answer questions a potential client may have. You are producing the brochure for others, not for yourself. So make it clear to your planners: the brochure must tell the prospective client what he wants to know about you.

What does the client want to know? He wants to know:
   —WHO you are,
   —your firm's CAPABILITIES,
   —your SCOPE of operations,
   —your EXPERIENCE,
   —your ACHIEVEMENTS,
   —your AREAS OF WORK, and
   —your SPECIALITIES.
Don't make the mistake of thinking all you need do is produce a brochure and business will start rolling in. The brochure is a tool, but only a door opener!

You'll have to get the business yourself, possibly in oral conversation over a desk.

Follow These Steps!

To get a good and effective brochure for your firm, follow these steps:

1. Write to CEC for a copy of "Preparation of a Consulting Engineers' Firm Brochure."
2. Retain a professional.
3. Make certain you have good pictures.
4. Have planning sessions where you
   a. Hold a frank discussion to review your organization.
   b. Review the scope of your work.
   c. Break down your categories of professional services.
   d. Start selecting projects to discuss under each category.
   e. Determine the amount of copy, choice of photographs, choice of art work.
   f. Start working out fundamentals—page size, shape, paper stock, binding, colors.
   g. Hire a photographer to get pictures you need that are not in your photo library.

5. During the various steps, your professional will supply you with layouts, dummies, pasteups, proofs, silver prints, and—hopefully—the completed brochure. Thus, you have plenty of opportunities to evaluate, make changes, corrections and fairly well keep your finger on the brochure's progress. Remember, however, not to make TOO MANY changes. These are expensive. Make your decisions before you get the pasteups, before you get the silver prints. You'll save money.

Ordering the Finished Product

A good hint in brochure production is to ORDER ONLY as many bound or stitched copies as you need immediately. Ask the printer to supply the rest of the order "flat." This means you will receive unbound sheets of your brochure, and you can bind them as needed. It is much less expensive in reprinting to ask for two pages (front and back) than it is for an entire brochure. Another advantage of getting the sheets unbound is the flexibility you achieve in being able to tailor a specific brochure for a particular prospect who may be interested in only ONE of your specialities.

One expert, who has done many a brochure for member firms of CEC, offers a few facts to save time and money:

1. Establish the lines of responsibility at the outset.
2. Plot a step-by-step course based on the advice of specialists.
3. Set up deadlines for each phase.
4. Establish a budget, but allow for contingencies.
5. Do not expect miracles. This project will take a long time no matter how thoroughly you plan it.

IDENTIFYING PUBLICS

On a later page, the ACEC guide advises on identifying publics:

It is important that we identify our various publics and determine which thoughts we wish to convey. Let us look at the publics with which we communicate, and which bear upon our relationship with the client:

1. Direct representatives of the client.
2. The larger client.
3. The general public.
4. Our employees.
5. Our contemporaries.
6. Creditors.
7. Communities and government.
8. Suppliers.
9. The news media.

NEW ACEC BROCHURE GUIDE

Early in 1974 the ACEC published *The Brochure on Brochures,* a twenty-four-page guide on the subject. Even though its coverage of many points was necessarily brief, *The Brochure on Brochures* was the first significant attempt made by a professional society in the design field to provide assistance to its members.

THE BASIC PROHIBITIONS

Three basic themes underlie all the ethical codes of the professional societies of architects, engineers, and planners. The themes, which basically are prohibitions, may be summarized as follows:

- Brochures may not be indiscriminately distributed.
- They may contain only factual information about a firm, its staff, and its practice, that is, no exaggerated or self-laudatory statements; no testimonials from outsiders; and no misleading content with respect to the practitioner's participation in the projects described.
- Finally, and as a catchall prohibition, the brochure must in no way be derogatory to the dignity of the profession.

None of these points should come as a surprise to seasoned professionals. The brochure project manager, along with those who will be assisting with the planning and design, should review these general restrictions before getting too far into the project.

ETHICAL OVERKILL

Not long ago I had a call from the head of marketing for a large engineering firm in the Southwest, who was involved in completing a new brochure design for his organization. An aerial photograph had been made, covering some fifty or sixty blocks in a populous area, which showed over two dozen of the firm's completed projects. His question was whether they would risk violating ethical codes or other professional considerations by including the photograph in the new brochure. He believed it would be proper, but one of the principals questioned its propriety.

After assuring him that there was no apparent ethical transgression involved, I pointed out that all the picture really demonstrated was that his firm had done a sizable amount of work in a relatively small area, and that they apparently satisfied clients, since several of the buildings shown were done for a single client. I suggested that all of their buildings be identified by a number and a key be carried below the photograph.

A firm for which I once worked had designed, over a period of ten years or so, a dozen major buildings in a five-or six-block area, most of which could be seen from the windows of the principal's office. It was a standard ploy to take potential clients to a window at some point in an interview and, with a sweep of an arm, indicate the more than half-billion dollars worth of our work spread out in front of him. Eventually, a map was prepared of the general area, outlining a walking tour of our "city within a city." The map was later included in a brochure.

The point here is to not be overawed or intimidated by professional and ethical codes. The ACEC candidly stated: "A brochure is a sales tool." Seasoned professionals *should* know when their brochures overstep ethical limitations. If a truly sticky question arises, get a ruling *before* the brochure is printed!

ON OBSOLESCENCE

It is an unfortunate fact of life that a brochure for marketing design services begins its obsolescence the day the printer starts up the presses to print it. Up to that point corrections, deletions, updating, and other modifications could be made, albeit at vastly escalating costs as the process moves closer to press time.

The major project under construction at the time the comprehensives reach the printer (and which, because of its importance, was represented in the brochure by a rendering with a construction photo insert) possibly will be completed by the time the brochure is less than three months old. Another significant project, which was difficult to photograph because of unfinished landscaping, may well win a design award about the time the first shipment of the new brochures arrives in your office. And at least one of the staff members pictured and/or named in the section on person-nel will have left to go with another firm or to start his or her own.

These are all things which are apt to happen. If the brochure is properly designed, the obsolescence should not be apparent to clients and potential clients for at least the first year of its life. Most brochures will serve a firm well for two years, with three years about the maximum to expect. These considerations are tempered, of course, by the amount of flexibility inherent in the brochure form.

THE BROCHURE'S LIFE EXPECTANCY

The single, bound brochure normally will have the shortest potential life. The brochure format that uses individual project sheets, boxed or in a folder, may be updated continually, extending its life almost indefinitely. By the end of the third year the contents may bear little resemblance to the original, particularly if an aggressive replacement program has been pursued. A brochure system likewise has a longer shelf life than the single, permanently bound booklet.

USE OF OUTSIDE CONSULTANTS

At an early stage the makeup of the brochure design and production team must be settled on. Some firms that have the in-house capability have no need for outside consultants. A large design firm may even print its entire brochure in its own print shop.

Other firms, where full-scale research, writing, graphics, photogra-phy, and printing facilities are not maintained in-house, may use outside consultants for every phase of brochure production. There are several consulting firms that specialize in the production of annual reports and brochures for a wide variety of product and service organizations. Per-haps a half-dozen consultants work only or primarily with the design profession. Most of these specialty operations are located in New York City, for obvious reasons. Some have their headquarters on the West Coast.

SOURCES OF CONSULTANTS

Advertising agencies, public relations firms, and graphic design specialists all have turned out successful brochures for design firms. They have also been a source of some mediocre—even bad—brochures, which only goes to point up the importance of the consultant selection process.

Look carefully at examples of brochures they have done for other architect-engineer (A-E) or planning firms. Then, talk to the designers who were in charge of the brochures you saw—to make sure they are still on the agency's staff and to get a feel for how well you might work with one of them. Ask to see samples of several brochures designed for architects, engineers, or planners. If the brochures all seem to have come from the same mold—the "cookie cutter" approach—you are best advised to look elsewhere.

NO SHORT CUTS TO QUALITY

One consultant advertises that he needs only a few hours to research a design firm, using tested methods, preparatory to designing that firm's brochure. The "tested methods" usually involve someone filling out a detailed questionnaire. If the questionnaire is tailored to your firm, the results could be acceptable. Then, on the basis of a few hours of on-the-spot research, the brochure is designed and produced in the consultant's home office. It is highly questionable whether or not an outsider could absorb enough about a firm in a day or less to enable him to produce a truly customized professional brochure—and the last thing a seller of a highly individualized service such as design should want to project to potential clients is the appearance of a mass-produced brochure.

If you are going to use an outside consultant, the fee will be a significant portion of the total costs of the brochure. Be as certain as possible in advance that that fee will be earned. If the advertising or public relations firm really is interested in building up a clientele of design professionals, chances are that some staff members will be familiar with this book. Ask if they have read it. A negative answer should not rule them out, of course, but a negative answer, coupled with a promise to read it, should count in their favor.

A word of caution about using an advertising agency—if the agency's current clients are predominately in the products field, rather than in service-selling, the search should probably be pressed further. An agency staff oriented to hard-sell promotion of consumer products is going to be difficult for a design professional to work with.

WHO AND WHERE TO ASK

First, ask around within your own firm for leads on consultants; someone in the next office might come up with a very good lead. The chances are you've seen at least a few brochures you like from other design firms—ask one of the principals who the designer was. If it was done in-house, forget it; but if an external consultant was involved, get the name and address. Local, state, and national offices of professional societies may have some good recommendations. If the local AIA or NSPE chapter retains public relations consultants, talk to them.

Occasionally, you may see a brochure from a supplier or a contractor that seems especially well done. Ask who designed it. The Public Relations Society of America has local chapters in many cities. Find out who the chapter president is and ask for the names of some qualified consultants.

If there is a school of journalism or communications in your area, talk to some of the faculty. One or more of the instructors may do consulting work on a free-lance basis—or may be able to recommend an outstanding graduate student. They also should know something about local advertising and public relations firms.

After the decision has been made and a consultant has been retained, get a contract that spells out in advance the duties and responsibilities, schedule of planning and production, consultant's fee, and some kind of estimate of the overall cost of the project.

FEES

Fees charged by brochure consultants range all over the map, which is a source of some confusion and concern to many of their would-be clients. An all-inclusive fee, covering the total package and specifying the delivery of x thousand brochures by a certain date, usually can be worked out. In such cases the client is, in effect, relinquishing some control over the brochure in exchange for a guaranteed product and delivery date—and relief from most of the thousand-and-one details of putting a brochure together.

If some of this sounds vaguely familiar to practitioner readers, it should. Design professionals should see all kinds of similarities between the selection of a brochure consultant and a client's selection of a design firm for a new building, bridge, or master plan. Just as some A-E firms will assure potential clients that they are the best possible choice for their projects—because they've never done a similar or even related structure, and therefore can come to the job unprejudiced and with no preconceived solutions—so will some brochure consultants earnestly explain that their greatest advantage is they have never done a brochure for an architect, engineer, or planner. Principals of A-E firms are in a particularly good position to evaluate such arguments. In my own experience, retaining a consultant who has had no previous experience with even related brochures is asking for trouble at worst, and a lot of lost time at best. But the chances are pretty good that a consultant who has designed A-E brochures can be found in your area.

Public relations and advertising firms usually add a markup to the cost of goods and services purchased for a client. The markup may range from 10 percent to more than 20 percent, so have a clear understanding on this point before signing a contract. If the client provides goods (photographs, art, and so on) and services (typesetting, printing, and the like), there obviously is no markup charged. Some consultants will waive all or certain markups—the best solution is to ask questions and get definite answers beforehand. Outside consultants and suppliers are not bound to volunteer information on cost savings to clients. It's a caveat emptor world.

Even if the job is handed over to experienced external consultants, clients should not expect that to be the end of their involvement. They must be prepared to put in many hours with their consultants over the next six to eight months—reviewing, suggesting, rewriting, and approving. Here again we find a strong resemblance to the preliminary and schematic stages of building design.

Whether the decision is to do the brochure with your own staff, or to bring in a consultant, someone must be put in charge. The job requires a project manager.

AVOID THE COMMITTEE APPROACH

The American Consulting Engineers Council, in its *The Brochure on Brochures*, suggests that "policy and conceptual decisions should be made by a committee, including principals and the individual who is personally responsible for the brochure." The committee approach is all right, if there is no particular hurry for a new brochure—otherwise, forget it.

We will get into planning in detail in Chapters 5 and 17. Suffice it to say here that a *small* group from management (avoid even the word "committee," if possible) must meet at the outset to set up guidelines and agree on specifics, such as budgets and schedules. It is assumed that the brochure project manager will have been named far enough ahead of the initial session so that he or she can provide a good meeting agenda and come prepared with at least some facts and figures on costs and timing.

Ordinarily, a management group of two to five persons is sufficient to sign off on the project manager's early planning recommendations. Thereafter, the group should serve as an advisory board (when asked), and as a review board as certain stages are reached. Naturally, if an outside consultant has been retained at this point, he or she sits in on the first meeting of the management group. From that point on, the onus is on the project manager and the consultant.

A PRIORITY PROJECT

This is not to say, of course, that various members of top and middle management will not be called on for occasional and specific contributions—and a clear understanding should be established that all such requests have the standing of a priority order.

REFERENCE

[1]*Architect's Handbook of Professional Practice*, The American Institute of Architects, Washington, D.C., 1971, p. 8.

Chapter 3
WHY MOST BROCHURES ARE INEFFECTIVE

IT CERTAINLY IS NO SECRET that brochures are among the major marketing tools of design professionals. If your firm's brochure gives a potential client a favorable impression of your company (and of the firm's services), it passes the first test of tone and design.

CONSIDER OBJECTIVES AND AUDIENCES

The importance of giving consideration to the desirable objectives and probable audiences for a brochure is a point that will be stressed throughout this book. One reference suggests asking these questions in the very earliest planning stages:

Are the tone and design appropriate?
Does it whisper when it should shout?
Or does it shout when it should whisper?[1]

Every design element, including typography, photo selection (and cropping), white space, arrangement, color, and illustrations, must harmonize with and balance every other element if the overall effect on the reader is to be favorable.

BROCHURES MUST REFLECT THEIR PRODUCT

A sales brochure for earth-moving equipment should give its readers a feeling of strength, durability, and dependability. A general capability brochure for an architect, engineer, or planner should give a feeling of a high degree of professionalism and quality design. Most clients believe that a firm with a properly organized, well-designed brochure is more than likely to be an outstanding firm. Obviously, that is the impression any brochure should project and nurture.

Remember that a brochure generally will be regarded by its recipients as the sending firm's best effort.

QUALITY COUNTS

A truly excellent brochure or an outstanding building is not achieved through an amateurish, half-hearted, save-every-penny-possible approach. In a series on producing office brochures for the Building Industry Development Services' *Jobletter*, we quoted a financial public relations consultant on the subject of corporate annual reports:

> Review 100 randomly selected corporate annual reports, and you'll find a general level of quality which reflects the efforts of the nation's finest designers, illustrators, and printers. Now picture a security analyst or shareholder seeing these reports, each one better than the next. When someone suggests that yours be designed in the mailroom to save a few dollars, tell him your company couldn't afford it.[2]

CLIENT SURVEY RESULTS

What do potential clients want to see in a brochure? In a recent survey of major corporate buyers of A-E services, a number of significant points were developed—most of them concerning brochures from architects, engineers, and planners.

The questionnaire recipients represented an equal number of the largest potential building clients in the United States—development companies, mail order companies, utilities, airlines, department store chains, broadcasting organizations, oil companies, insurance companies, and the manufacturers of a variety of consumer products.

GENERAL EFFECTIVENESS OF BROCHURES

The respondents were asked to rate the general effectiveness of A-E brochures they receive, on a 1-to-10 scale:

Excellent		Good		Fair		Mediocre			Bad
10	9	8	7	6	5	4	3	2	1

The overall rating for all brochures was 4.2—or about a mediocre plus! This consolidated rating was estimated conservatively to cover at least 5,000 brochures, to which the corporate representatives had been exposed. All were unanimous in that they have never selected a design firm solely on the basis of its brochure—which is possibly fortunate for all concerned.

HOW SELECTION LISTS OF FIRMS ARE COMPILED

Another question asked for the primary sources of design firm names used to make up a selection, or interview, list. The answers follow:

- 90%—A-Es previously used

- 80%—Letters of interest and brochures on file
- 50%—Recommendations from others involved in corporate planning (external)
- 40%—Recommendations from planning staff (internal)
- 30%—Articles in professional journals
- 20%—Other, including lists jointly prepared by the corporation and reliable local sources, such as banks, local AIA chapter, and so forth, recommendations from local plant or division personnel, and, of course, knowledge of firms interviewed for previous jobs

The weight given to brochures alone in making up interview lists varies from 10 to 50 percent, with most answers falling into the 20 to 25 percent range. On the average then, one-quarter of the interview selection process is based on your brochure.

Without exception, the corporate buyers of design services agreed that the optimum format (dimensions) for an A-E brochure is 8½ x 11 inches. One respondent added, "any size fitting a legal file."

PREFERENCE AS TO TYPE OF BROCHURE

Respondents also were asked to indicate their preference in brochure types, from among the following:

1. A single, bound brochure
2. A brochure system (identified in the questionnaire as "a series of smaller brochures, highlighting specific building and client types")
3. Individual sheets on projects and the firm, assembled in a box or pocketed folder
4. Other (explain)

There was less than universal agreement in these answers. About 40 percent opted for the single, bound brochure; just over 40 percent favored a brochure system; 14 percent liked the individual project sheets, boxed or in a folder; and the remainder suggested various other approaches, but none in significant enough numbers to list here.

SELECTION CONSIDERATIONS

Perhaps the most interesting answers were to a question which asked the corporate representatives to rank thirteen considerations they might use in selecting design firms for interview. The consolidated rankings, in order of most important to least important, follow:

1. Firm's past experience related to the project
2. Staff size
3. Staff background (education, experience, honors, and so on)
4. Firm's location (proximity to project)
5. Accuracy of cost-estimating procedures
6. Postconstruction follow-up
7. Engineering experience
8. Satisfaction of past and present clients

9. In-house specialities (interiors, planning, and the like)
10. Design awards won by the firm
11. Firm's prestige (regional or national)
12. Articles about the firm and its work in the architectural and engineering press
13. Articles about the firm and its work in the general press (news magazines, newspapers, and so on)

In addition, the respondents added these two important considerations:

14. Present workload for all clients
15. Firm's record for meeting schedules

Please note that each of the above points can be covered in a brochure, in supplemental material, or in the letter of transmittal—or in all three. It wouldn't be a bad idea to use the fifteen items as an internal checklist every time brochures, letters, and enclosures are sent to a prospective client.

PREVIOUS SURVEY RESULTS

Compare the above rankings with those from a marketing survey of several years ago, as reported on page 33 of *How to Market Professional Design Services*. In that survey respondents were asked to rank seven considerations for selecting a design firm. Again, from most to least important:

1. Total service capability
2. Engineering know-how
3. Design creativity
4. Past projects of the firm
5. Postconstruction follow-up
6. Proximity of the firm to the project
7. National prestige of the firm[3]

Related past experience, staff size and experience, nearness to the project, and accurate cost control would seem to have moved ahead of all other considerations—at least among the business-oriented corporate representatives who made up the latest survey group.

SPECIFIC CRITICISMS

The corporate respondents were asked to note the major faults and shortcomings of brochures from design professionals. In general, the comments zeroed in on the following concerns:

- Oversized formats (larger than 8½ x 11 inches)
- Too theatrical
- Too philosophical
- Too flowery (not in business language)
- Too much information
- Poor design
- Poor organization

- Too superficial
- Poor response to client interests
- Not clear as to outside consultants used

One executive complained that brochures never mention a firm's provisions for continuity if the principal is injured or dies! Another asked for *brief* backgrounds of the people who would work on *his* job. ("If I hire I. M. Superarchitect, it is not Mr. Superarchitect who will be checking the shop drawings.") And still another client representative added this provocative note under the first list of thirteen considerations in selecting firms for interviews: "These items (prestige of the firm, design awards won, and articles about the firm in the trade and general press) would probably be important to a client who has had little personal experience with A-Es and uses prestige, awards and publicity as a crutch to defend or justify a firm's selection. Serious clients are not concerned with a design firm's public image."

SOME SOLUTIONS

In my experience, most of these specific criticisms have at least some validity, so let's take a few moments for comments on a few of the comments.

Oversized formats. This references back to an earlier point in the questionnaire, where every respondent agreed that the optimum format is 8½ x 11 inches. The brochure may be laid out along either dimension, but whether it is 8½ or 11 inches in width, the second dimension should not exceed the companion measurement.

Meeting this objection is a relatively simple matter of judgment. Do *you* have file space in *your* office for oversized brochures from suppliers or consultants, and would you go to a lot of trouble to find a way to store a brochure 14 x 16 inches in size? Then why subject a potential client to jumbo format brochures?

Emphasize costs and schedules in the language of business. Whether or not you agree that the purpose of your brochure is to dispel a professional image of monument builders, if there is an interest in corporate work it seems sensible to talk about your firm and its practice in businesslike terms. If projects are illustrated by photographs, include the year of construction and the total cost whenever this is not considered proprietary information by the client. At least occasionally, give the estimate and bid figures. Some brochures devote a page to a dozen or so selected projects, listing the name of the client and/or the project, year of construction, estimate, and final costs in total and by square foot.

Superficiality. This was one of the most frequent criticisms, and it is one of the hardest to overcome. Comments such as "too general," "not to the point," "not responsive to clients' interests," "useless puffery," "not clear," and "not specific," would all seem to add up to the fact that brochures do not hit the mark. Short of preparing a special brochure, aimed at a specific corporate client, there does not appear to be any complete solution here.

"Flexibility" is a kind of buzzword today in brochure production, but it does have its place. The brochure system, defined as "a series of smaller brochures highlighting specific building and client types," offers one fairly flexible method of being reasonably responsive to the client's interests and experience. The boxed folder, with separate sheets or minibrochures on individual projects, is another feasible approach to customizing material for a potential client.

One expert expressed the problem of customizing brochures in the following manner:

> Architects who are NOT increasingly concerned with [publications for clients, including the preparation of brochure-type special presentations for business development purposes] are not really much interested in doing much architecture, for it is a fact of the current architectural scene that word-and-picture communication, in a brochure *tailor-made for a specific prospective client*, has become an essential prerequisite to being seriously considered for most major commissions, whether public or private. "THE office brochure" is being supplemented if not superseded, in serious business development efforts, by an *ad hoc* series of brochures especially developed to respond to the increasingly searching specific questions about a firm's qualifications which are being asked by today's increasingly sophisticated clients of all architectural firms who wish to be seriously considered for an important project. . . .
>
> The basic concepts and principles do not require the expenditure of vast sums of money on lavish printing or production techniques, nor are they applicable only to elaborate or special publications; they can and should be applied to the whole family of publications which are produced by architects in the doing of architecture, from the simplest to the most elaborate, and from those produced to GET work to those (feasibility studies, master plan reports, and all the rest) produced in the DOING of work. . . .
>
> Alas, this reviewer can testify from long experience as an architectural editor, architects' publications all too often come out as though making them look good and making them work as communication were mutually exclusive objectives. The preparation of reports and brochures is an editorial process for which most architects are not equipped either by training and experience or by professional staff and consulting resources. Now that such publications are assuming a more and more critical role in architectural practice, architects need to provide themselves with both staff and consulting expertise in editorial services and graphic design; and, if they are to use such resources effectively, they also need to familiarize themselves with the kinds of problems involved, and with the range of possible solutions.[4]

Any brochure in preparation should be reviewed carefully and thoroughly in dummy form (before it goes to the printer), and the text and illustrations checked for relevance and specificity.

"TYPICAL" BROCHURE ARRANGEMENT

From a 1974 survey of perhaps 200 brochures, the AIA arrived at this "typical" brochure arrangement:

Philosophy
Types of service
Consultants
Personnel (biographies)

Project list
Project descriptions (sampling)
Reprints

Note that "philosophy" was not one of the corporate representatives' requirements for brochure information. If design philosophy must go into the brochure—and it often must to satisfy one or more of the firm's principals—try to make it as inconspicuous as possible.

BURYING PHILOSOPHY

Since most readers tend to flip through a brochure from back to front, while concentrating on the right-hand pages, it generally is safe to position text or photographs you want to play down on the left-hand pages. It's better to exclude them entirely, of course, but brochure design and production, like diplomacy, is the art of the possible. If owners or senior partners believe their philosophy of design is unique in the world, chances are it will appear somewhere up front in the brochure.

Frank R. Harris, a public relations consultant, gives this related example of Murphy's law at work (If anything can go wrong, it will): "Following delivery of photographs to be included in an important brochure, which required chartering a plane to southern Mexico to shoot, the managing partner decides he likes the vacation snapshots taken by his wife better."[5]

CORPORATE ANNUAL REPORTS

Familial relationships abound between brochures for design professionals and those issued annually as a report to a corporation's shareholders. In both cases, the honest, factual approach is best, coupled with a careful cultivation of the art of understatement.

The Potlatch Corporation's *Annual Report Guidebook* (an excellent reference on the general subject of brochures) points out that a survey of shareholders found general dissatisfaction with annual reports. Unlike our corporate buyers of design services, however, the shareholders offered few specific recommendations for change.

Elsewhere in the Potlatch *Guidebook* (address given at the end of this quotation) there is a roundup of ideas and suggestions for the corporate annual report from various designers. Practically all the suggestions have direct application to general capability brochures for architects, engineers, and planners.

- Annual reports should have dignity, quality and professional appearance.
- An unusual theme concept is one of the basic considerations in making an attractive annual report. It should reflect the good taste of the people who put it together.
- Some recent reports are venturing out under different formats to present their information, even departing from traditional 8½ x 11 size. Among those few who ventured to different sizes are both large and small corporations, but they all keep the size within easy to file limits!
- One of the good qualities of an annual report cited by several graphic

designers is what might be called its "architecture." The really outstanding ones have a predominant feeling of horizontal or vertical line. A poorly designed annual report lacks unity, continuity, and a sense of control. This continuity and simplicity of design may be far more important than an intriguing, adventuresome, new experience on every spread.

• It appears that some of the reports currently coming out may be "overdesigned" in the search for uniqueness and individuality, but others seem to err in the opposite direction: they are simply stodgy and dull, and do not invite readership.

• A well-designed annual report should visually entertain the reader as well as inform him. It should have striking graphics, bold color, use interesting papers in contrasting but complementary colors and textures.

• The report should have a carefully coordinated message and design concept, a theme that is interpreted graphically in the appearance of the report and also texturally and esthetically in the paper, ink, and illustrations that are chosen to carry it. Well-designed annual reports make good use of white space—as important as the areas covered by illustration or typography.

• Style trends vacillate between use of photography and illustration. Presently, there seems to be a discernible trend back to good illustration, but the use of photographs, which began with the rise of *Life* and *Look* magazines, still continues strong, and is favored by many as contributing to believability. There seems to be a trend toward fewer, better, and larger photographs or illustrations to give strength and impact.

The Potlatch booklet concludes with a list of questions to be asked while planning and designing an annual report (or any type of brochure, for that matter). Certain of the questions have a direct relationship to design firm brochures, and we strongly recommend that any brochure project director write for a copy of the *Annual Report Planner*, containing the *Guidebook* and much other useful information. (Potlatch Corporation, Northwest Paper Division, Cloquet, Minnesota 55720.)

Your general capability brochure is your showcase—so put your best foot forward and try not to stumble.

THE FIRST A-E BROCHURES

An A-E brochure does not have to be very old by modern standards to qualify as a historic curiosity. When do you think brochures came into general use as a marketing tool for design professionals? The question is essentially rhetorical, since few design firms can claim to maintain adequate archives. The oldest true general capability brochure we've unearthed is that used by the Chicago firm of Holabird & Roche (1882–1925), the predecessor firm of Holabird & Root.

Our definition of a "true" brochure is one intended for at least minimal distribution.

An album of project sketches used by Boston's Henry Hobson Richardson around 1870 is in the files of his modern-day successors, Shepley, Bulfinch, Richardson and Abbott, but it does not qualify as a brochure under the definition since it was used only to talk from in interviews. Mr. Richardson did not leave the leather-covered, gold-stamped album with

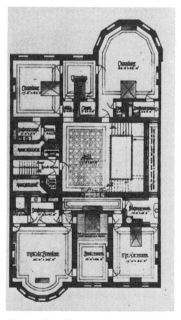

Figure 3-1. Some pages from Henry Hobson Richardson's sketchbook, which the famous designer used to talk from in nineteenth-century meetings with clients and prospective clients.

clients or potential clients. Views of this ancestor of today's brochures are shown in Figure 3-1.

An interesting detail of the Holabird & Root brochure is the back-of-the-book advertisements for contractors and suppliers. It was published by Architectural Catalogs on Lexington Avenue in New York City. Representative pages are shown in Figure 3-2.

STANDARD FORMS 254 AND 255

Not included in this chapter are user comments and criticisms of the U.S. Government Architect-Engineer and Related Services Questionnaire—Standard Forms 254 and 255, as completed and furnished to potential clients in both public and private sectors by design and consulting firms. A discussion of these specialized forms will be found in Chapter 16.

SUMMARY

We conclude this chapter with a few personal observations on why most brochures are ineffective. These observations are offered after reviewing several thousand efforts from as many firms of architects, engineers, planners, and other consultants over the past two decades.

My own average rating of brochures from design professionals—on the same 1 to 10 scale used by the corporate clients surveyed—would be closer to 3.5 than the clients' composite rating of 4.2. Perhaps 20 percent of all brochures can be characterized as having fully and faithfully accomplished their twin missions of presenting and representing the firm to prospective clients.

Far too many principals are prone to view their brochures as a vehicle for a kind of ego trip. By the time one cuts through the wordy philosophy, ducks around the narcissistic "I"s, chops away the professional jargon, and wades through lengthy and often meaningless passages of unrelated rhetoric, one emerges wondering where the poor client is meant to fit into the grand scheme.

A number of marketing consultants—and most clients—hold that brochures are a valid index of the firm's design approach and philosophy—as valid as the deportment of its staff and the appearance of its offices and work areas. At the beginning of this chapter we suggested that a brochure is usually regarded as the best effort of its sender. Ergo, to most clients, a sloppily designed and produced brochure means an undesirable approach to design and implementation of client projects.

Figure 3-2. Eight representative pages from the Holabird & Roche brochure of 1925, as compiled and published by the Architectural Catalog Company, New York City. The supplier advertising pages were in the back of the publication. Presumably most, if not all, of the brochure's cost was covered by advertising revenue.

By the same token, conspicuous extravagance in brochures should be avoided as the plague. Gold-plating may backfire, as when the client is a school board on a modest or tight budget. Unusual or dazzling techniques of design and production do not guarantee readership or interest, nor are effective brochures necessarily based on a lavish use of color or expensive printing and photography. This is not to say that certain cosmetic touches—even tricks and gimmicks—may not improve the overall impact of the brochure, but all such devices should only be applied over the firmest of foundations.

REFERENCES

[1]*Short Course in the Graphic Arts*, The Mead Corporation, Dayton, Ohio, 1972, vol. I, p. 5.

[2]*b.i.d.s. Jobletter*, Building Industry Development Services, Washington, D.C., July 1973, p. 7.

[3]Gerre L. Jones, *How to Market Professional Design Services*, McGraw-Hill Book Company, New York, 1973, p. 33.

[4]Jeanne M. Davern, "Design for Communication," *Architectural Record*, August 1974, pp. 43–44.

[5]Gerre L. Jones, op. cit., p. 32.

Chapter 4
FREE IDEA SOURCES

ALERT BROCHURE PROJECT MANAGERS WILL be continually on the lookout for ideas to incorporate into the next brochure for their firms. There are four primary sources for no-cost ideas:

1. Other professional brochures
2. Industry publications
   a. Printing and paper companies
   b. Construction industry brochures
3. Government publications
4. Corporate annual reports

These by no means exhaust the possibilities. Once into designing a brochure, and committed to doing an outstanding one, project managers should find that they are reading or scanning all kinds of publications with an eye for unique layouts, especially attractive photographs and other illustrations, and better or more interesting ways of turning a written phrase.

OTHER PROFESSIONAL BROCHURES

Reference was made in Chapter 2 to two AIA publications, *You and Your Architect* and *How to Find, Evaluate, Select, Negotiate with an Architect*. Neither of them is illustrated, and some readers may find the graphics a little overpowering (particularly in *You and Your Architect*), but the text offers some ideas worth adopting or adapting.

Ask Fellow Professionals. In the main, design professionals seem hesitant to ask other architects, engineers, and planners for copies of their office brochures. Under the "nothing ventured, nothing gained" theory, I have requested many brochures over the years and recall only one refusal—from a relatively obscure firm in the Southwest.

Assembling a library of brochures from other design firms through individual requests to the firms' principals may seem like a formidable undertaking to some offices. If the idea of putting together one's own collection is not appealing, for whatever reason, there are other ways in which sizable numbers of brochures may be reviewed.

Brochure Libraries. Some marketing and publications consultants have amassed respectable brochure libraries. Our own firm's collection, consisting of brochures from client firms and friends in the profession, contains more than 800, with new or replacement brochures added every week or so.

In the previous chapter we recommended that all prospective consultants be asked for samples of other brochures they have designed. If the decision is to use outside consultants, once they have been retained, ask them to bring all related publications from their shops to the first planning meeting. They should be able to leave the brochures in your office for at least a couple of weeks, giving the design and production team an opportunity to study them.

National, state, and local chapter offices of professional organizations should have at least a few members' brochures in their files. Ask them. Don't overlook the libraries of nearby schools of architecture, engineering, and planning. Some offices routinely forward copies of their general capability brochures to schools of design—usually with recruitment in mind. (This, incidentally, is an audience to consider as one of the "publics" for your own brochure when it's finished.)

Brochure Research. In 1973 the College of Architecture and Planning at Ball State University received a university research grant to investigate changing patterns in the architectural profession. Part of the study, directed by Prof. Uwe F. Koehler, involved assembling an exhibition of professional brochures from architectural offices.

The purpose of the exhibition, according to Professor Koehler's report, was the following:

- To survey the types, variety, and formats of professional brochures
- To define the marketing value of brochures for architectural offices
- To demonstrate how architects see their organizations and their architecture
- To show examples of graphic design and layout

Brochure Types. The brochures in the Ball State exhibit were classified into two major types—the office brochure and the selling brochure. The study report described the office brochure as "containing general material and information, covering the following aspects: History of the firm, representative examples of work, a list of clients, the range of services available, biographies of key personnel, awards, work procedures, and design philosophy."

"The office brochure," the report continued, "is sent to friends, contacts, and prospective clients. It also serves as a recruiting and orientation aid for prospective staff, and is a general public relations tool."

A "selling brochure," on the other hand, was characterized as "containing specific material and information aimed at a prospective client relative to a particular building project. It usually is individually prepared and responds to the information needs of the prospective client. Examples of work concentrate on the building type in question; biographical data concentrate on personnel who possibly will be involved in the project. Frequently, selling brochures are used in connection with the office brochure."

To clear up or to avoid any confusion that the above citations from the Ball State University analysis might engender, most offices attempt to combine the two brochure types—general and selling—into one publication or into a series of related booklets.

How Many Brochures—When?   A general capability brochure (defined as an "office brochure" in the Ball State study) normally is used for an initial contact or in response to a potential client's request for information. If the brochure has a flexible format (looseleaf and bound with plastic or metal spiral, or consisting of separate sheets boxed or in a folder), then the first response may be somewhat customized by the sequence in which the pages or individual sheets are assembled.

Depending upon the importance of the client and the size and significance of the project, one or more supplemental booklets ("selling brochures") may be produced for the potential client during the selection and marketing phases, leading up to the interview. It usually is desirable to have something to leave when the interview is over—and this is the point at which a good selling brochure, customized for the client and to the project, may have its most telling effect.

It is difficult to generalize on this subject because no combination of design firm, potential client, and project ever brings together exactly the same set of factors and interests. An organized, professional marketing plan, based on thorough and painstaking intelligence gathering, will dictate the total sales approach. This will include the type and number of brochures deemed necessary and productive in any given case.

The Special Brochure.   To cite a personal experience: I once discovered, by walking out the area, that a prospective corporate headquarters client had an odd-shaped site almost exactly corresponding to one for which our firm had designed another corporate headquarters several years before. Both were long narrow sites, bisected by feeder roads that could not be closed.

Being familiar with the earlier job, I took about two dozen photographs of the prospective client's site. I knew all the shots would correspond closely to the pictures in our files of the previously completed structure. The new views then were matched with the old, not to demonstrate that we had a stock solution for odd-shaped sites, but that we had solved an almost identical site problem before, and, by implication, would be that much ahead of any other firm under consideration.

In this situation, the client received three brochures from our firm: a general capability brochure as soon as we knew of the project, the special photo brochure just described, and a "leave behind," specially assembled sales brochure at the conclusion of the interview. In this instance it worked, but that's certainly no guarantee for any other prospective job.

Brochure Formats.   The Ball State study showed that most offices use single brochures, either permanently or spiral bound. A few firms use a box or folder to hold loose sheets and/or small booklets, and around 20 percent have some combination of looseleaf, permanently bound, and spiral-bound brochures.

The spiral-bound brochure is perhaps the most practical for most firms. Loose sheets—one or two to a project—are printed and stored unassembled. As the need for a brochure arises, the loose sheets are assembled and bound with a plastic or metal binder. Some aspect of customizing usually is present in the assembly. If the potential client wants an office building, for example, information on all such projects and any others that relate to the building type are placed toward the front of the brochure. This is a form of what magicians call "forcing"—a kind of psychological ploy to impress clients by forcing on them *first* all of a firm's work that is similar or related to their project.

Some firms that use the looseleaf approach furnish brochure order forms to principals and other staff members involved in client development. Each loose project sheet has a corresponding number on the form, and by just checking off thirty to forty numbers a somewhat customized brochure is ordered. A fully customized product may be assembled by using figures instead of checkmarks. Figure 4-1 shows how this method works.

Combination brochures bring together two or more formats. An example would be a combination of looseleaf and permanently bound booklet. Several methods have been devised to allow the not very esthetic plastic or metal spiral bindings to be covered in the final assembly of the brochure. (See Figure 4-2.)

INDUSTRY PUBLICATIONS

A wide variety of brochures about papers, type, ink, and printing production are published by individual suppliers to the printing trade and by their trade associations. Many of the better publications that relate to brochure design and production are referred to throughout this book. Others are listed in the bibliography.

Printing and Paper Companies.   If you use a consultant for your brochure, he or she will be familiar with most of the trade literature—and should have fairly complete files of the publications. If you are doing the brochure totally in-house, ask your printer to get for you copies of such publications as the Potlatch Corporation's *Annual Report Guidebook*, Mead Papers' *Short Course in the Graphic Arts*, and the Kimberly-Clark

HRS ARCHITECTS-ENGINEERS—Brochure Order Form

___ ABC High School	_6_ Charlotte Museum
_1_ XYZ Jr. High	___ Hamlet City Museum
_3_ Smith Hospital	___ M & N Factory
_2_ Central City Hospital	___ J & R Factory
_5_ Berlin Hotel	_8_ Newell Candy Co.
___ Mid City Hotel	_9_ Reinhold Recreation Park
_4_ Jones Hotel	___ Tunlaw Park
___ Beverly Apartments	_10_ Kelly Lake
___ Wendy Apartments	___ Stone City Airport
___ Putnam Office HQ	_7_ Robinson Village

Instructions: Place an "x" or a number on the line at the left of project photos wanted in the brochure. If numbers are used, the brochure will be assembled in the sequence indicated by the numbers.

Figure 4-1. Internal brochure order form for customizing brochures.

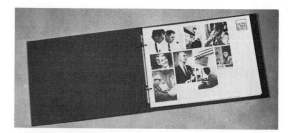

Figure 4-2. There are a variety of methods to disguise or hide plastic and metal brochure bindings. The usual way is to bring a second or false cover back around the metal or plastic, giving the brochure the appearance of a hardbound book.

Corporation's several booklets on printing fundamentals, type, paper, and color printing.

One of the most helpful of all the industry-generated publications is International Paper Company's 191-page *Pocket Pal*, now in its eleventh edition. The *Pocket Pal* sells for less than $2, and is worth many times its cost. If you catch your printer at the right moment, you may be given a complimentary copy. Otherwise, it can be ordered from the International Paper Company, 220 East 42d Street, New York, N.Y. 10017.

Construction Industry Brochures.   We are not talking here about the *Sweet's Catalog* type of sales material, but rather about the more elaborate publications distributed by direct mail or left by salespersons from the larger suppliers or distributors of building materials. Industry associations, such as the American Iron and Steel Institute, also have well-done publications that may serve as idea starters. (See Figure 4-3.)

Nor should the external publications of other design firms and consultants be overlooked in putting out a dragnet for ideas. Dames & Moore's bimonthly publication, *elements*, is always well laid out and makes excellent use of color. *Context*, published on an irregular schedule by E. I. du Pont de Nemours & Co., Inc., Wilmington, Delaware, has equally high standards of design, photography, and writing. Figure 4-4 shows sample pages and covers from *Context; elements* is illustrated in Chapter 19.

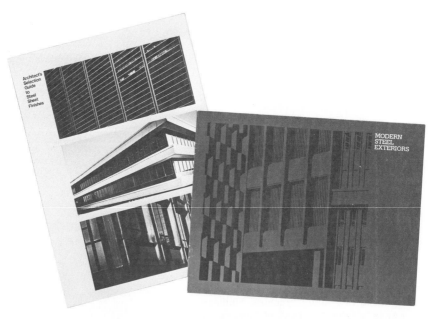

Figure 4-3. Supplier associations publish many excellent booklets, as illustrated by these two from the American Iron and Steel Institute, Washington, D.C.

Figure 4-4. Du Pont's *Context* magazine consistently displays high standards in layout, photography, and writing. The brochure designer can find many useful ideas in such publications.

Still another good magazine for your idea file is the monthly magazine of the Brick Institute of America, formerly known as the Structural Clay Products Institute. An example of a manufacturer's publication is PPG Industries' booklet, *Glass and the Future* (See Figure 4-5).

DON'T FORGET GOVERNMENT PUBLICATIONS

Somewhat related to the foregoing examples would be government publications, such as the U.S. Department of Housing and Urban Development's (HUD's) brochure on the winners of its biennial awards program. The Fifth Awards Program booklet, shown in Figure 4-6, certainly is not outstanding for its printing production, but the layout, general text, and mode of project identification and description are worth reviewing. HUD makes an initial free distribution of the brochure; additional copies may be obtained for $1.25 each from the U.S. Government Printing Office, Washington, D.C. 20402.

By now the point should have been made—stop routinely throwing away those colorful booklets and pamphlets from manufacturers, distributors, and industry associations, after a quick back-to-front flip through. Look at them with a layout person's eye and file the good to outstanding ones for future reference.

Figure 4-5. PPG Industries' *Glass and the Future* is another example of a good supplier publication. The use of charts and color photographs is worthy of study.

Figure 4-6. The Department of Housing and Urban Development (HUD), among many United States government agencies, has some publications very similar to brochures for the design profession. This is HUD's Fifth Biennial Awards for Design Excellence booklet.

CORPORATE ANNUAL REPORTS

Undoubtedly the most fruitful source of free ideas is the annual flood of corporate reports published in late spring and early summer. Just a dozen or so annual reports from large corporations such as General Motors, Eastman Kodak, Xerox, and General Electric can form the nucleus of an excellent idea file for the design professional's general capability brochure, particularly in the areas of photography, layout, graphics, use of color, and paper selection.

Each year, between the end of April and the beginning of June, annual report cooperative advertisements appear in such publications as the New York *Times*, *Forbes*, the *Wall Street Journal*, and *Barron's*. By simply checking off the list of corporations on the form provided and mailing it to a central distributor, up to several hundred annual corporate reports may be amassed—a free idea file representing the best efforts of some of the highest-paid designers, writers, artists, photographers, and production people in the country.

Alternatively, one may request copies of the reports through a friendly stockbroker. Any corporation in which you hold stock automatically sends a copy of its report, of course.

One of the advantages of using corporate annual reports as an idea source is that no copyrighted material is involved. This is not to say that one may—or should—make and use copies of the photographs or artwork. First of all, the reproduction would be less than acceptable, but, second, the odds are good that at least some of the material was shot by commercial photographers not in the company's employ—and the photographers may still own certain rights to the pictures.

However, brochure project managers may freely adapt the ideas—composition, for example—to their requirements. Layout is another area where plagiarism is the rule rather than the exception.

Let's look at a few examples. The Xerox Corporation consistently wins graphic industry awards for its annual reports. For some years now, the emphasis in the Xerox reports has been on people—its employees, and clients who use its products. Figure 4-7 shows sample pages from the 1969 report.

Figure 4-7. These photographs from the Xerox Corporation's 1969 annual report would be appropriate in any general capabilities brochure. (Reproduced with permission of the Xerox Corporation. Left above and below by René Burri, Magnum Photos, Inc.)

Figure 4-8. *(a)* **The cover of the Xerox 1971 annual report shows the company's concern with people.** *(b)* **The school photograph and** *(c)* **the picture of an engineering laboratory, from the 1973 annual report, are outstanding in their portrayal of the subject matter.**
(Reproduced with permission of the Xerox Corporation.)

Sample pages from later Xerox annual reports, covering the years 1970–1973, are shown in Figure 4-8.

General Motors, in the photographs in its 1973 report to its stockholders, intermixed regular rectangles, rounded-corner rectangles, circles, and many silhouettes. (The latter are often referred to as "COB'ed" illustrations, COB standing for "cut-out background.") (See Figure 4-9.)

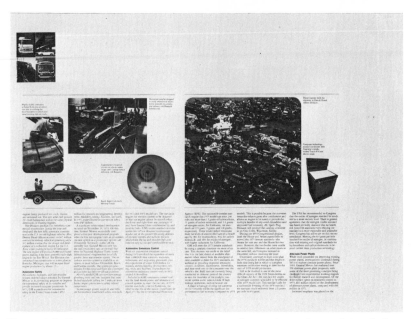

Figure 4-9. General Motors, in its 1973 annual report, used a variety of photographic shapes to illustrate its products and people. (Reproduced with permission of General Motors Corporation. Major photography shown: Burt Glinn, Magnum Photos, Inc.)

The covers of six annual reports from other corporations are shown in Figure 4-10—those of Philip Morris, Incorporated, The Signal Companies, IBM, Eastman Kodak Company, International Paper Company, and the 1964 annual report of Charles Pfizer & Co., Inc. The Pfizer report is included because it marked the first use on an annual report of 3D photographs printed by the Xograph process. Xograph, developed by Cowles Communications and a subsidiary of Eastman Kodak Company, achieves a three-dimensional effect through the parallax stereogram principle. It is the only 3D process that can be printed in multimillion press runs on automated equipment. The Pfizer Xograph is a model of disease-producing organisms controlled by the antibiotic Terramycin.

Little has been heard of Xographs in recent years. The photographs are time-consuming to set up because of the necessity to calculate aim points and planes of depth. The original camera was a 6-foot cube and had to be moved to shooting locations by truck. The optimum size picture in the early days (1964) of Xograph was 8½ x 6½ inches.

We could continue with examples of outstanding corporate annual reports, but it would only belabor the obvious: that the publications can be an endless source of ideas. And the price is right.

There are also a number of sources of commercial photographs and illustrations (the kind whose use one pays for), and we will cover them in Chaper 15.

Figure 4-10. Covers from six corporate annual reports: top row, left to right, Philip Morris, Inc., Charles Pfizer & Co., Inc., and the Signal Companies. Bottom row, left to right, Eastman Kodak Company, International Paper Company, and IBM. The Pfizer cover used a three-dimensional Xograph representation of disease-producing organisms.

Chapter 5

WHERE TO START

PLANNING, CONCEPT, AND PRELIMINARIES FOR a brochure are not unlike the same considerations for any design project in the office. Because design is an intellectual exercise, or process, it is similar to many other disciplines. Inspiration and "instinct" should have no greater role in the design of a brochure than they do in the design of a 50-story office tower or a 400-bed general hospital.

It goes without saying that the first step is to select a project manager from within the design firm. This holds true whether you plan to retain an outside consultant (or consultants), or to do the entire job in-house.

The next steps in producing an effective brochure are to define its broad objectives and to identify its publics. The working out of these problems has a bearing on the overall approach and design, which in turn affects the final cost of the brochure. And don't be fooled into thinking the objectives are self-evident or as simple as "getting more work."

THE BROCHURE REPRESENTS YOU

Review the characteristics and objectives of *your* firm that seem to set it apart from other firms. Realize that while a brochure is not a substitute for personal contact, it must sometimes serve as practically the only representative of your office during one or more cuts by the client—particularly if the client is far away or has made it clear that no visits are wanted until interviews are scheduled with the surviving three to six firms.

Many federal agencies now use computers in making their initial, or gross, sort of A-E firms for projects. The computer data for each design firm is derived entirely from its brochures—usually general capability and Standard Form 254. If the information in the brochures is incomplete or badly organized, the computer printout can reflect only that, and a firm may consistently lose out on consideration for major projects as a result.

ACCENTUATE THE UNUSUAL

Plan to play up any unique or unusual systems, services, specialties, or procedures offered by your firm. These might include:

1. Comprehensive services
2. Economic feasibility analyses
3. Value engineering
4. Schedule maintenance
5. Project review and control
6. Construction management
7. CPM (Critical Path Method) and other computerized or computer-assisted operations
8. Environmental impact studies
9. Postconstruction maintenance programs
10. Unusual staff capabilities, such as members who are psychologists, sociologists, educators, former hospital administrators, former law enforcement officials, specialists in zoning laws and building codes, artists, attorneys, and so forth.

ELIMINATE THE NEGATIVE

By the same token, if you lack certain specialties or services in-house, don't be apologetic about it. Make it clear that it is the firm's practice to bring in the very top consultants and specialists, as indicated and required by a client's project. Smaller firms often can turn their lack of internal expertise into an asset by explaining that outside consultants bring original thinking and a fresh approach to engineering and design problems.

Other potential negatives must also be countered: by omission, implication, or other means. We will assume that the average principal has had enough experience in such matters, in interviews and presentations, to be able to come up with positives to offset any negatives.

IDENTIFYING PUBLICS

It usually is a fairly simple matter to zero in on the publics you want to reach. These normally include potential clients—both public and private—past and present clients, your own staff, consultants worked with, and a new but growing public for some firms—shareholders when the A-E has gone public.

Don't overlook suppliers, banks, and professional schools—the latter for purposes of recruiting. And don't forget the list of publics in the ACEC public relations guide (Chapter 2).

SCHEDULING

As stated before, there are three obvious routes to getting a brochure produced: by an internal staff team; by an external consultant team, including a graphics designer, illustrators, photographers, writers, and possibly a printing consultant; or by some combination of internal staff and external consultants. Any of the methods requires an inordinate amount of time from one or more principals, acting as general coordinator and project manager. For the present, we will assume that most of the production will be done in-house.

Start planning early. If the brochure should be ready six months from today, *now* is not too early to rough out a day-to-day schedule. Allow plenty of time for writing, editing, photography, and printing. Start *now*, whatever your method. For example, some designers resort to false deadlines in their "public" schedule to keep the timetable functioning smoothly. Some work forward from *now* until the day of delivery, then schedule a start at the appropriate time; others work backward from the day of delivery. It is not a bad idea to set up a simple PERT (Progress Evaluation and Review Technique) production flow chart to help everyone keep on schedule. See Figure 5-1 for a sample brochure production timetable.

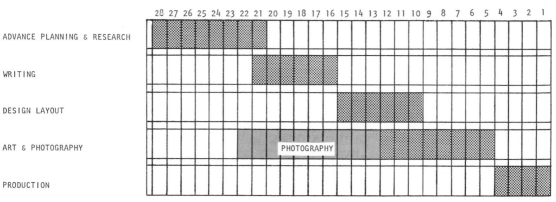

Figure 5-1. This brochure production timetable is in the form of a flowchart for a production period of twenty-eight weeks (approximately seven months), from appointment of a project manager to delivery of the finished brochure. Note that the photography is scheduled to proceed concurrently with other activities in the early weeks.

SAMPLE PLANNING SCHEDULE

The following detailed schedule for getting from initial planning to brochure distribution is based upon a schedule published by Graphics Institute, Inc., and covers a period of approximately seven months. Beginning in mid-August, for purposes of illustration, the schedule goes as follows:

August 17–September 15

    1.   Review and analyze previous brochures.

2. Discuss and evaluate your practice and your professional objectives.
3. Set a timetable for the brochure, and circulate it.
4. Plan and develop an overall theme.
5. Pick your design and graphics consultant.
6. Have the designer submit recommendations for cover design, graphic topics, format, colors, photos, illustrations, and budget.

September 15–October 15

1. Review, discuss, and make decisions regarding the designer's proposals.
2. Round up ideas and developments from principals, associates, and department heads.
3. Tentatively decide on the distribution list: past, present, and potential clients, employees, media, opinion leaders, and so forth.
4. Set the budget for the complete brochure.

October 15–December 1

1. Develop a copy outline and a design approach.
2. Schedule and shoot any special pictures needed.
3. Prepare a preliminary dummy to show styling, color, handling of graphics, photos, and illustration—and submit it to management.

December 1–December 22

1. Revise the preliminary dummy and copy outline, based on management's review.
2. Prepare a first draft of the text.
3. Anticipate and discuss possible production problems with the designer and the printer.

December 22–February 15

1. Prepare a final draft of the text, charts, and graphics.
2. Prepare a comprehensive dummy with all elements in place or indicated, and submit it for management's review.

January 15–February 15

1. Make changes and revisions, as dictated by management's review.
2. Prepare all final artwork, charts, and graphics.
3. Have the text typeset.

February 15–February 28

1. Engrave the art and charts if the brochure is to be printed by letterpress. Prepare the mechanicals if the report is to be printed by offset lithography.
2. Review the final press proofs and authorize printing to begin.

March 1–March 15

1. Supervise the printing and binding.
2. Make the initial distribution to employees, community leaders, suppliers, and the media.

Prepare a dummy of the brochure as soon as possible and get general agreement on the approach from the principals and any others who will have an input or veto down the line. The expense of starting all over again just before the material is due at the printer's is not to be believed. We will get into the cost factors of changes after the material goes to the printer in a later chapter.

PHOTOGRAPHS

Arrange early for photographs known to be required, whether they are to be shot today or four months from now. Photographers and nature both work to a schedule, and if you don't want a project blanketed in snow it must be photographed in the spring or summer. Be specific with the photographer about requirements; few are gifted with ESP and even fewer will think exactly as you do about what to show in a picture. Some projects—usually the most important ones—will not be landscaped until the last moment. Crank those deadlines into the schedule.

Interior photographs of principals, staff, and the office may be made almost anytime. Get those out of the way early; the more egotistical subjects will never be satisfied with the first results. Just remember, a good photo schedule will help prevent expensive overtime for retakes and lab work. Backups further down the production line can result in even more expensive overtime costs for retouchers, plate makers, and pressworkers.

BUDGETS

Budgeting is one of the more difficult aspects of brochure planning, but architects and engineers should not have to be sold on the necessity for establishing and sticking to a budget.

Make it realistic. If this is not the first brochure for the firm the past cost experience should be helpful. Get estimates (not bids at this point)—on the basis of a preliminary dummy—for the photography, typesetting, and printing (we are still proceeding on the assumption that design, writing, and graphics will be done internally).

Printers' estimates will be based on their equipment and how it adapts to your job, their standards of service and production, and their desire or need for the job.

When total cost is of major importance, remember that significant economies can be effected, without sacrificing the desired quality, by decreasing the number of pictures, pages, and colors of printing inks. The deletion of extras and gimmicks—such as die-cuts, embossing, fold-outs, end sheets, and over- and undersized pages—offers other possible ways to economize.

Since the finished brochure will be heavy on illustrations, printing by offset lithography normally will be the least expensive and most satisfactory. Faster presses, cheaper plates, and the ability to make last-minute changes economically are all reasons for the great majority of professional brochures being printed by offset. For the curious, a description of the most common printing processes, including letterpress, offset, and gravure, is given in Chapter 18.

INITIAL RESEARCH

In the production timetable (see Figure 5-1), we allocated eight weeks to advance planning and research. Planning an effective and productive brochure requires a long lead time for research, and a lot of time can be saved by putting the research phase on a continuing basis—that is, you are always getting ready for the next brochure.

This year-round approach to research means maintaining a continually updated file of anything and everything that might be of help in planning and producing a brochure—photographs; news releases; articles about the firm, its personnel, and its projects; job histories; design competition entries; letters from clients; speeches; and so on.

Part of the research should include a thorough study and evaluation of the firm's last brochure, to pick out its strengths and weaknesses. In looking for areas of needed improvement, subject it to a page-by-page critique of graphics, paper, content, typography—every element over which the designer has control.

Concurrent with the merciless evaluation of your own past and current efforts, review a number of brochures from other design firms. Suggested sources for these brochures are given in Chapter 4.

A brochure project coordinator must keep abreast of fashions in brochure design—formats, use of charts and diagrams, layout modes, photomechanical techniques, and the like. The practice mix, as illustrated by project photographs and descriptions, also is subject to some "fashion" influence. A few years ago it would have availed no firm to include information about its construction management capabilities. Today, if you offer construction management services, you tell about it in the brochure. The same is true for any involvement in the design of facilities for pollution control, or environmental impact studies. Be as specific as possible. Give facts and figures—don't generalize and don't overstate the firm's involvement and experience.

JOB HISTORIES

A few paragraphs back, job histories were mentioned as being of possible help in researching the text for a brochure. As we explained in *How to Market Professional Design Services*, the problem is to develop a format for a firm's job histories that will serve the needs of as many staff members as possible, such as administrators, planners, programmers, designers, draftsmen, accountants, specification writers, estimators, and promotion and marketing staffs.

For writing project descriptions and furnishing accurate building dates and costs for project photographs in the brochure, the best information source *should* be the job history. If your firm does not now have a procedure to ensure the prompt compilation of these histories, plus a format to make it relatively simple to extract the necessary facts, give a high priority to instituting a workable job history system.

MISCELLANEOUS PLANNING TIPS

- The basic ingredients for an effective brochure include
  competent, imaginative graphics;
  reasonably literate, professional writing;
  good quality paper and printing.
- Graphs and charts can be particularly effective in presenting financial information and a record of professional growth. They are especially useful in showing trends; for example, the rise in construction costs, or where the client's building dollar goes.
- The use and development of a theme that carries throughout the brochure can be helpful. A good central idea usually is more interesting and serves to unify sometimes unrelated material and art.
- Brochures reach new audiences every time they are revised and reprinted. Therefore, just because certain aspects of your firm's operations have been covered thoroughly in previous brochures does not mean that they can be dropped or slighted in subsequent publications. A brochure is not a newspaper, with a constant requirement to drop old facts and add new ones. To much, if not most, of its audience, the brochure will be brand new.
- Figures and percentages usually are preferable to generalities.
- In writing, clear and simple English is best. The brochure text might be tested with a readability formula.
- At least subtly, your firm should be related to the design profession—according to its standing, size, design awards, and so forth.
- Your brochure should be interesting. Too many brochures are just plain dull.
- Half sheets irritate some readers. Foldouts (multiple sheets folded and bound as one) are all right if they serve a real purpose. They can also add a lot to a brochure's cost.
- Adequate spacing among elements and large clear type are a must. Unusual type may look nice, but it seldom adds to readability. (See Figure 5-2.)
- Paper and inks must not glare.
- Two- or three-column pages make for easier reading than one column.
- All headings should be descriptive and relate to the overall brochure theme. Action headings are desirable, wherever possible.
- A listing of executives of a firm should also include the names (and photographs, if possible) of the marketing staff with whom prospects will meet and correspond. Prospects want to feel they are getting the atten-

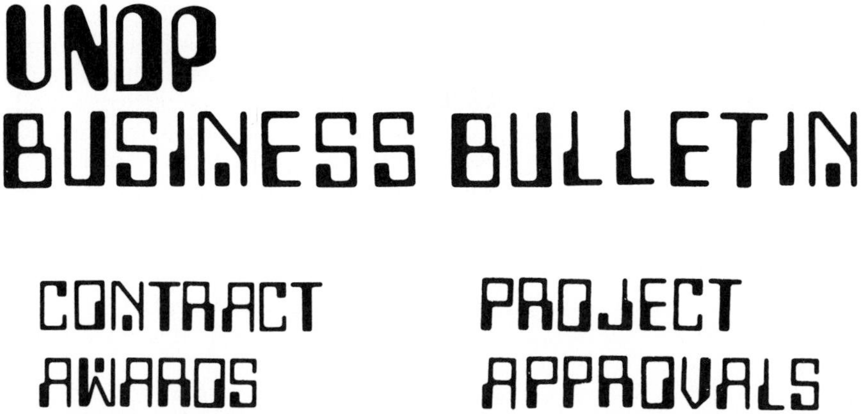

UNDP
BUSINESS BULLETIN

CONTRACT AWARDS

PROJECT APPROVALS

Figure 5-2. This unusual type is from the masthead and column headings of the United Nations Development Program's *Business Bulletin,* a monthly newsletter published by the UNDP in New York City. Several specialty typefaces, imitative or suggestive of computer printouts and type designed to be read by computers, have become available in recent years. Unfortunately, what is readable to computers may border on the illegible to humans—and humans will be reading your brochure.

tion of top management, but if they cannot find any reference to the business development representatives in the material that is sent or left, they may well conclude they're getting second- or third-class treatment.

Chapter 6
LAYOUT AND FORMAT

Layout: the manner in which anything is laid out; arrangement; specifically, the plan or makeup of a newspaper, book, page, advertisement, and so forth, so that all elements follow a desired format.

Format: the shape, size, binding, type, paper, and general appearance of a book, brochure, magazine, and so forth.

SCHEMATICS ARE TO THE ARCHITECT and drawings are to the engineer as the layout is to creative staffs and production departments. A layout may be considered the working drawing by which writers, artists, photographers, and printers generally chart their courses in the preparation of a brochure. The layout has been called the foundation on which the creative artists and the technicians build.

YOU DO THE LAYOUT

All compositions more complex than ruled forms or straight text matter should go to the printer with comprehensive layouts. The cost of any printing job is in direct ratio to the amount of work the printer must do. When printers are given a handful of photographs, a dozen sheets of badly typed copy, and a few scribbled notes on placement, they must make a layout themselves before proceeding with the job. Their ideas of what your brochure should look like may be widely divergent from what you have in mind. Properly executed, detailed layouts demand less of the printers' time and should result in a better and less costly final product.

Good layout, as more than one expert has pointed out, is double insurance: against waste in production and aginst poor design.

Headlines, illustrations, copy, borders, and white space are the major elements of a layout with which we will deal in this chapter.

Seven Principles of Composition. In illustration work there are seven generally accepted principles of composition: balance, proportion, rhythm, movement, unity, clarity, and simplicity. While these principles are basic to the composition of illustrations (drawings, paintings, charts, photographs), they also apply to layout.

Balance. Balance is perhaps the most important of the seven principles, with proportion running a close second. Balance, to attract attention and maintain interest, may take one of two forms—formal (symmetric) or informal (asymmetric). The two forms sometimes are referred to as bisymmetric (formal) and occult.

F. H. Wills, in his excellent book, *Fundamentals of Layout*, points out:

> In all creative work, measurements judged by the eye are more reliable than those arrived at with a ruler, for the reader's reaction will also be a product of his feelings. The eye for which you are creating your layout can easily be deceived. You must always make allowances for this quite justifiable deception in all your calculations. You will acquire from experience a sense of aesthetic fitness and a feeling for proportion.[1]

The optical center of a page, for example, is not the same as the geometric center. A photograph or block of text with equal amounts of white space above and below it actually will seem to be sited below the middle of the page.

Page Proportioning. Wills also refers to formulas for proportioning pages, as discovered and perfected by such masters of book design as Gutenberg, Didot, and Bodoni. These guides generally specify that the length of the type line should be two-thirds the width of the paper, and that width ratios of 2:3:4:5, 2:3:4:6, or 2:3:5:6 are most pleasing to the eye for the inside, top, outside, and bottom margins respectively. (See Figure 6-1.)

But, as was pointed out earlier, the eye is more reliable than the ruler in most cases, so use any such mathematical relationship as a beginning and a guide—never as an inviolable rule.

Still on the subject of books and text-only pages, keep in mind that the size of type is governing in establishing most text widths within the page. Brochure text usually is set in 8- to 12-point type, with at least 2-point leading between lines for legibility.

Watch Line Lengths. Typographers are in general agreement that lines more than 20 picas (3.33 inches) wide become difficult to read, even with proper leading. A good rule of thumb on how wide to set body type

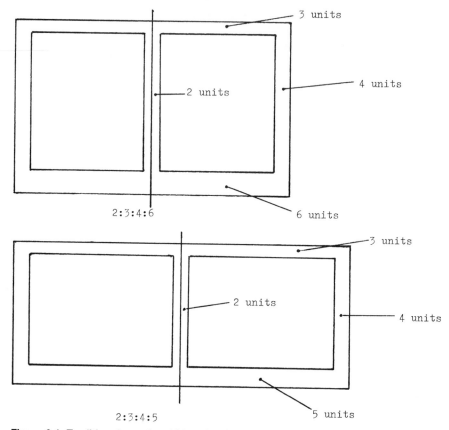

Figure 6-1. Traditional margin-width ratios for books.

for a brochure is not to exceed two alphabets (52 characters) in length of the typeface, regardless of size. For 6-point type this corresponds to an average line width of 14 picas (2.33 inches); for 8-point type, an average width of 16 picas (2.67 inches); for 10-point type, an average width of 18 picas (3 inches); and for 12-point type, an average width of 21 picas (3.5 inches). But in some typefaces (News Gothic Bold Extended, for example), two alphabets of 12-point type would require 30 picas (5 inches). These and related points will be covered in greater detail in Chapter 7, on typography.

Formal versus Informal Balance. Formal, or symmetric, balance is depicted on the left of Figure 6-2. It is achieved through the placement of visual elements (mass, shape, and lines) on an imaginary vertical center line, or by creating a mirror image of each element which appears on one side of the center line in exactly the same position on the other side of the center line.

Formal balance projects a feeling of conservatism and dignity and, although it is easier to plan, usually it is too static to hold a viewer's interest. Formally balanced graphics, therefore, should be as simple as possible in order to be grasped during only a brief attention span.

If we move the vertical and horizontal lines away from a perfect geometric balance, as in the right side of Figure 6-2, the result is informal balance—a more interesting but more complex form of layout. Balance must be maintained for the eye between left and right sides and the top and bottom halves of the rectangle. A large element on the left is balanced by a smaller, usually darker, element on the right. Since there are no formulas to apply to informal balance, the person doing the layout must, as Wills suggests, "acquire from experience a sense of aesthetic fitness and a feeling for proportion." He then continues:

> When informal balance is employed the units are often of different shapes, sizes and color (degree of blackness), and are not distributed equally on both sides of a vertical axis. Yet the composition, as a whole, balances because the sum of the weight of printed matter and white space on either side of the line is equal in its appearance to the eye. Informal balance is much more difficult to use than formal balance and, since no definite rules can be made for it, successful execution depends upon the layout man's skill. Informal balance is livelier and holds greater interest than formal balance. It gives greater opportunity for originality, action and "punch." The informal layout especially calls for experimentation with rough sketches to arrive at the correct effect.[2]

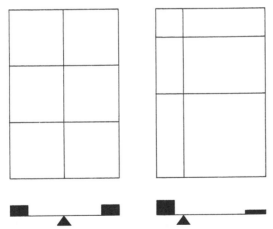

Figure 6-2. Formal (symmetric) balance is represented by the left figure; informal or asymmetric balance by the right. In formal balance all visual elements are placed on an imaginary vertical center line, or every mass, shape, and line on one side of the center line is duplicated by its equal on the other side. Thus, one side of a formally balanced composition is a mirror image of the other side. Informal balance is a much more complex composition in that the left side must balance the right, and the top half must appear in balance with the bottom half. A large, heavy element on one side of the center line is balanced by a smaller element placed farther from the center on the opposite side. The more elements used in informal balance, the more difficult balance becomes.

Proportion: The Golden Division of a Line. Proportion, the second element of a layout, adds variety and interest to a composition. Proportion is concerned with how the various elements of the layout relate to one another and to the whole. Let's look at the proportioning of a straight line:

_____

Divide the line a short distance in from the right:

_____|_____

This division does practically nothing for the eye and the smaller section of the line to the right is lost. If we divide the line into equal halves

_____|_____

we achieve equilibrium and an uninteresting ratio. Which half does one look at? Dividing the line into thirds

_____|_____|_____

gives more dynamism, a kind of rhythm, and considerably more interest than the division into halves. Finally, divide the line between the one-third and one-half divisions:

_____|_____

The ratio of the smaller part to the larger is equal to the ratio of the larger part to the entire line.

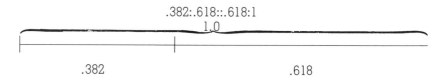

.382:.618::.618:1

1.0

.382   .618

Known variously as "the golden division of a line," "the golden mean," "the line of golden proportion," and "the golden ratio," this proportion has specific application to composition and layout. The ratio is sometimes mistakenly stated as 3:5 or 3/8:5/8, rather than the correct .382:.618::.618:1, as in our illustration. Obviously, the ratio 3/8:5/8::5/8:1 is not a true one.

Emil Ruder, in his *Typography*, calls the proportion "The Golden Section," gives the ratio as 3:5::8:13 (again, an untrue proportion), and correctly points out that it "may be right for one work but wrong for another."

Layout in Spreads. Any brochure, pamphlet, booklet, or book must be laid out or composed as the graphic unit or entity in which it will be viewed, for example, as a unit of two facing pages, called a "spread." Figure 6-3 illustrates the golden division rule applied to trial layouts for two 2-page spreads. In these examples the areas are divided from both sides and from top and bottom by the golden division, resulting in a

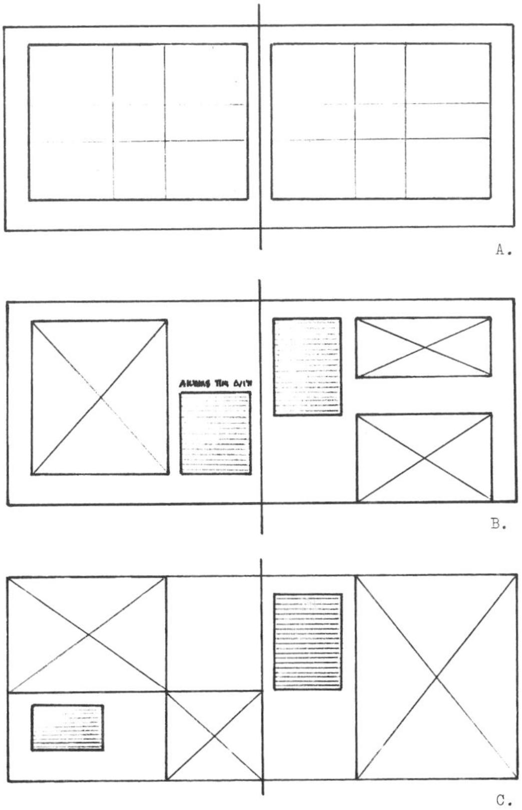

Figure 6-3. The golden division rule can be applied in different ways. *(a)* Here the golden division grid is applied to a double-page spread for an 8½ × 11 inch brochure in a horizontal format. Side margins setting off the graphic area are in width ratios of 2:3:4:5 units. All measurements are at one-quarter scale. *(b)* This trial layout is for three photographs, a headline, and two copy blocks. The lower right illustration is a "bleed" photograph, appearing to project beyond the bottom edge of the page. *(c)* This sketch is for the same elements, less the headline. In this example all illustrations are bleed photographs.

golden division grid. Figure 6-4 shows the relationship of the golden division, optical center, and mathematical center of a page.

The brochure or book designer may well feel pity for his or her counterpart in the magazine field. Intruding throughout the average magazine and contributing to the disruption of a horizontal sense and philosophy are the ubiquitous advertising pages. Usually with little or no control over where ad pages fall in the publication's makeup, the magazine designer often is faced with a form of working in the dark in laying out up to several hundred pages for an issue.

In *Editing by Design*, Jan V. White referred to this problem:

> Think in terms of horizontal spreads, instead of vertical single pages. The normal magazine shape is vertical; the text in its columns is vertical; so the temptation is to subdivide the space in vertical slivers. But, once the readers get beyond the front cover and have opened up the issue, they see a horizontal shape interrupted by the gutter in the middle. However, they perceive only one page at a time, because they are used to seeing pages split away from each other and because the available space is normally organized as two contiguous vertical elements. (One automatically thinks of an

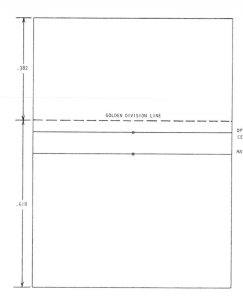

.382

GOLDEN DIVISION LINE

OPTICAL
CENTER

MATHEMATICAL
CENTER

.618

Figure 6-4. The relationship of three imaginary page divisions—golden division, optical center, and mathematical center—all of which have an effect on layout and balance, is shown here. The center of balance (optical center), to those with normal vision, appears to be slightly above the page's mathematical center.

ad as a single-page vertical element—and the same holds true for frontispieces, chapter openings, and so forth.) It is incumbent upon the editor and designer to break out of this straitjacket wherever opportunity allows; hence, they must conceive of the two-page spread as a large horizontal module with a minor interruption down the middle, instead of as two smaller vertical modules that happen to be glued together in the middle.

The resulting effect on the reader is of a broadened, widened, more expansive aura in the product as a whole; and—when big pictures are used—a feeling of enormous enclosure, like the experience of the audience at a Cinerama presentation.[3]

Golden Division Grid.   The grid based on the golden division rule originally was developed as a diagram to help artists locate the four strongest points of a composition on their canvas. The center of interest may be constructed at any of the four interior crossing points, or along any of the division lines.

There is, of course, nothing magic about using the golden division rule to set up grids for brochure layouts. It may be of some help in getting one's thoughts organized when beginning a layout. Several sketches of additional layout ideas (see Figures 6-5 and 6-6) will be found at the end of this chapter.

The Other Composition Principles.   There are five remaining principles of composition—rhythm, movement, unity, clarity, and simplicity.

Rhythm.   Rhythm normally is obtained by repetition and progression (Edgar Allan Poe's "The Bells"). Repeating or alternating lines, masses, directions, weights, angles, and intervals in an orderly manner gives rhythm. Progression may be achieved by slight variations in value, size, and shape.

Movement.   Movement across a layout may be in any direction, but the normal route is generally clockwise, beginning in the upper left corner and progressing to lower right. Intermediate paths of eye (and interest) movement may occur within a layout, but the ultimate goal is to lead the viewer to the center of interest. This effect sometimes is called "linear suggestion," since curved or diagonal lines both suggest motion and indicate direction of movement.

Notice the advertisements in a magazine; check how the layout designer and the artist deliberately lead a reader across and down through an advertisement. This may be done through a combination of headlines, illustrations, and an attractive combination of masses (type blocks, logos, art work, and so forth). If your eyes stray away from the page before you've absorbed the message, the layout probably lacks movement.

Unity, Clarity, and Simplicity.   These are closely related principles of composition. If a layout appears to fall apart the elements are not a unified whole, and the effect will be disturbing to most readers.

Importance of Clarity.   Occasionally, a layout seems to have been put together as a committee exercise—too many typefaces and sizes, not enough separation of similar tonal values, type reverses too small to be legible. All of these are signs that clarity was sacrificed in an attempt to gain some hoped for effect, which obviously did not come off.

"Keep it simple" should be on a wall plaque right alongside the ubiquitous "Think" in a designer's office. A layout's primary goal in life is to command attention. And the simpler the layout is, the greater the odds that someone will look at it. Eliminate all elements that can be omitted without destroying the central message.

Three Steps in Layout.   Three kinds of layouts usually are done on the way to the final printed product: thumbnail sketches, roughs, and comprehensives. The final stage, mechanicals, or camera-ready copy, will be covered in Chapter 11.

Thumbnails may be likened to preliminaries in the design process. Normally done at small—even miniature—scale to work through design and layout ideas visually, thumbnails are quick sketches by the layout artist. They should be in the same proportion and shape as the full-size layout. Studying a series of thumbnail sketches for a simple layout problem will illustrate how details of composition, balance, movement, and other design factors evolve.

When one or more promising thumbnails have been done, the ideas are transferred to a full-scale, more detailed rough sketch. A rough (sometimes called a visual) falls somewhere between the preliminary sketchy thumbnail and the comprehensive layout. Design faults too small to be picked up in the thumbnail are corrected and refined in the rough.

The more detailed comprehensive pretty accurately shows what the finished product will look like. Tones, colors, and details are carefully drawn—sometimes almost to the point of being finished artwork. When the client is able to visualize the final product from a rough, the comprehensive often is omitted.

Fit Type First. Fitting copy into the layout can be one of the more difficult problems in laying out a brochure. It is best to keep type matter the same width throughout the brochure—for reasons of cost as well as aesthetics. Illustration size usually is more flexible than body type blocks, and varying or adapting the measurements of photographs and drawings to the amount of type that must be dealt with is more satisfactory and effective than ever-changing type line widths. The prime goal of brochure illustrations should be to liven up the layout, rather than to dominate or mold it.

Ground Rules. Technically, the preliminary planning of a brochure breaks down into three major areas, or requirements. The first is establishing broad objectives. In Chapter 1 we established these objectives by answering two questions:

1. Whom are we talking to—or who will receive the brochure?
2. What are we trying to sell—or what must the brochure accomplish?

A second requirement is that of determining the brochure's contents: theme, headlines, amount of copy, quantity, size, kind of illustrations, and kinds of composition—text, machine, display, hand-set, hand-lettered, and so forth.

The final requirement is that of determining the physical details. This covers items such as the size and number of pages, colors needed (hues and number), quantity of brochures needed, type of cover (self-cover or separate), kinds and grades of paper, binding, inserts, die-cuts, mailing envelopes or cartons, and so forth.

The second area (contents) is closely related to layout, while the final area involves considerations of format (refer to the definition of "format" at the beginning of this chapter).

Printers' Estimates. If you would like to startle a printer, drop by the plant and ask something like, "How much will 3,000 brochures cost?" That question is just about as meaningful as "How long is a piece of string?" or "How high is up?"

Some of the first questions in reply to your question will be about size, number of colors, and number of pages involved, but until you furnish much more in the way of specifications, any pricing can only be a guesstimate. Estimating printing costs has become the next thing to a science. Every step in major printing firms is governed by job standards. Exact costs for practically all details are known and may be applied to almost any job. (An estimator's worksheet is reproduced in Chapter 13.)

Photoengravings, artwork, cold-type composition, and pasteups usually are estimated on a per-word, a square inch, or a unit scale.

Tempering Estimates.   The main variables in printers' costs concern press availability and individual worker productivity. Estimates vary or are tempered for several reasons, including customers' credit ratings, their desirability as new or continuing accounts, and what the printers' competition is doing.

Dr. Gerald A. Silver, in his book *Printing Estimating*, explains it this way:

> After the printing job has been estimated the estimator may want to temper his figures. Tempering the estimate is the bringing to bear on the final quotation a judgement of all of the subtle, marginal, abstract and intangible elements which have not been assessed in dollars and cents. It means adjusting the quotation from the theoretical to the practical. It could mean the difference between a successful sale or a loss of profit.
>
> After the estimator has prepared his figures he must ask himself certain questions. Will the customer be hypercritical in his quality and delivery demands? Will there be reruns on the job? How much time and additional expense will be involved in closing the transaction? Is the price consistent with previous prices? Can a loyal, long term account be developed?
>
> There are no simple guideposts to help the estimator answer these questions. Yet they may materially affect the price quoted to the customer.[4]

Once you have the ground rules established and committed to paper—objectives, contents, and physical details—you are ready to make up a comprehensive layout or dummy for a printer's estimate. The more completely you spec the layout, the more accurate you can expect the estimate to be.

FORMAT CONSIDERATIONS

Most of the remaining chapters deal with subjects directly or indirectly related to format, so at this point a quick preview of format considerations will suffice.

Size and Shape.   If a brochure is intended to be kept for reference (and most are), it should fit into standard file folders. Although legal size folders will accept a 14-inch dimension, it is advisable to keep the larger dimension to around 11 inches. The maximum shorter dimension should be approximately 9 inches. This does not rule out the increasingly popular square format, in 8½-inch or 9-inch dimensions.

If pockets are included in the brochure's format, to carry loose project sheets or article reprints, the overall cover dimensions may be increased by ¼ inch or so to accommodate the inserted material more neatly. Pockets may be placed on either or both inside covers.

The cost of a brochure obviously is affected by its size. Design your cover and page sizes to be cut from stock paper sizes with a minimum of waste. The proper number of pages, within certain restrictions, is whatever it takes to meet the brochure's objectives.

Paper.   The kind, grade, weight, and finish are all primary considerations in paper selection; other factors include opacity, receptivity to ink, uniformity of color, and foldability.

Color.   The range in number of ink colors is from one- (usually black) to four-color process work, in which practically every color in the rainbow may be reproduced. The use of colored stock for cover and/or inside can add additional color to the brochure. The selection of colored stock should be made with the image to be conveyed in mind. Remember, graphic arts experts do not usually run four-color process work on colored stock.

Type.   The primary objective of type is legibility. Legibility suffers when the type is too small, too large, too fancy, insufficiently leaded between lines, or the type line is too long (remember the two-alphabet-width rule of thumb), or is reversed against a distracting background.

Illustrations.   "Almost all persons today see good design regularly: on television, in their newspapers and magazines, in packages, automobiles, homes and interiors, etc. Whether they consciously recognize fine design is immaterial. They are surrounded by it, and any departure establishes a negative image of the product, the service, or even the corporation represented by shoddy design."[5]

In other words, every potential reader of a brochure is a critic. The chances are that most potential clients will have been exposed to more good design—in books, news magazines, annual reports, and the like—than the average person.

Don't let poor photographs, drawings, and charts be a handicap to your brochure's overall image. The many photographic and photomechanical techniques and processes available to the designer today, used in moderation and with taste, can impart a distinctive emphasis and flair to the pages of a brochure.

Binding.   Modern binding methods are almost as numerous and varied as typefaces and paper grades. Book-type bindings include side-wire, saddle-wire, sewn soft-cover, sewn case-bound, and perfect bindings. There also are plastic bindings (both spiral and riveted), and a variety of metal bindings—screw, spiral, and riveted. Select the method that most nearly meets your budget and aesthetic requirements.

REFERENCES

[1]F. H. Wills, *Fundamentals of Layout*, Dover Publications, Inc., New York, 1971, p. 16.

[2]*Copy-Fitting Manual*, Baumwell Graphics, Inc., New York, 1966, p. xlii.

[3]Jan V. White, *Editing by Design*, R. R. Bowker Company, New York, 1974, p. 20.

[4]Gerald A. Silvers, *Printing Estimating*, American Technical Society, Chicago, 1970, p. 132.

[5]*Short Course in the Graphic Arts*, The Mead Corporation, Dayton, Ohio, 1973, vol. 2, p. 2.

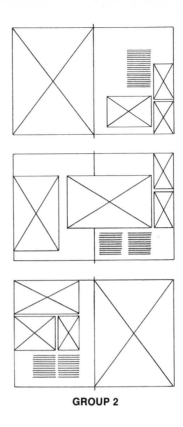

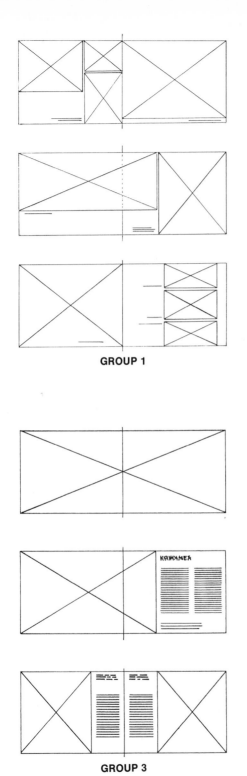

GROUP 1

GROUP 2

GROUP 3

Figure 6-5. Thumbnail sketches of various layouts for brochure spreads are shown here. Group 1: spreads for a brochure in a horizontal format. Group 2: three sample spreads for a vertical format. Group 3: The top thumbnail shows total photo coverage of a spread, bled on four sides. In the center thumbnail a gutter-jumping illustration is used, with head, text, and caption on the right. The bottom layout illustrates formal balance of photos, captions, and text blocks. Compare the center and bottom layouts for visual interest.

Chapter 7
TYPOGRAPHY

MANY TYPOGRAPHERS TEND TO WREATHE their profession in a sort of enigmatic mystique. One anonymous typographic mystagogue wrote:

> Typography has character and spirit—sometimes intangible and invisible as the force of gravity, but like the force of gravity, the character is ever present. The force we see—the only force—is in the effectiveness of type in printed, finished form. If type is right, it accomplishes our purposes; if it is wrong, it is often detrimental. What gives type its character? By what magic formula do type designers work? The answer is in those elements that built lasting monumental works, and still inspire strides of science and architecture.

Professor Cabibi comments:

> The study of type and its many forms and functions is highly specialized and requires much research on the part of anyone who would use the various styles to their fullest extent. Type can express atmosphere and impart definite character and feeling. It can also emphasize the physical construction and expressiveness of a layout and the message it portrays. Typefaces can express nearly all the characteristics attributable to humans.[1]

Be that as it may, typography *is* one of the most important elements in a successful piece of printing. Much of the effectiveness of type depends upon the knowledge and skill of the designer. A great deal also depends upon the plates, presswork, and paper. Before getting into specifics, a brief backward look at the history of type and printing is in order.

HISTORICAL ORIGINS

Although Johann Gensfleisch zum Gutenberg usually is credited with the invention of movable type, around 1440, it was in use in China by the middle of the eleventh century. Pi Sheng, a Chinese alchemist, produced the first known movable type about 1040, in the Ch'ing-li period. Pi Sheng's type was compounded of a glue and clay mixture, hardened in a kiln. Upon his return to Venice from China in 1295, Marco Polo reported on the advanced stage of the printing arts in China.

Not long after Pi Sheng made his baked-clay movable type, Korean printers, using wooden type as models, began sand-casting metal type, fonts of which made their way to China and Japan. The oldest known text was printed from bronze type in Korea in A.D. 1397.

EVOLUTION OF ROMAN LETTERS

The Roman alphabet we use today had its origin in the hieroglyphics of ancient Egypt, of around 2500 B.C. After the Egyptians developed their symbols into a cursive form (script typefaces which imitate handwriting), the Phoenicians adopted the form and produced a formal twenty-two–letter alphabet. In the course of time the Phoenician alphabet was transmitted to the Greeks, and by them to the Romans. The Roman capital alphabet evolved and was passed down to modern times practically intact. Its longevity is due to the fact that its letters are based on well-defined principles of proportion and geometric truths—the elements of the circle, ellipse, and vertical, horizontal, and diagonal lines.

As we have seen, Gutenberg's work with movable type and his development of a practical printing press occurred around 1440. His forty-two-line Bible was printed some four years later. A recent estimate has it that modern electronic phototypesetters, some of which have theoretical performance rates of more than 10,000 characters a second, easily could duplicate Gutenberg's five-year Bible typesetting chore in about an hour.

SPREAD OF PRINTING

As letterpress printing spread across the face of Europe from Italy (1465) to the British Isles (1476), it revolutionized communication on the Continent, effectively bringing an end to the Middle Ages.

The first press in the New World was set up in Mexico City in 1539. In 1638 the first printing press in the Colonies was established in Cambridge, Massachusetts. Harvard College obtained its own press about 1650, marking the beginning of the oldest continuing press operation in America—the Harvard University Press. One of the first books printed at Harvard was an Indian edition of the Bible, which, in one sense, closed the Mainz-to-Cambridge printing circle in a matter of just over 100 years.

As migration and settlement moved south, then west, across America, the printing trade followed. By the early 1800s the first press was in operation in St. Louis.

TYPE AND LETTER NOMENCLATURE

Including all sizes, weights, and styles, there are over 10,000 typefaces available today in the United States. Omitting type set by photocomposition, each letter, figure, and punctuation mark is a separate piece of type, 0.918 inches high. Type nomenclature is shown in Figure 7-1. Letter nomenclature is shown in Figure 7-2.

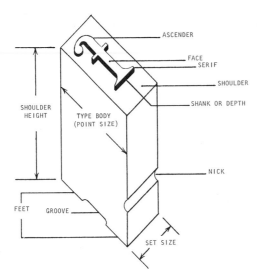

Figure 7-1. Nomenclature of a piece of type.

TYPOGRAPHIC STANDARDS

Standard sizes and heights of typefaces were unknown to Gutenberg. Not until Didot, who died in 1836, was there a generally recognized and used system of measurement. Didot's system was the first to be based on point size.

The typographic point system used in the United States and other English-speaking countries is called the American point system. In this system, a point is 0.013837 inches, or approximately 1/72 inch. In 1886, the United States Typefounders Association adopted the basic measurement of 83 picas set to equal 35 centimeters. The Didot, or French, system is the most widely used system throughout the rest of the world. A Didot point is 0.0148 inch and a pica in that system (known as a "Cicero") is 0.1780 inch.

Twelve points constitute one pica in the American system (0.1667 inch), and six picas approximate one inch (0.9960 inch). The square of any point size is called an *em*. The em is used as a surface measurement unit and to determine composition charges. Inches are not used in expressing type-form measurements.

In the same point size, types may show a considerable variance in the height of their printing surface, owing to differences in the length of ascenders (the upper parts of the b, d, f, h, k, l, and t) and descenders (the lower parts of the g, j, p, q, and y), and the main body height. Type size is measured from the top of an ascender to the bottom of a descender.

Still another descriptive term used by typographers for type images is "ex-height" (also known as "x-height" and "z-height"). The ex-height is the height of letters without either ascenders or descenders, such as x, z, a, r, m, n, and o. A designer can impart an appearance of leading by using a typeface with a small ex-height. A large face, conversely, can be obtained from type of the same point size when it has a large ex-height design. The latter faces should be leaded generously for legibility.

In noting type-form dimensions on layouts and copy, first give the line length in picas (for example, 18 picas or 18 p.), then the depth of the copy, also in picas. Thus

18 x 26 picas
10 Bod. Bk.
lead 2 pts

in the margin of a page of copy tells the typesetter the material will fill a block 18 picas wide by 26 picas deep, and is to be set in 10 point Bodoni Book type, with 2-point leading between lines. The type size, face, and leading also could have been written 10/12 Bod. Bk.

Paper, on the other hand, is always dimensioned in inches—width first, then length. If these basic rules are followed in instructing typesetters and printers there should be no room for confusion about the desired measurements of any elements of the layout.

Many typefaces look alike to the layman. Even experts sometimes have trouble differentiating between type look-alikes. A few lowercase letters—a, e, g, p, and t—are distinctive in most faces and offer the best keys to identifying a type. By studying the size, shape, and position of the lowercase g—the hook off the top loop, the top loop, the line joining top and bottom loops, and the lower loop—one can usually identify the typeface.

TYPEFACE CLASSIFICATION

Not all authorities agree on the number of typeface categories, or even on which face belongs in a given group, but these eight classifications generally are accepted by a majority of typographers. Examples follow each classification:

- *Oldstyle:* Garamond, Caslon
- *Modern:* Bodoni, Scotch Roman
- *Transitional:* Century, Baskerville
- *Square serif:* Clarendon, Stymie
- *Sans serif:* News Gothic, Futura
- *Script and cursive:* Lydian Cursive, Commercial Script
- *Text letters:* Old English, Engravers Text
- *Decorative types:* Comstock, Caslon Openface

Nowhere will the designer or layout artist—tyro or old pro—find a set of rules or charts that tells when to use which typeface. No catalog or text exists to say which faces blend with or oppose others. Typography, as one expert has said, is largely a matter of feeling and spirit. Mechanical or mathematical selection of type is no more feasible than the creation of a painted masterpiece by consulting a table showing which colors harmonize with each other. When designers have a sensitivity for the "feel" of various faces, the problem will resolve itself as they naturally avoid unharmonious elements.

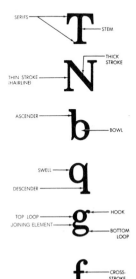

Figure 7-2. Nomenclature of a letter.

Since the basic function of a piece of printing is to deliver a message, the message should determine the various elements of the printed form—size, paper choice, copy, illustrations, and art techniques. A vastly different layout would be appropriate for selling air conditioners at reduced prices than would be for selling wealthy buyers on the virtues of owning a Lincoln Continental or a Cadillac.

Color, in stock and inks, affects the legibility of type faces. Some faces that are easily read as black type on white paper become impossible to read when color is introduced into ink or stock, or both. Always check samples of the selected typeface on the same stock, and in the same colors, as will be used for the final product.

> In combining type faces, it is generally safe to assume that the members of one group of designs will go reasonably well with another; by the same general rule, they will not be harmonious with members of another group. A delicate, feminine type such as Garamond has nothing in common with blocky Beton; free, open-air-loving Bookface is uncomfortable in the company of citified Cairo. Only the broadest outlines can be used as general guides. Serious, open-minded study of the history and development of various faces is essential for combining type faces sympathetically and well.[2]

On the same subject, here is another comment:

> Remember that the main purpose of type is to be read. In the selection of type for any particular job, the choice must necessarily be built around legibility. To a large extent the legibility of printed matter depends upon the size and style of the type used, the paper upon which it is printed, the width of the measure in which type is set, the leading between lines, and the amount of margin or white space around the type matter.[3]

While there seem to be at least two schools of thought on the matter among educators, psychologists appear to be in general agreement that reading is a process of word and phrase recognition, as opposed to letter-by-letter identification. One is generally on safe ground, therefore, in selecting from among the more popular typefaces—those most familiar to the eye from reading newspapers, books, and magazines. The chief key to word recognition seems to be in the formation of the upper sections of lowercase letters. See Figure 7-3 for an illustration of this.

It might be instructive in this context to look at the typefaces used by three of the largest-circulation magazines in the world: *Reader's Digest*, *National Geographic*, and *TV Guide*.

For body type the *Digest* uses 11-point Monotype Granjon on an 11-point base, unleaded. (See Figure 7-4.) A nice characteristic of Granjon is that, set solid, it has the appearance of being leaded. Granjon has been described as a bookface worthy to rank with Caslon for usefulness and with Centaur for beauty, and as being sharp enough for publicity, yet clear enough for a dictionary. The basic headline face in the *Digest* is 30-point Baskerville. Note that the initial letter is sunken and repeats the Baskerville headline type.

Initial letters usually are used to typographically brighten up all-text pages, although many brochures use them in shorter copy blocks. Two types of initial letters are in common use—sunken (as in the *Digest* and

it's only a matter of seconds

clean and simple

(a)

REPORTS AVAILABLE

structuring
communities

(b)

Figure 7-3. Upper and lower sections of lowercase letters illustrate an interesting point. *(a)* When only the upper parts of letters are shown, the words are still decipherable. But the average reader, when presented with only the bottom sections of letters, will find the words difficult to make out. Alternately cover the bottom and top halves of the examples to see the effect. *(b)* But some typefaces seem inherently difficult to read, almost as if the artist and designer conspired to keep the message a secret.

Highway Robbery—Via the ICC

Set up to protect the public, the Interstate Commerce Commission today actually throttles competition in the trucking industry and drives up the price of everything from tuna fish to television sets

BY MARK FRAZIER

A TRUCKFUL of furniture, en route from Dallas to San Diego, detours 800 miles out of its way—adding 12 hours to the trip and squandering 160 gallons of fuel. Reason: arbitrary federal regulations.

• In Atlanta, Ga., a trucking company announces plans to lower rates on truckloads of tire treads bound for Ohio to save its customers $400 a trip. But it is prevented from making the cut. Reason: arbitrary federal regulations.

• Along the main interstate routes between Milwaukee, Wis., and Birmingham, Ala., trucks roll along with trailers empty, even though depots at both ends of the line would gladly give them cargo. The truckers

are permitted to haul freight one way only, and must make the 1000-mile return trip empty. Reason: arbitrary federal regulations.

Responsible for these and hundreds of other interstate-trucking regulations is the Interstate Commerce Commission. Every day, its regulatory roadblocks prevent the speedy, efficient transport of the goods we buy and sell. Economists totaling the bill say that ICC edicts cost consumers from $5 billion to $10 billion a year in higher prices for everything from tuna fish to television sets—as much as $200 a year for the average U.S. family.

Few would have predicted such a destructive role for the ICC when it was set up in 1887. Its handful of em-

72

the *National Geographic*) and raised. The two types are also referred to as "cut-in" and "upstanding." Instead of cutting into two or three lines at the beginning of a paragraph, as for a sunken initial letter, the raised initial uses space between paragraphs to accommodate its extra height. There is a third, less common, type of initial known as free-standing. It usually is placed in the left margin, upstanding, and is followed by a lead-in line to the copy block.

An old rule held that the top of a sunken initial should align with the body type ascenders in the top line, but the *Digest* does not follow that system. There are no particular rules as to the size of initial letters, but they are usually at least twice the height of the body type. Three times the body type height is a more pleasing proportion in most cases. The bottom of a raised initial is aligned with the bottom of body type caps and small caps on the line in which it appears.

In *Editing by Design* Jan White points out that the graphic flavor imparted to a page by initials requires care in their handling.

1. The typeface chosen [for the initial] must be harmonious with the body type in design.
2. The alignments must be precise, or the product looks shoddy.
3. There must be no gap between the initial and the rest of the word. [This can get very tricky in the case of A and L.][4]

The *Geographic* used 10-point Oldstyle No. 7 on an 11-point base for its body type. (See Figure 7-5.) Headline type choices are from Modern No. 20, Helvetica Ultracompressed, or Fiedler Monotype Gothic, ranging in size from 30 to 44 points. The Helvetica and Fiedler Gothic are sans serif typefaces.

TV Guide, with a circulation in excess of 20 million, has probably a greater total readership than any other publication in the world. Body copy for the articles in the *Guide* is Helvetica Light ⅞, or 8-point type on a 9-point body—the same as 8-point type with 1-point leading. (See Figure 7-6.) Headline type for articles varies; it is often special or handlettered. Program listings in the *Guide* use a special 8-point typeface developed for the magazine. All copy is set by electronic phototypesetters.

None of this is to say that a brochure designer should specify Granjon or Oldstyle or Helvetica because they are used in these three well-read publications. But keep in mind that a fair-sized body of prospective clients are familiar with *Reader's Digest*, the *National Geographic*, and *TV Guide*— and might relate favorably to familiar typefaces.

OTHER TYPOGRAPHIC CONSIDERATIONS

One classification of typefaces concerns the variations in width and depth in the same point size. These variations are due to differences in

Figure 7-4. Sample page from the *Reader's Digest* showing body type and headline face. Note the sunken initial letter. (Reproduced with permission of the *Reader's Digest*)

Vermont
A STATE OF MIND
AND MOUNTAINS

By ETHEL A. STARBIRD
NATIONAL GEOGRAPHIC STAFF

Photographs by
NATHAN BENN

"LOOKIN' for Poultney, y'say?" The old man shuffled closer to the car. "Well, you're in it now. 'Less ya want East Poultney. Which is where Poultney used to be. When Poultney was West Poultney, that is."

I knew I had crossed the line into my home state. This is the kind of conversational web Vermonters delight in weaving.

Did he know the way to the Greeley place?

"N'body by that name 'round here," he assured me. "Better try up to East Poultney. May be one of them city folks that keep movin' in."

Horace Greeley was, indeed, a city man, but he was raised a country boy, in New Hampshire and then in West Haven, Vermont. In 1826—at the age of 15—he sowed the seeds of his journalistic career apprenticing on the *Northern Spectator*, a Poultney newspaper. East Poultney has

Figure 7-5. Sample page from the *National Geographic* magazine showing headline, body type, and sunken initial letter. (Courtesy of the *National Geographic* magazine and the National Geographic Society)

design of the face, and are called expanded, normal, condensed, and ultracondensed. Another related variant is the set width. Typefaces are available in narrow, medium, and wide set, and each offers certain advantages when properly used. Narrow set faces, for example, can reduce the length of a type block or the number of pages in a brochure without affecting the overall design. (See Figure 7-7.)

Word and letter spacing are generally automatic in body type, that is, machine imposed and justified. Spacing in headlines and in other all-capital words, as for emphasis or effect, will vary according to the design and the eye of the designer and typographer. The width of the capital E of the font and size selected is often used to obtain correct spacing between words in all-capital lines. However, in the close-spacing style of today, one-half the width of the capital E is the more usual space. Open areas between certain capitals, such as an F at the end of one word and a T at the beginning of the following word, are spaced optically. Letter spacing in words set in all caps almost always is an optical exercise.

Type series and type families are two other terms a designer must know. The Craw Modern series, from 6 to 48 point, is shown in Figure 7-8.

Figure 7-9 illustrates the type family of the ITC Souvenir face—light with italic, medium with italic, demibold with italic, and bold with italic.

Finally, Figure 7-10 contains showings, in 10-point size, of 35 different typefaces. This review is for both familiarization and reference purposes.

Don't forget that some typefaces are made by more than one foundry, which can lead to important variations in the width of the same typeface and size. In some cases, it may be important that the designer specify both typeface and manufacturer.

COPY FITTING

Copy fitting is the careful organization of three elements: copy, type, and area. To fit copy accurately and to mesh these three elements, certain information must be at hand:

1. Number of characters in the copy
2. Character count of the selected typeface and size

Figure 7-6. A spread from *TV Guide* for the week of February 8, 1975, showing head and body types. This spread also illustrates the line outline method of identifying large groups of individuals in a photograph (Chapter 10). (Reproduced with permission of *TV Guide* magazine. Copyright © 1975 by Triangle Publications, Inc., Radnor, Pa. Photograph by Roger Prigert)

Narrow set	MTSERWBQGPAJ	abcdefghijklmnopqrstuvwxyz and cccccccccc
	MTSERWBQGPAJ	abcdefghijklmnopqrstuvwxyz and cccccccccccc
	MTSERWBQGPAJ	abcdefghijklmnopqrstuvwxyz and cccccccccccccc
Medium set	MTSERWBQGPAJ	abcdefghijklmnopqrstuvwxyz and ccccccc
	MTSERWBQGPAJ	abcdefghijklmnopqrstuvwxyz and ccccc
	MTSERWBQGPAJ	abcdefghijklmnopqrstuvwxyz and ccccccc
Wide set	MTSERWBQGPAJ	abcdefghijklmnopqrstuvwxyz and ccccc
	MTSERWBQGPAJ	abcdefghijklmnopqrstuvwxyz and cc
	MTSERWBQGPAJ	abcdefghijklmnopqrstuvwxyz and ccccc

Figure 7-7. Examples of variations in typeface widths and heights—narrow set, medium set, and wide set.

3.   Dimensions of the area in the layout to be filled

Any two of the three will give the third.

Some type catalogs carry character-count tables on the specimen type pages. The tables list by size and in a variety of pica widths the average number of characters that will fit into a line. A complete showing of letters, figures, and symbols for Garamond, followed by a character-count table for Garamond in 6- to 14-point sizes, from 1 to 42 picas in width, is shown in Figure 7-11.

COPY-FITTING EXAMPLES

As an example, the typed paragraph in Figure 7-12 was made on an *elite* typewriter, which counts out at 12 characters to an inch (2 characters per pica). A *pica* typewriter has 10 characters to the inch.

The designer wants the copy set in 10-point Garamond, 14 picas wide. How many lines will it take?

Actually, two good copy-fitting techniques are available to the designer. One requires only the character-count tables, as illustrated in Figure 7-11. There are 10 lines of typed copy. Draw a light vertical line down the right edge of the sheet at a point that averages out long and short lines. In this case, the average is about 49 characters per line. Multiply the 10 lines by 49; the answer is 490 characters.

CRAW MODERN

6 Foundry   TYPE FACES HAVE BOTH DIFFERENCES and similarities. To become pro

8 Foundry   PRINTED MESSAGE, ONE MUST ALWAYS strive to practice the

10 Foundry   FACES AT EVERY AVAILABLE opportunity. A person

12 Foundry   LEARNING SHOULD NEVER hesitate to ask

14 Foundry   PROBLEMS ARISE. YOU will find that the

18 Foundry   PEOPLE WITH EXPERT advic

24 Foundry   HAPPY TO HELP you.

30 Foundry   CONSCIOUS effort

36 Foundry   WHO WOULD 1

48 Foundry   BECOME m

Figure 7-8. The Craw Modern type series, 6 to 48 point.

Find the 14-pica column in the top line of the Garamond character-count table in Figure 7-11. Read down to the 10-point line; a 14-pica measure will set 40 characters to the line. The character count, 490, divided by 40, equals 13 lines of type 14 picas wide. If the type is to be set solid (no leading), then the depth is 10 points times 13 lines, or 130 points. This is equal to 10.83 picas (1.8 inches).

A more involved problem would be a manuscript averaging 55 characters per line, with 25 lines on each of 8 pages. Multiply 55 by 25 by 8, for an answer of 11,000 characters. In this case the designer has decided he

ITC Souvenir Light with Italic

abcdefghijklmnopqrstuvwxyz
ABCDEFGHIJKLMNOPQRSTUVWXYZ1234567890

abcdefghijklmnopqrstuvwxyz
8 *ABCDEFGHIJKLMNOPQRSTUVWXYZ1234567890*

abcdefghijklmnopqrstuvwxyz
ABCDEFGHIJKLMNOPQRSTUVWXYZ1234567890

abcdefghijklmnopqrstuvwxyz
9 *ABCDEFGHIJKLMNOPQRSTUVWXYZ1234567890*

abcdefghijklmnopqrstuvwxyz
ABCDEFGHIJKLMNOPQRSTUVWXYZ1234567890

abcdefghijklmnopqrstuvwxyz
10 *ABCDEFGHIJKLMNOPQRSTUVWXYZ1234567890*

abcdefghijklmnopqrstuvwxyz
ABCDEFGHIJKLMNOPQRSTUVWXYZ1234567890

abcdefghijklmnopqrstuvwxyz
11 *ABCDEFGHIJKLMNOPQRSTUVWXYZ1234567890*

abcdefghijklmnopqrstuvwxyz
ABCDEFGHIJKLMNOPQRSTUVWXYZ1234567890

abcdefghijklmnopqrstuvwxyz
12 *ABCDEFGHIJKLMNOPQRSTUVWXYZ1234567890*

abcdefghijklmnopqrstuvwxyz
ABCDEFGHIJKLMNOPQRSTUVWXYZ1234567890

abcdefghijklmnopqrstuvwxyz
14 *ABCDEFGHIJKLMNOPQRSTUVWXYZ1234567890*

Figure 7-9. Complete ITC Souvenir type family.

ITC Souvenir Medium with Italic

abcdefghijklmnopqrstuvwxyz
ABCDEFGHIJKLMNOPQRSTUVWXYZ1234567890

abcdefghijklmnopqrstuvwxyz
ABCDEFGHIJKLMNOPQRSTUVWXYZ1234567890

8

abcdefghijklmnopqrstuvwxyz
ABCDEFGHIJKLMNOPQRSTUVWXYZ1234567890

abcdefghijklmnopqrstuvwxyz
ABCDEFGHIJKLMNOPQRSTUVWXYZ1234567890

9

abcdefghijklmnopqrstuvwxyz
ABCDEFGHIJKLMNOPQRSTUVWXYZ1234567890

abcdefghijklmnopqrstuvwxyz
ABCDEFGHIJKLMNOPQRSTUVWXYZ1234567890

10

abcdefghijklmnopqrstuvwxyz
ABCDEFGHIJKLMNOPQRSTUVWXYZ1234567890

abcdefghijklmnopqrstuvwxyz
ABCDEFGHIJKLMNOPQRSTUVWXYZ1234567890

11

abcdefghijklmnopqrstuvwxyz
ABCDEFGHIJKLMNOPQRSTUVWXYZ1234567890

abcdefghijklmnopqrstuvwxyz
ABCDEFGHIJKLMNOPQRSTUVWXYZ1234567890

12

abcdefghijklmnopqrstuvwxyz
ABCDEFGHIJKLMNOPQRSTUVWXYZ1234567

abcdefghijklmnopqrstuvwxyz
ABCDEFGHIJKLMNOPQRSTUVWXYZ1234567

14

ITC Souvenir Demi with Italic

abcdefghijklmnopqrstuvwxyz
ABCDEFGHIJKLMNOPQRSTUVWXYZ1234567890

abcdefghijklmnopqrstuvwxyz
ABCDEFGHIJKLMNOPQRSTUVWXYZ1234567890

8

abcdefghijklmnopqrstuvwxyz
ABCDEFGHIJKLMNOPQRSTUVWXYZ1234567890

abcdefghijklmnopqrstuvwxyz
ABCDEFGHIJKLMNOPQRSTUVWXYZ1234567890

9

abcdefghijklmnopqrstuvwxyz
ABCDEFGHIJKLMNOPQRSTUVWXYZ1234567890

abcdefghijklmnopqrstuvwxyz
ABCDEFGHIJKLMNOPQRSTUVWXYZ1234567890

10

abcdefghijklmnopqrstuvwxyz
ABCDEFGHIJKLMNOPQRSTUVWXYZ1234567890

abcdefghijklmnopqrstuvwxyz
ABCDEFGHIJKLMNOPQRSTUVWXYZ1234567890

11

abcdefghijklmnopqrstuvwxyz
ABCDEFGHIJKLMNOPQRSTUVWXYZ1234567890

abcdefghijklmnopqrstuvwxyz
ABCDEFGHIJKLMNOPQRSTUVWXYZ1234567890

12

abcdefghijklmnopqrstuvwxyz
ABCDEFGHIJKLMNOPQRSTUVWXYZ123456

abcdefghijklmnopqrstuvwxyz
ABCDEFGHIJKLMNOPQRSTUVWXYZ123456

14

ITC Souvenir Bold with Italic

abcdefghijklmnopqrstuvwxyz
ABCDEFGHIJKLMNOPQRSTUVWXYZ1234567890
abcdefghijklmnopqrstuvwxyz
ABCDEFGHIJKLMNOPQRSTUVWXYZ1234567890

8

abcdefghijklmnopqrstuvwxyz
ABCDEFGHIJKLMNOPQRSTUVWXYZ1234567890
abcdefghijklmnopqrstuvwxyz
ABCDEFGHIJKLMNOPQRSTUVWXYZ1234567890

9

abcdefghijklmnopqrstuvwxyz
ABCDEFGHIJKLMNOPQRSTUVWXYZ1234567890
abcdefghijklmnopqrstuvwxyz
ABCDEFGHIJKLMNOPQRSTUVWXYZ1234567890

10

abcdefghijklmnopqrstuvwxyz
ABCDEFGHIJKLMNOPQRSTUVWXYZ1234567890
abcdefghijklmnopqrstuvwxyz
ABCDEFGHIJKLMNOPQRSTUVWXYZ1234567890

11

abcdefghijklmnopqrstuvwxyz
ABCDEFGHIJKLMNOPQRSTUVWXYZ12345678
abcdefghijklmnopqrstuvwxyz
ABCDEFGHIJKLMNOPQRSTUVWXYZ12345678

12

abcdefghijklmnopqrstuvwxyz
ABCDEFGHIJKLMNOPQRSTUVWXYZ1234
abcdefghijklmnopqrstuvwxyz
ABCDEFGHIJKLMNOPQRSTUVWXYZ1234

14

10 POINT AIRPORT BLACK

ABCDEFGHIJKLMNOPQRSTUVWXYZ
adcdefghijklmnopqrstuvwxyz
$1234567890

10 POINT ALTERNATE GOTHIC #2

ABCDEFGHIJKLMNOPQRSTUVWXYZ
abcdefghijklmnopqrstuvwxyz
1234567890 (&.,:;!?'"''-*$¢%)

10 POINT BALLOON BOLD

ABCDEFGHIJKLMNOPQRSTUVWXYZ&
1234567890$.,;?!

10 POINT BASKERVILLE

ABCDEFGHIJKLMNOPQRSTUVWXYZ
abcdefghijklmnopqrstuvwxyz
1234567890

10 POINT BODONI BOOK

ABCDEFGHIJKLMNOPQRSTUVWXYZ
abcdefghijklmnopqrstuvwxyz
1234567890$?!

10 POINT BOOKMAN

ABCDEFGHIJKLMNOPQRSTUVWXYZ
abcdefghijklmnopqrstuvwxyz
1234567890$?!

10 POINT BRUSH

ABCDEFGHIJKLMNOP2RSTUVWXYZ&
abcdefghijklmnopqrstuvwxyz
1234567890$¢ .,;?!( )%

10 POINT BULMER

ABCDEFGHIJKLMNOPQRSTUVWXYZ&
abcdefghijklmnopqrstuvwxyz
1234567890$.,-';;?!

10 POINT CALEDONIA

ABCDEFGHIJKLMNOPQRSTUVWXYZ
abcdefghijklmnopqrstuvwxyz
1234567890$?!

10 POINT CASLON

ABCDEFGHIJKLMNOPQRSTUVWXYZ
abcdefghijklmnopqrstuvwxyz
1234567890

10 POINT CENTURY

ABCDEFGHIJKLMNOPQRSTUVWXYZ
abcdefghijklmnopqrstuvwxyz
1234567890$?!

10 POINT CHELTENHAM

ABCDEFGHIJKLMNOPQRSTUVWXYZ
abcdefghijklmnopqrstuvwxyz
1234567890$?!

10 POINT CLOISTER BLACK

𝕬𝕭𝕮𝕯𝕰𝕱𝕲𝕳𝕴𝕵𝕶𝕷𝕸𝕹𝕺𝕻𝕼𝕽𝕾𝕿𝖀𝖁𝖂𝖃𝖄𝖅&
abcdefghijklmnopqrstuvwxyz
1234567890$.,;?!

10 POINT COOPER BLACK

ABCDEFGHIJKLMNOPQRSTUVWXYZ
abcdefghijklmnopqrstuvwxyz
1234567890 $

10 POINT COPPERPLATE

ABCDEFGHIJKLMNOPQRSTUVWXYZ
1234567890$

10 POINT CRAW MODERN

ABCDEFGHIJKLMNOPQRSTUV
WXYZ&   1234567890$¢ .,;?!%
abcdefghijklmnopqrstuvwxyz

10 POINT EGMONT MEDIUM

ABCDEFGHIJKLMNOPQRSTUVWXYZ&
abcdefghijklmnopqrstuvwxyz
1234567890$.,-';;?!

Figure 7-10. Showings, in 10 point, of thirty-four of the most popular typefaces.

10 POINT FUTURA LIGHT
ABCDEFGHIJKLMNOPQRSTUVWXYZ&
abcdefghijklmnopqrstuvwxyz
1234567890$.,;?!()

10 POINT GARAMOND
ABCDEFGHIJKLMNOPQRSTUVWXYZ
abcdefghijklmnopqrstuvwxyz
1234567890$?!   1234567890

10 POINT GARAMOND ITALIC
ABCDEFGHIJKLMNOPQRSTUVWXYZ
abcdefghijklmnopqrstuvwxyz
1234567890 $

10 POINT GOUDY
ABCDEFGHIJKLMNOPQRSTUVWXYZ&
abcdefghijklmnopqrstuvwxyz
1234567890$.,-':;?!

10 POINT HELVETICA
ABCDEFGHIJKLMNOPQRSTUVWXYZ
abcdefghijklmnopqrstuvwxyz
1234567890$?!

10 POINT HELVETICA ITALIC
ABCDEFGHIJKLMNOPQRSTUVWXYZ
abcdefghijklmnopqrstuvwxyz
1234567890$?!

10 POINT LYDIAN
ABCDEFGHIJKLMNOPQRSTUVWXYZ&
abcdefghijklmnopqrstuvwxyz
1234567890$¢ .,;?!

10 POINT LYDIAN CURSIVE
ABCDEFGHIJKLMNOPQRSTUVWXYZ&
abcdefghijklmnopqrstuvwxyz
1234567890$¢ .,;?!

10 POINT OLDSTYLE #1
ABCDEFGHIJKLMNOPQRSTUVWXYZ
abcdefghijklmnopqrstuvwxyz
1234567890 $

10 POINT OPTIMA
ABCDEFGHIJKLMNOPQRSTUVWXYZ
abcdefghijklmnopqrstuvwxyz
1234567890$?!

10 POINT P. T. BARNUM
ABCDEFGHIJKLMNOPQRSTUVWXYZ&
abcdefghijklmnopqrstuvwxyz
1234567890$.,;?!

10 POINT STYMIE LIGHT
ABCDEFGHIJKLMNOPQRSTUVWXYZ&
abcdefghijklmnopqrstuvwxyz
1234567890$

10 POINT STYMIE BOLD
ABCDEFGHIJKLMNOPQRSTUVWXYZ&
abcdefghijklmnopqrstuvwxyz
1234567890$

10 POINT TIMES ROMAN
ABCDEFGHIJKLMNOPQRSTUVWXYZ
abcdefghijklmnopqrstuvwxyz
1234567890$?!

10 POINT VENUS LIGHT
ABCDEFGHIJKLMNOPQRSTUVWXYZ&
abcdefghijklmnopqrstuvwxyz
1234567890$.,;?!()

10 POINT VENUS LIGHT EXTENDED
ABCDEFGHIJKLMNOPQRSTUVWXYZ
abcdefghijklmnopqrstuvwxyz
1234567890 $

10 POINT VENUS MEDIUM ITALIC
ABCDEFGHIJKLMNOPQRSTUVWXYZ&
abcdefghijklmnopqrstuvwxyz
1234567890$.,;?!( )

COMPLETE SHOWING

A B C D E F G H I J K L M N O P Q R S T U V W X Y Z a b c d e f g h i j k l m n
o p q r s t u v w x y z fi fl ff ffi ffl & $ 1 2 3 4 5 6 7 8 9 0 . , - : ; ! ? * '' ' ( ) [ ]
% ½ ⅓ ⅔ ¼ ¾ ⅕ ⅖ ⅗ ⅛ ⅜ ⅝ ⅞ † ‡ § ¶

	1	10	12	14	16	18	20	22	24	26	28	30	32	34	36	38	40	42
6 Point	3.70	37	44	52	59	67	74	81	89	96	104	112	118	126	133	141	148	155
8 Point	3.20	32	38	45	51	58	64	70	77	83	90	96	102	109	115	122	128	134
10 Point	2.85	29	34	40	46	51	57	63	68	74	80	86	91	97	103	108	114	120
12 Point	2.50	25	30	35	40	45	50	55	60	65	70	75	80	85	90	95	100	105
14 Point	2.30	23	28	32	37	41	46	51	55	60	64	69	74	78	83	87	92	97

Figure 7-11. Complete showing of Garamond in 10 point, with a character-count table for the face in 6 to 14 points, from 1 to 42 picas wide.

Anyone who has used "copy-fitting systems" based on word count knows from experience that such methods are both inaccurate and misleading. We recommend and use a more positive method based on character count. The character count of typewritten manuscript is easily determined, and with the help of the copy-fitting tables at the bottom of each page showing machine-set composition it is equally simple to determine the space that will be occupied after setting in type.

Figure 7-12. This figure shows how copy fitting is done, using a sample paragraph typed on an elite typewriter. Draw a light vertical line down the right edge of the copy at a point that averages out long and short lines. In this example the average line is 49 characters long. Publications, advertising agencies, and others producing a volume of typed copy for printers, use layout page forms with copy-fitting lines preprinted. An example of such forms is found in Chapter 9.

wants to use 12-point Garamond, leaded 2, and set 22 picas wide. Referring again to the table in Figure 7-11, the appropriate characters-per-line figure is 55. To determine length, divide 55 into 11,000; the answer is 200 lines of type. This figure translates into 233.33 picas (38.88 inches). (Don't forget to multiply 200 lines by 14 points—12-point type plus 2-point leading. The answer, 2,800 points, is divided by 12 points to get the answer into picas and 72 points to come up with the inch equivalent.)

REVERSE COPY FITTING

It is possible, of course, to begin with the desired dimensions of a copy block and work backward to find out how much copy is required to fill the predetermined block.

Let's assume the designer wants a block of text 18 picas wide by 36 picas deep. Further, he wants to use 10-point Garamond, leaded 1 point. From the character-count table, 10-point Garamond set 18 picas wide requires 51 characters per typewritten line. Set up the typewriter space guide accordingly. The 36 pica depth is 432 points. Divide by 11 (10-point type leaded 1) to get 39.2 lines. Thus, if you write to fill a space 51 characters wide by 40 lines long, the typewritten copy should fill an 18 x 36 pica copy block in the brochure.

The accuracy of this method is quite high, although certain variables should be taken into account. Copy containing a number of short paragraphs and lines will affect the accuracy, as will excessive tabular material, which is often set line for line. It is advisable to calculate these lines separately when using this method of copy fitting.

INTERNATIONAL TYPOGRAPHIC COMPOSITION ASSOCIATION COPY-FITTING SYSTEM

The second copy-fitting technique uses a system developed by the International Typographic Composition Association (ITCA). This system accommodates new typefaces as they are introduced, as well as photocomposition type styles.

In 1964 the ITCA sponsored a copy-fitting project. The initial step was to make a comprehensive study of the frequency of use of the letters of the alphabet. This analysis of a wide variety of printed material found that in every 600-character sampling the following frequency of letter usage occurred:

e—60	r—30	m—12	k—4
t—42	h—25	w—11	j—2
a—40	d—21	y—11	q—2
i—38	l—21	p—10	x—2
o—34	u—19	b— 8	z—1
n—34	c—16	g— 8	
s—34	f—12	v— 6	

spaces and punctuation—97

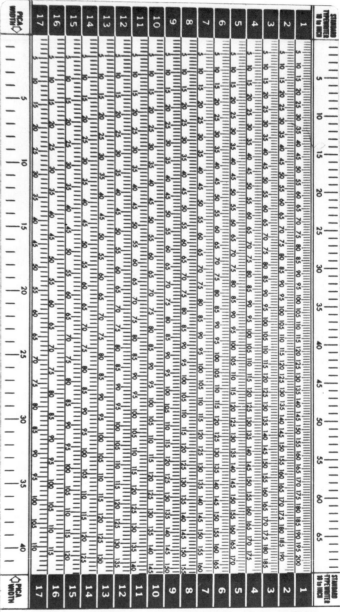

Figure 7-13. Front *(a)* and back *(b)* faces of the ITCA Copy-Fitting Gauge, shown slightly reduced.

(a)

ITCA COPY-FITTING GAUGE

For use with the official copy-fitting system of the International Typographic Composition Association

❶ Select the type face and size to be fitted. ❷ Find its ITCA number in the Manual ❸ Locate that number on this gauge (in reverse at both ends of the scale) ❹ With a pica ruler, measure along the applicable scale to the desired pica width. Here you will see the average number of characters that will fill one line of type. ❺ Read the ITCA Copy-Fitting Manual for more information.

(b)

These findings became the basis of a computer program that eventually enabled ITCA to compile character-count data for some 15,000 typefaces and sizes listed in their *Copy-Fitting Manual*.

The complete ITCA system consists of the *Manual* (or the ITCA numbers from the *Manual* carried in a printer's type specimen catalog) and the ITCA Copy-Fitting Gauge, as shown in Figure 7-13. The *Copy-Fitting Manual*, with the sturdy plastic gauge included in a back pocket, is available from Baumwell Graphics, 461 Eighth Avenue, New York, N.Y. 10001, for around $8.

At the top of the gauge is a typewriter character counter. Standard (pica) characters (10 to an inch) are on the front and elite characters (12 to an inch) are on the reverse side. Use the gauge to measure several lines of typed copy, average the count, and multiply by the number of lines in the manuscript.

In the ITCA *Manual*, or from the printer's type specimen book, find the ITCA number for the face and point size wanted. American Type Founders Alternate Gothic No. 3, for example, appears in the *Manual* as:

Alternate Gothic No. 3

Pt. size	ITCA no.
6	4
8	8
10	16
12	20
14	26
18	29
24	33

MORE COPY-FITTING EXAMPLES

We will use 10-point Alternate Gothic No. 3 to illustrate the ITCA system. On the front of the Copy-Fitting Gauge (see Figure 7-13) find the ITCA number 16 in the reverse figures at either end of the gauge. The horizontal scale for number 16 shows how many characters in the selected type will fill one line in any measure up to 42 picas (pica width is the bottom line on the gauge). In our example, typed copy averaging 60 characters in line length will set 21 picas wide in Alternate Gothic No. 3.

To determine how to fill a given area, using the ITCA system:

1.   Count the number of manuscript characters in the copy, using the copy-fitting gauge as described above. Say the character count is 600.

2.   Refer to the ITCA number and then to the gauge to find the number of type characters of the selected typeface and size that will fit into the chosen line length of 21 picas. Note that 10-point Alternate Gothic No. 3, 21 picas wide, requires 60 characters per line.

3.   Divide the findings from (2) above into the findings from (1) ($^{600}\!/_{60}$) to

find the number of type lines the manuscript will make—in our example it will be ten lines.

4. Multiply the number of type lines by the depth (point size) of each line, leading included, to determine the total depth of the printed copy. We are using 10-point type, unleaded, so ten lines will be 100 points, or 16.67 picas.

SOLVING COPY-FITTING PROBLEMS

The layout has been made, copy has been written, and now the copy must be fitted to the blocks in the layout. The typeface, Bodoni, has been selected, but not the size or the amount of leading.

The copy contains 1,800 characters and must fit into a layout area 20 picas wide by 28 picas (336 points) deep. The ITCA *Manual* listing for Monotype Bodoni No. 175 appears as follows:

Monotype Bodoni No. 175

Pt. size	ITCA no.
5	3
6	8
7	11
8	13
9	15
10	18
11	21
12	24
14	28
18	32

Try 11-point Bodoni to see if it will fit. The appropriate ITCA number is 21. On the gauge find 20 picas on character-count scale 21. (See Figure 7-14.)

The scale tells us that 49 characters will fill a 20-pica line. Dividing 49 into the total characters—1,800—shows that the copy will make thirty-seven typeset lines. That many lines of Bodoni 11-point type, unleaded, will fill an area 34 picas deep, or 6 picas longer than the allotted space allows.

Now, try a smaller type size—in this case 9-point Bodoni (ITCA number 15) is the best solution. According to the gauge, 59 characters will fill each 20-pica line. Dividing the 1,800-character total by 59 shows the manuscript will take thirty lines of type and allow for 2-point leading between lines.

Solutions to other copy-fitting problems are illustrated in the *Copy-Fitting Manual*.

CALIFORNIA JOB CASE

Type for hand composition is kept in California job cases, which were

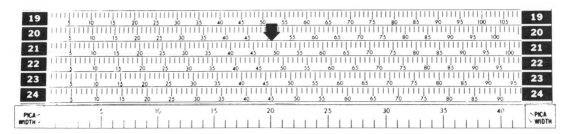

(a)

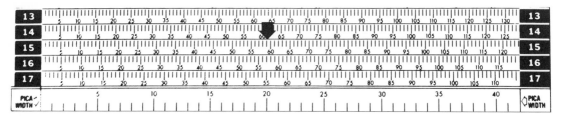

(b)

Figure 7-14. Using the ITCA Copy-Fitting Gauge (scales 21 and 15) to solve the copy-fitting problems in the text.

first used to move type to the West during the California gold rush. The left two-thirds of the case (see Figure 7-15) has sections for lowercase letters, figures, punctuation marks, some ligatures, and em spaces. The right side holds capital letters, the dollar sign, ampersand, and the remainder of the ligatures.

The lowercase letters were originally arranged in the case according to frequency of use. Uppercase letters are in alphabetical order, except for J and U.

California job cases are almost a curiosity in modern printing plants, but appear to have been taken over by nostalgia buffs. An advertisement in the *Wall Street Journal* in mid-1974 called the cases "authentic Americana" and suggested converting them into "unique cocktail tables, seed pictures, storage trays, and picture frames. These many compartmented drawers are ideal for memorabilia display in den, nursery, workshop, home, or business. Add legs and a glass top and you have an eye-catching conversation piece." The price for cases "as-is," $12.95; cleaned and finished, $29.50.

PHOTO COMPOSITION

One reason the California job case has become a rarity is the trend in typesetting and printing plants to replace hot type and hand composition with phototypesetting equipment. The newest (third generation) photo-typesetter is the extremely fast, all-electronic cathode ray tube (CRT) equipment. Type characters are generated on a screen much as a television picture is formed.

The Linotron 1010 is a CRT phototypesetting system capable of electronically composing and photographing an entire 8½ x 10 inch page at a time, at speeds of up to 10,000 characters per second.

A refinement of the 1010, the Linotron Lexical Graphical Composing Printer (LGCP), composes complete book-size pages in combinations of type, line art, halftones, and continuous tone art. Processing such a page requires up to ten seconds.

This brief discussion of the status and impact of alphanumeric phototypesetters is not to discourage the serious student of typography and printing production. Any summary at this stage must of necessity be tentative.

TYPOGRAPHY CHECKLIST

1. Is the type face too small for legibility?
2. Is the text line short enough for reading ease? Remember the two-alphabet maximum for line lengths.
3. Is the typeface so large as to be distracting to the reader?

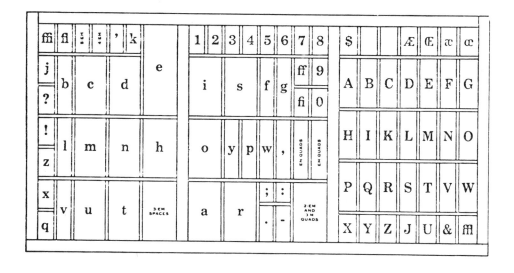

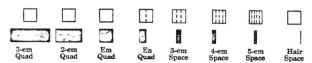

Figure 7-15. California job case, with em and en quads and em spaces shown below the job case.

4. Is sufficient leading between lines called for?
    a. Is the leading consistent in the proof?
5. Is the typeface for body text a serif or sans serif face?
    a. If sans serif, why?
6. Are all type reverses legible and the background contrasty enough for good readibility?
7. Are any type blocks to be set in all capitals?
    a. If so, why?
8. If you are overprinting type on color, is the contrast between the type and background colors right?
9. Are heads and subheads properly letterspaced?
10. Was the proof carefully read to pick up broken letters; transposed letters, words, or lines; and all typos?

COPY PREPARATION CHECKLIST

Preparing copy for the typographer

1. Type copy double-spaced on one side of 8½ x 11 sheets.
2. Keep typed lines 4 to 5 inches wide. Use of specially prepared copy sheets can be of assistance in copy fitting. Such sheets are marked off by light vertical lines into different widths, corresponding to various column widths. A wide left column is left blank for the typographer's production marks; a wide right-hand column is for the author's typesetting instructions.
3. Number all sheets consecutively. Type "MORE" at the bottom of each page but the last. Type "END" when copy is completed.
4. Prepare a carbon copy for yourself, as insurance against loss of the original—which goes to the typesetter.
5. Type inserts for already prepared copy on strips of paper and paste them on the page of copy beneath the place where they are to be inserted; use rubber cement. Paste down one edge only so the strip can be folded back. Key all inserts clearly with key letters or numbers on both the insert and the copy. Inserts may also be typed on a full-sized sheet of paper and added as an "A" page. On the original copy show where the insertion goes by noting "Insert A (page number)." On the insert print boldly, "This is Insert A."
6. Type statistical tables and similar material on separate sheets. Locate the position of this matter in the prepared copy with key letters or numbers.
7. Check copy carefully for uniform style, punctuation, spelling, capitalization, and accuracy of facts. Corrections made in the manuscript are much less costly than author's alterations in type.
8. If clippings, book pages, or other previously printed matter are to serve as copy, paste them on standard 8½ x 11 sheets.

Underlining copy for the typographer

1. One line under copy: set in *italics*.
2. Two lines under copy: set in SMALL CAPITAL letters.

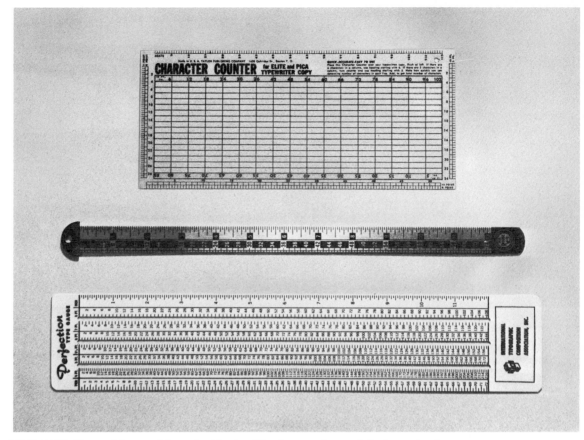

Figure 7-16. Three of the most important tools of the typographer and designer: top to bottom, character counter, line gauge, and type gauge.

3. Three lines under copy: use CAPITAL letters.
4. Four lines under copy: use *ITALIC CAPITAL* letters.
5. One wavy line under copy: use **bold face** type.

Marking position of the copy for the typographer

1. *Flush left, ragged right:* all lines are aligned on the left side of the column but not on the right. Sometimes known as "ragged right."
2. *Flush right, ragged left:* all lines align on the right side of the column but not on the left. (Seldom used; considered difficult to read.)
3. *Flush left and right:* all lines even on both sides.
4. *Centered:* copy of irregular line lengths centered in the column with equal left and right margins for each line. Usually increases composition costs; often loses legibility.
5. *Indented:* spaced in from margins but not necessarily centered.

The four most popular types of indentions are hanging indention, half-diamond indention, squared indention, and diagonal indention.

Specifications for the typesetter

1. *Width*. Length of line to be set, in picas.
2. *Size*. Type size and whether to be set solid or leaded. If the latter, how much leading, in points. Example—10-point type on 12-point slug (or with 2 points of leading) is shown $^{10}\!/_{12}$.
3. *Name and number of typeface*. From type books.
4. *Weight*. Light, medium, bold, or extra bold.
5. *Style*. Roman, italic, wide (extended), condensed, or extra condensed.

TOOLS OF THE TRADE

In addition to character-count tables and type specimen catalogs, there are several other tools to assist designers, typesetters, and printers in their craft. As illustrated in Figure 7-16, these include the type gauge, line gauge, and character counters.

REFERENCES

[1]John F. J. Cabibi, *Copy Preparation for Printing*, McGraw-Hill Book Company, New York, 1973, p. 6.
[2]*How to Select Type Faces*, Intertype Company, New York, undated, unpaginated.
[3]John F. J. Cabibi, *Copy Preparation for Printing*, McGraw-Hill Book Company, New York, 1973, p. 91.
[4]Jan V. White, *Editing by Design*, R. R. Bowker Company, New York, 1974, p. 86.

Chapter 8
THE FIRST LAYOUT

THIS CHAPTER WILL DRAW UPON certain of the material discussed in Chapters 5, 6, and 7, as we begin translating theory into practice. At some point, if the production schedule outlined in Chapter 5 is to be met, the brochure design team must move resolutely from the planning and research stages into the first, or trial, layout stage. Writing, an equally important early stage of brochure production, will be covered in Chapter 9. As a rule, writing should proceed concurrently with the research and layout stages.

ART AND COPY PREPARATION

The two basic steps in art and copy preparation of a printed piece are the following:

1. Layout and design
2. Preparation and assembly of all elements for reproduction by the printer

"Art and copy," to printers, means all materials—type, diagrams, drawings, color negatives, and the like—supplied to them for reproduction.

In Chapter 6 we listed a four-step layout procedure:

- Thumbnail sketches
- Roughs
- Comprehensives
- Mechanicals

Technically, the first two steps may be combined under the term "rough"; the second two steps are usually referred to as working, or finished, layouts.

Thumbnail layouts, of which, in the developmental phases, up to several dozen may be sketched for a single two-page spread, are primarily for exploring arrangements of the various elements on a page and in a spread in the quickest possible manner.

As the layout work progresses to the first full-size roughs, crystallization of the designer's ideas begins to take place. Some guidelines on type sizes and illustration sizes and formats should begin to emerge from the early full-scale roughs.

Comprehensive layouts are made after satisfactory rough layouts have been completed and approved. The comprehensive usually is quite detailed, closely resembling the finished job as the designer envisions it. Figure 8-1 shows a headline segment of a comprehensive.

Figure 8-1. Headline segment of a comprehensive layout.

DUMMY PREPARATION

At some point a blank-paper, full-size dummy of the brochure is made up. If a printer has been selected by this time, he or she will usually furnish one or more blank-page dummies from the stock to be used for the finished brochure—or at least one of the stocks under serious consideration. It sometimes is helpful to transfer the comprehensive layouts to the pages of the dummy, as yet another check on how the finished product will look. The dummy in this form, once approved, will be of aid in all following production stages—and it is especially valuable for the typesetter and the printer.

One designer describes the use and importance of the dummy in this way:

> For a printed piece of work involving a number of pages, a dummy is compulsory. To prepare a dummy, secure a number of pieces of the stock to be used. Cut these to a size that, after folding once, will be the untrimmed page size of the booklet. Prepare a piece of cover stock of the same size (after folding). [But note that if the brochure is to be a "self-cover"—the inside pages and the cover all of the same stock weight, finish, and color—then references to separate cover stock are not applicable.]

Assemble the cover and sufficient folded sheets, and staple them once through the fold, near the top. Number the pages in the lower outside corners consecutively, beginning with "1" on the first right-hand page.

Cut a number of pieces of stock, each the final untrimmed page size of the booklet. These page-size pieces will serve as layout sheets for the pages of the booklet. (Page proofs may be used, instead.) When laid out, these single pages will be attached to the dummy pages—the outside cover will be clipped to the outside cover of the dummy; the title page clipped to page 1, if it's desired there; and remaining pages clipped where desired in the dummy. On each single page, indicate the actual page number it will carry when printed.

Each page should be laid out completely for the job. Ruled lines should be drawn to indicate the space to be occupied by the body type. Display type, ornaments and illustrations should be indicated in their actual size, and in the exact position. Dimensions must be given for the width and depth of the printed page and the location of the page numbers and running heads. If the page has more than one column, the width of the columns and the spacing between columns must be specified.

Type faces, sizes and length of line must be indicated.

Trim lines should be drawn on the cover (and pages) to indicate the appearance after trimming head, foot and outside edge of the printed and folded booklet.

Indicate all margins to show how much white space will remain at the head, gutter (next to the fold), foot, and fore-edge.

In short, the dummy must be made to look as much like the finished work as possible. Yet, while still in the planning stage, individual pages may be shifted about, added, or eliminated without much trouble. Once the dummy is approved, the pages can be made up and production can start.[1]

PREPRINTED PLANNING SHEETS

There are at least two kinds of preprinted forms that make brochure planning and production a simpler, more organized operation. One was mentioned in the copy preparation checklist in Chapter 7—copy sheets for text material, marked off by light vertical lines into predetermined column widths. (See Figure 8-2.)

The second form is for thumbnail sketches; a small-scale version of the two-page spread in the full-size layout. Down the left side of the page are miniature pages for spreads, showing column widths, margins, or other grid overlays for the designer. On the right side is room for notes on each spread. As an idea is discarded during planning, an "x" is drawn through the thumbnail sketch and its notes, as at the bottom of Figure 8-3.

Some designers use a third preprinted form, which shows the entire brochure, in spreads, on a single sheet. A form with twenty miniature spreads should accommodate most brochures. (See Figure 8-4.) Jan White, in *Editing by Design*, cautions that this sheet is for broad planning, space allocation, organizing—but *not* for designing the magazine or brochure.

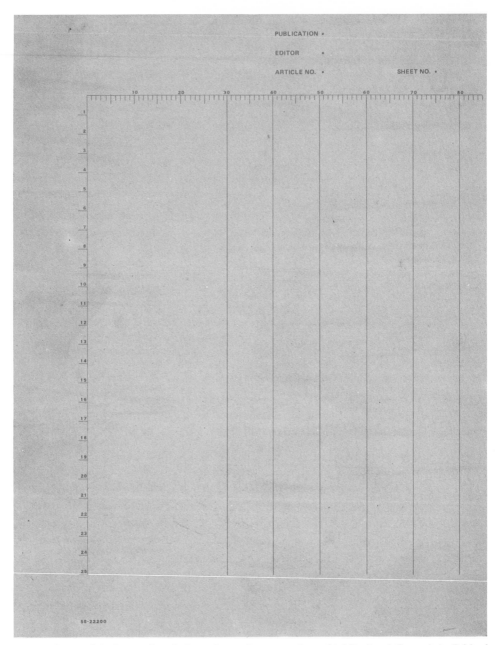

Figure 8-2. A preprinted sheet for typing copy, from *Architectural Record*. Individual double-spaced lines are numbered down the left side of the page; widths of typed columns are marked off at ten-space intervals across the top of the page. (Courtesy of *Architectural Record*)

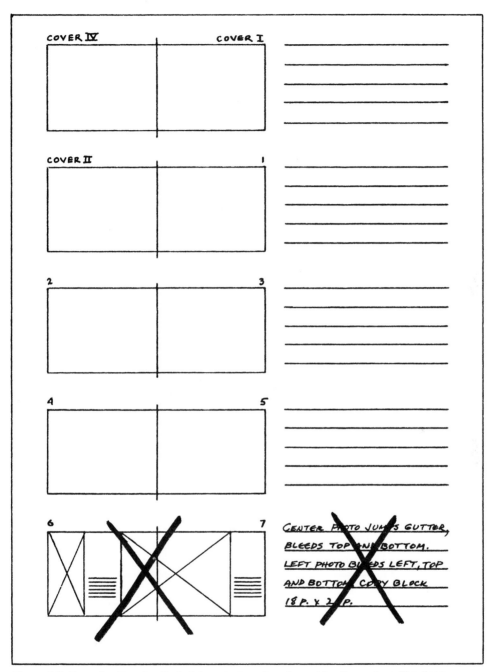

Figure 8-3. Form for thumbnail sketches designed and used by the author. The lines to the right are for brief notes on each spread.

Figure 8-4. *Architectural Record's* **layout sheet—a preprinted thumbnail sketch form. Such sheets should be used primarily for broad planning and space allocation. They are too small to accommodate any real design.** (Courtesy of *Architectural Record*)

FORMAT AND LAYOUT

The selection, assembly, and placement of the internal elements of a brochure are normally a matter of fairly personal choice, but there are a few tested solutions to keep in mind.

It has become traditional to devote the first page or two to a statement of the firm's (or the principal's) objectives and design philosophy. This may or may not be accompanied by original or purloined definitions of architecture and engineering. If kept reasonably brief, this introductory section should not intrude too much on the basic purpose of the brochure—which is to provide information about completed projects which may relate to the potential client's interests and requirements.

Some firms opt to produce a project catalog, which it is presumed will overwhelm the reader by the sheer volume of project photographs and descriptions. Other offices—the majority, actually—adopt a sampling approach, wherein one project is used to represent many others of similar type, size, cost, location, and the like. Larger firms are practically forced to follow the latter course; otherwise their completed brochures would be as large as the Manhattan telephone directory.

The projects selected to be shown should demonstrate several desirable attributes, such as the ability to solve difficult problems, to meet deadlines, to work with a variety of consultants, and to work within established budgets. Obviously, the projects should convey a feeling for the firm's design outlook, aesthetic abilities, and staff accomplishments.

In Chapter 3 we mentioned an AIA study of a large number of architects' brochures. One of the survey findings was a "typical" brochure arrangement:

Philosophy
Types of service
Consultants
Personnel
Project list
Project descriptions (sampling)
Reprints

In the American Consulting Engineers Council's (ACEC's) "The Brochure on Brochures," typical segments of an engineering brochure are given as:

Table of contents
Letter from the president
Introduction
History of the firm
Principals/officers
Key personnel
Services
Facilities
Projects
Clients

The ACEC suggests that the first segment, a table of contents, is seldom necessary and can even be a hindrance to partial or full customization of a brochure. Nor is the president's letter particularly recommended—a personal letter of transmittal is preferable in most cases. The ACEC also recommends incorporating the history segment into the introduction. With these three reservations or modifications met, the ACEC brochure contents essentially match up with the AIA brochure survey results.

INTRODUCTIONS

Even though an interested prospect probably will not be turned off completely by a boring, irrelevant, repetitive, and wordy introduction to a brochure, there is little point in taking the chance. A prospect may be inclined to shrug off tendentious writing and faulty syntax on the premise that a design professional really is not expected to be a trained writer. Why not surprise the potential client with something approaching good— even outstanding—composition?

A good introduction should be low key (soft sell) and interesting, and as brief as possible. Remember, its main purpose is to get the prospect's attention and lead on into the remainder of the brochure. An example of a low key approach to getting a client in the proper frame of mind is found in the introduction to the brochure of the Toledo architectural firm Angel & Mull & Associates. Titled "A Moment, Please, For Reflection," the text reads:

> In today's business world, where time measurements are computed in infinitesimal fractions of a second, it may seem grossly inexact and somewhat imperious to ask for a "moment" for reflection. However, we believe this to be important—especially when one has an important decision to make.
>
> The selection of an architect is one of the most important of all the decisions to be made on any building project. If your architect is in consonance with your primary objectives, your path will be easier and more pleasant. It is unreasonable to expect that good architecture can result from an architect-client relationship which is not built on a firm community of opinion.
>
> The question arises: What is good architecture? It is certainly more than a well-functioning building, constructed within the budget; although these are very important considerations.
>
> Good architecture is a combination of all the available human and material resources at one's disposal to produce a structure which serves its utilitarian needs well and makes life richer for having been created. Good architecture is created for people, and especially for the people who dwell within.
>
> It was said long ago that "Well-building hath three virtues: Firmness, Commodity and Delight." We believe this to be just as true today. One could say that a definition of what is not good architecture is that which possesses only one or two of these three essentials.
>
> Assuming that the client wants to create good architecture, how does he select an architect who will be certain to produce this result? This is difficult to answer, but certainly the more important characteristics of that architect would emerge from a personal appraisal, an examination of his qualifications, and some contact with his past clients. It must be recognized that there are many competent architects. It is the client's obligation to find the architect best suited for the specific project.

One word regarding responsibility: It should be firmly kept in mind that a building influences many people and the adjacent community for many years, and the client therefore bears a heavy responsibility to produce the best architecture possible.

Another introduction I like is in the brochure of the New Jersey consulting engineering firm of Kammerer, Symes & Associates, Inc.

What is a
Consulting
Engineering Firm?
It is a firm that offers knowledge and skill in engineering to its clients.

However, when most people think of an engineer, they picture a man with a thousand mathematical equations in his head, standing over a set of engineering drawings with a slide rule in one hand and a pencil in the other.

True, this is a part of engineering, but it is only a small part. Engineering, and the services of a consulting engineering firm, is much more than this.

Engineering is an art.

It is an art just as truly as the art of a painter, a writer or any other creative professional.

True engineering creates from nature, utilizing and improving upon it. It is the art of planning for the use of land and air, and the use and control of water.

It is the art of directing great sources of power in nature for the benefit and convenience of man, without disturbing the delicate ecological balance.

Finally, it is the art of experience with the practical needs of life tempered by common sense in the application of scientific knowledge.

Just as the artist relies upon his creative process, the engineer depends upon his engineering cycle.

This cycle includes:

- *Conception*—Conceiving and developing new ideas.
- *Experimentation*—Trying these ideas out to determine if they are workable.
- *Design*—Development of a model or plan based upon the results of the experimentation.
- *Building*—Construction of one or more of the items proposed by the design.
- *Testing*—Close scrutiny of what has been built to see if it conforms to the highest standards.
- *Improvement*—Examining test results for the possibility of any improvements.

The services of a consulting engineering firm must incorporate all of these. Kammerer, Symes & Associates offers its clients the art of engineering, along with extensive professional experience.

The Boston-based firm of Shepley Bulfinch Richardson and Abbott traces its lineage directly back to the New York City office that Henry Hobson Richardson established in 1866. Here is the introduction to Shepley Bulfinch Richardson and Abbott's brochure—a classic of understatement:

Shepley Bulfinch Richardson and Abbott, one of the nation's few long established practices, offers a complete range of expert architectural services to its clients. The Firm is proficient at master planning, surveys and feasibility studies.

Our offices in downtown Boston, located on six floors of a landmark building designed by us in 1889, are modern and well-equipped. As well as our own computer and a time-shared terminal to a more complex unit, we have ample drafting studios, a large model shop, facilities for graphic design and macro-photography, projection and meeting rooms, in addition to a fully staffed Interior Design Department.

Most important, we are proud to have already offered more than a century of uninterrupted service. Our longevity attests to our reliability and to the confidence of our many continuing clients. From such early works as Boston's Trinity Church to the present, our unique traditions have guaranteed, and will continue to guarantee, a quality of Architecture unbroken by the passing of generations.

An example of a short, sweet historical update appeared in the brochure of the Ballinger Company:

The Ballinger Company is one of the oldest architectural and engineering partnerships in continuous practice in the United States. Since its founding in 1878, the firm has designed more than 3,250 buildings of all sizes and types. Industrial and commercial firms, government agencies, and others have invested more than one and one-quarter billion dollars in those buildings.

Short and sweet; brief and simple. All text in a brochure should be written with those concerns foremost.

The preceding examples are not cited as the only or even necessarily the best ways of getting a reader into the brochure, but the approach seems to work for these firms.

SPACE PLANNING AND ALLOCATION

It may seem a little strange to consider that space allocation is at least as important a planning function in brochure design as it is in designing a building. A vital early step in preparing the first layout is to set down on paper the order of the segments or sections of the brochure and the number of pages to be allocated to each. Space allocation normally precedes thumbnail sketches.

A typical guide to segment ordering and page allocation might look like this. (Remember, a bound brochure, or any printed publication, for that matter, normally is laid out in multiples of eight pages, plus the cover. A brochure has four covers: Cover I, outside front; Cover II, inside front; Cover III, inside back; and Cover IV, outside back.)

- Cover I—Firm name, address, and logo
- Cover II—Photo of offices (exterior)
- Page 1—Introduction, brief history
- Page 2—Partners (informal photos) and biographies
- Page 3—Remainder of principals, same as page 2
- Page 4—Other key personnel; photos and biographies
- Page 5—Organization chart for firm

- Page 6—Listing of services
- Page 7—Photo page, illustrating services and specialities
- Pages 8 through 17—Photos and descriptions of representative projects to more fully illustrate scope of services
- Page 18—Photo of partners in a client meeting
- Page 19—List of clients by project types
- Pages 20 and 21—Representative listing of projects
- Page 22—Photo of a major project
- Page 23—List of awards won by firm
- Page 24—Information on branch offices and on how to get additional information on firm
- Cover III—Pocket for reprints and list of current projects
- Cover IV—Aerial photo of large development project (residential, shopping center, educational complex, or the like; inset of firm name and full address.

PHOTO INVENTORY

While space and page allocation may be done "on spec," with photo subjects noted in general or even in fairly specific terms, it makes more sense to know exactly what photos are available (or are apt to become available) before the planning gets very far along.

If yours is a relatively new firm, or a small firm that is getting its first real brochure together, your choice of pictures is likely to be rather limited. If the principals had major responsibility for projects in other firms, at the job captain level or above, then it may be possible to obtain project photos from previous employers to use in the new brochure. Be certain that the captions for all such photos make it clear that this is work done while in another office.

O'Dell/Hewlett and Luckenbach, of Birmingham, Michigan, successfully solved the problem of getting out a transitional brochure for a new firm in a novel manner. The brochure basically consists of pages of simulated contact prints of 35-mm film strips. The positioning of the strip prints on the pages is the basic graphic treatment. (See Figure 8-5.)

The small photos purposely do not give much in the way of detail, but their number and the arrangement impart a feeling of considerable activity.

Brochure designers should familiarize themselves with the on-hand inventory of photographs. In a well-organized firm, pictures of all completed work should be in clearly marked files. A review of the slide files may turn up some views not in the black-and-white photo file. If it is not possible for a photographer to reshoot and duplicate the 35-mm slide pictures on regular black-and-white film, whether because of time, distance, cost, or other factors, then it may be necessary to make enlargements from the slides. Get this process under way early, since it involves an internegative and some color slides will not give acceptable black-and-white enlargements. In Chapter 10 we will get into much more detail about all types of brochure illustrations, including photographs.

Figure 8-5. The cover and representative pages from a brochure used by O'Dell/Hewlett & Luckenbach of Birmingham, Mich. Intended as a stopgap publication, when the firm was new, the many small photographs impart a feeling of activity and production.

THEME DEVELOPMENT

There were several references in Chapter 5 to the importance of developing a central theme for a brochure, both to unify sometimes unrelated material and art, and to impart additional reader interest. It is not always possible (or even desirable) to attempt to work the design of a brochure around a central message, but where it can be brought off in a logical manner results are usually above average. Some designers strive for a special theme effect wherein the headlines alone tell a story. In such cases, the body copy must serve as a reinforcer to the theme established in the headlines.

Figure 8-6. (Left) Cover and representative pages from the Free Europe, Inc., annual report. The simulated teletype tape on the cover, which reads "Toward A New Europe," is repeated in smaller scale throughout the report as a graphic theme. (Below) The same general idea showed up almost eight years later on the cover of a Department of Defense publication about automated data personnel management in the military. Again, the punched tape was repeated on inside pages.

Figure 8-6 shows the cover and inside pages of a twenty-four-page (plus cover) annual report for Free Europe, Inc., that I produced some years ago. The cover design, which is explained on page one of the report, is a five times enlargement of a piece of teletype tape, machine-punched to read "Toward a New Europe," the report's theme. Repetition of the punched tape on each spread carried the theme graphically through the report. While this example has no direct relationship to a brochure for a design professional, it does illustrate the application of a central theme, in words and/or graphics.

Another method of unifying a brochure by graphics is to use a full-page photograph on Cover II or page 1, or both, and then repeat an enlarged detail from that photograph in approximately the same position on each spread, à la the punched-teletype tape symbol.

TYPES OF SERVICE

Services offered by a firm may be covered in various ways. The Chicago architectural-engineering-planning firm of Holabird & Root includes two sheets in its loose-leaf brochure system under "Basic Organization." The information, in outline form, provides a complete listing of Holabird & Root's services to clients.

CONSULTANTS

The point here is to give the impression of a full team approach to any project. When specialties are not available internally, list them and give names of consultants used in the past few years. Make it clear that the list is only a sampling. It also is advisable to convey the idea that your firm always is open to client suggestions for consultants, that is, that you are not irrevocably tied to any one consultant or group of consultants on the list.

PERSONNEL

Biographies of principals and senior staff people are normal elements of a general capability brochure. When they are written with a little imagination and flair, and kept brief, lean, and relevant, this section can be made into interesting reading; otherwise, it will stimulate little but boredom in the average reader.

The people factor is always important. Staff background, education, experience, honors, and length of experience with the firm may tell a potential client something about the caliber of your people and the continuity of their service—but don't get carried away with biographical material. Candid photographs of principals and staff in natural working conditions usually are far more interesting than posed, studio-type portraits.

PROJECT LIST

Some organization of project listings is desirable. One firm, with heavy experience in the medical and educational fields, breaks down its project list into fourteen classifications:

Master plans and study reports
Teaching facilities
Dormitories
Student commons
Music buildings
Libraries
Museums and art buildings
Physical education facilities
Laboratories
Medical schools
Hospitals and medical research facilities
Projects for official agencies
Office and commercial buildings
Religious buildings

The firm's project listings take up twenty-one pages of the umbrella brochure in a four-brochure system.

Another example of project classification:

Government buildings
Public use and cultural centers
Education buildings
Campus planning and research institutes
Museums
Hospitals
Religious buildings
Theaters
Housing
Hotels
Factories
Urban planning
Commercial buildings

Figure 8-7 shows how projects in such a list could be illustrated with miniature photographs. This method would not add much to the space required for a printed project list.

Still another firm broke its list of projects into the following divisions:

Industry and research buildings
Commercial buildings
Government buildings
Medical and welfare buildings
School, church, and community buildings
City planning/urban design/land planning
Interior design

These classifications could also become the titles for individual booklets within a brochure system.

Keep in mind that unless yours is a new firm and needs to list literally every project that can be claimed, the project list should contain "typical" or "representative" projects. Many firms use "Representative Projects" as the main heading for this section. For psychological reasons, never use the title "Partial Listing of Projects."

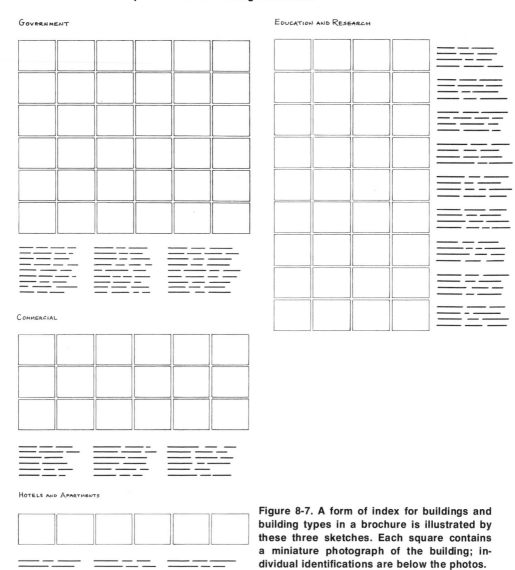

Figure 8-7. A form of index for buildings and building types in a brochure is illustrated by these three sketches. Each square contains a miniature photograph of the building; individual identifications are below the photos.

PROJECT DESCRIPTIONS

Remember that many potential clients are interested in such mundane matters as the address of the project and the name of the client, the cost (total and square foot), dates of construction, and identification of consultants and the general contractor. Partly for this reason, some firms also indicate in the caption for the project photo how many other projects have been done for the same client, and over what time span, as: "Sixth project for the XYZ Company since 1952."

An increasingly popular method of illustrating projects in a brochure is the case history approach. A combination of drawings, photos, and text is used to show the development of a single representative project, from programming through schematics, preliminaries, models, working drawings, specifications—to the finished structure. One or more such case histories may be used to illustrate each building type and specialty.

By now, design professionals should know better than to use renderings or model photos of projects in a brochure if there is any way to avoid it. If, however, there *is* no way to avoid it, and if the project is under construction, inset a progress photo into the rendering. If the building was never built, but is considered important enough by someone to be shown in the brochure, justify its inclusion in the caption or text.

Few things will stir up more heated debates with architectural photographers than the subject of including people in project photographs, but it is a point that must be resolved—seemingly, every time around. My personal philosophy is that many photos are enhanced by the inclusion of a few human-scale figures, but it is not a universally accepted view. Some designers go to an inordinate amount of trouble to carefully place scaled-down human figures in their building models to show scale and traffic patterns. These same designers then demand photographic studies without a person in view. Before the Apollo missions these pictures were sometimes referred to as "moon shots." Now one would have to journey out a few hundred thousand miles farther into space to find an equally untracked planet, devoid of humans.

THE IDEAL BROCHURE

The most common faults to be found in existing brochures have been covered in this and previous chapters. What, in brief, are the qualities of a good brochure? One consultant gives this list:

Brevity

Clarity

Straightforwardness

Plain talk, with short sentences and short words

Text and illustrations meant to give the reader a quick understanding of what your firm can offer

A feeling of restraint, leaving the reader with the impression that there is much more to say, but that you chose to give only a few of the more salient points in highlight form

As for appearance, the same consultant recommends that a brochure express sophistication, elegance, modernity, and simplicity—always taking care to avoid any suggestion of slickness or extravagance.

A final suggestion for putting together the first rough layout—include a brief list of the most important selection criteria, from the client's standpoint, and, just as briefly, cover highlights of the selection process. Whenever brochure designers continually put themselves and their firm in the client's shoes, their brochure should be a winner.

REFERENCE

[1]John E. Cogoli, *Photo-Offset Fundamentals*, McKnight & McKnight Publishing Company, Bloomington, Ill., 1967, p. 31.

Chapter 9
WRITING

SHERIDAN BAKER SAID, "RHETORIC IS the art of persuasion. Logic is the science of reason. Add grammar—the anatomy of discourse—and you have language in its three major constituencies."[1] And he added, "Writing well is a matter of conviction . . . Writing well is not easy. It does not come naturally, though your natural endowments will certainly help."[2]

T. S. Eliot once characterized each foray into creative writing as "a new raid on the inarticulate." Lord Keynes suggested that "words ought to be a little wild, for they are an assault of thoughts upon the unthinking."

READABLE WRITING

Design professionals are well advised to remember that all of us are lay persons as far as most subjects are concerned. As such, we are owed the courtesy of having a technical or difficult subject explained in simple terms at least the first time around.

Simplifying does not mean primerizing. Nor does it mean undignified, uncultured, ungrammatical writing. Schopenhauer advised, "Write the way an architect builds, who first drafts his plans and designs every detail. . . . The first rule of a good style is to have something to say; in fact, this in itself is almost enough." Many writers are guilty of contributing to a particularly vicious circle. Sloppy thinking sires imprecise language, which in turn begets new heights (or depths) of sloppiness in thinking.

DEFINING THE PROBLEM

Seemingly, even those who try to help stem the flood of flabby language encounter problems of their own along the way. The television newsman-analyst-anchorman-drama critic Edwin Newman wrote a book called *Strictly Speaking*, much of which should be considered as assigned outside reading for this chapter. Sad to report, Mr. Newman's real message takes up only about one-third of the book. As one reviewer wrote: "Edwin Newman . . . has written about 90 pages of engagingly surly and erudite prose about the misuse of English. Unfortunately, his book runs to 205 pages."

Overlooking Newman's tendency to engage in writing overkill on such subjects as political cant and his fascination with puns (especially his own) as a form of expression, the book is worth reading for its discussion of how and why language (just as a person) gets tired from overwork. On the basic problems with contemporary writing, and our general use and misuse of language, he says:

> The rules of language cannot be frozen and immutable; they will reflect what is happening in society whether we want them to or not. Moreover, just as libraries, which are storehouses of wisdom, are also storehouses of unwisdom, so will good English, being available to all, be enlisted in evil causes. Still, it remains true that since nothing is more important to a society than the language it uses—there would be no society without it—we would be better off if we spoke and wrote with exactness and grace, and if we preserved, rather than destroyed, the value of our language.[3]

Mr. Newman, a professional newsman who makes a pretty decent living from communicating, also demonstrates in his book that rebellion—even heresy—can pop up in strange places:

> The notion that the trouble between generations is caused by a failure in communication may have some merit, but it makes a large and not necessarily justified assumption: that there should be communication and that if there is, things will be better. I am not so sure. It may be that we have entered a time when some groups would do better to ignore each other than to communicate with each other. Not communicating saves energy; it keeps people from worrying about things they cannot do anything about; and it eliminates an enormous amount of useless talk.[4]

A VARIED PROGNOSIS

Arthur Schlesinger, Jr., the onetime Presidential speechwriter, takes a more pessimistic view of the current state of our language. "A living language can never be stabilized, but a serious language can never cut words altogether adrift from meanings. The alchemy that changes words into their opposites has never had more adept practitioners than it has today. . . . Social fluidity, moral pretension, political and literary demagoguery, corporate and academic bureaucratization and a false concept of democracy are leading us into semantic chaos."

Pulitzer Prize–winning writer Jean Stafford, in a 1970 lecture at Barnard College, commented: "The prognosis for the ailing [English] language is not good. I predict that it will not die in my lifetime, but I fear that it will be assailed by countless cerebral accidents and massive strokes and gross insults to the brain and finally will no longer be able to sit up in bed and take nourishment by mouth."

CURRENT, NATIONAL, AND RESPECTABLE

One routinely misused word (of many) that upsets Ed Newman and other defenders and advocates of good English is "parameter." Current dictionary definitions of the word are in general agreement that its broad meanings are "characteristic," "element," or "factor." A parameter may be a constant or any of a set of physical properties whose values determine characteristics or behavior—but a "boundary" it is not.

Samuel Johnson defined as linguistically correct those words and expressions which are "current, national and respectable." "Hopefully," which once meant "with hope," now is used by all except the purest of purists to mean "it is to be hoped that." At least one writer/editor (but not Edwin Newman) applauds this particular word evolution "because the word was needed."

We all know that under our laws no one has to prove his innocence, but traditional newspaper usage still calls for writing that a person pleads "innocent," rather than the correct "not guilty," to ensure against a printer or compositor accidentally losing the "not."

If your speaking and writing are notable for their euphemisms, redundancies, solecisms, banalities, jargon, and related linguistic anomalies, all is not necessarily lost. Early surgery and remedial therapy are indicated, assuming that a serious desire for a cure exists.

SIFT, SORT, SELL

An experienced writer suggests that all facts for expository writing should be sifted, then sorted, and, finally, sold to the reader.

Sifting means screening out concepts that are beyond or in any way alien to the reader's understanding and experience. If the reader cannot relate, he cannot understand. "Never be more exact than the occasion calls for," Aristotle once said, which does not mean to distort facts while sifting them. Plato advised: "Ask yourself, does my utterance correspond to the facts?"

Sort facts logically and avoid duplication by grouping them under main, related headings. Outline first, then rearrange the order as often as is necessary to present the facts in a form that the reader will understand.

> Remember, your reader doesn't *know* as much about your subject as you do; your reader doesn't *want* to know as much about your subject as you do; and of this you can be sure—your reader won't have your inclination to read your stuff.

Bait the reader's interest with live subheads and eye-catching titles. A good title with a live verb *sells* your readers on reading your writing. . . .

    Short paragraphs, short sentences, short words sell your ideas; they help surround your words with white space. White space is eloquent; ideas flourish in white space.[5]

President Lincoln immortalized 268 words at Gettysburg. All but seventy of them were one-syllable words. At least one historian has observed that Lincoln's commanding position in his party in 1860 was due "not to his policies, nor his course of action, but to his way of saying things. In every revolution, there is a moment when a man who can phrase it can lead it." Think about it.

Disraeli's remark "With words we govern men" apparently is borne out by most studies on management and leadership characteristics. Such research has found successful executives to be extremely open-minded, omnivorous readers, and fluent speakers and writers. In short, language facility is a key factor in leadership.

Several examples of unsifted, unsorted writing, which therefore did not sell, were given in *How to Market Professional Design Services*. The Chinese government spec writer who requested bids on "manually operated biquinary computers" (abacuses), and his U.S. Army counterpart who asked for bids on "aerodynamic personnel decelerators" (parachutes) demonstrate the confusion possibilities that can arise from muddy writing.

Planners have introduced their very own adaptation of English, which might be called "Planish." Planish is peppered with technical names for ordinary activities. Driving through a neighborhood and looking around becomes a "windshield survey in the field." Residents who move from a city are "gross out-migrants." Presumably, those who move in to take the place of GOMs are "gross in-migrants."

OSCARS FOR OBFUSCATION

But the all-time Oscar winner for cramming the most obfuscation and technical jargon into a single paragraph goes to the unknown writer of the following prose, taken from an internal report of the New York City Department of City Planning:

> Acceptance of the postulate framework and its resultant conceptualized statement diagramming the functioning of the education system within the community leads to an analysis of the components of the system as well as of the potential impacts and implications of the consequences of the process. This analysis is both prerequisite and part of the formation of a new methodological approach which is an objective of this work. . . . There are some aspects, whether because of their intrinsic value, or their extrinsic value as among all factors of the system, which must be dealt with in a cursory fashion.[6]

Directions for do-it-yourself Planish, Socialish, and Architectish will be found in the Wordsmanship System and the Architectural Innovator System charts on pages 28–30 of the just-cited *How to Market Professional Design Services*.

SCIENTIFIC GOBBLEDYGOOK

As a profession, scientists seem to be more inclined to obfuscate than the rest of us. *The Journal of Irreproducible Results*, a Chicago-based publication, regularly collects and publishes gems of scientific writing. The *Journal's* editors are particularly quick to pounce on examples of scientific doubletalk or revelations that belabor the obvious. A few offerings:

- "Most people who have been shot realize what has occurred"—from the *Archives of Dermatology*.
- "The lateral surface, lateral to the anterior border, is anterior, lateral, and also posterior above, for it extends from the anterior to the posterior border of the radial tuberosity, but it is largely lateral below; and the posterior surface, narrow and mostly medial above, expands and is truly posterior below"—from an anatomy textbook.
- "Fifty-four percent of the men and 22 percent of the women were able to move their ears. That the figure is twice as high for men can possibly depend . . . on the fact that men are even in childhood more interested in sports"—from the "Proceedings of the Eighth International Congress on Genetics."
- "The thermal conductivity of wood is affected little by species, except as species differ with respect to factors that influence thermal conductivity"—from the *Wood Handbook*.
- "Development of hydropower in the desert of North Africa awaits only the introduction of water"—from *Nuclear News*.

GREENSPAN CLEARS IT UP

Here is one final example of vivid writing, this one extracted from the Proceedings of the Financial Conference on Inflation, held in September 1974. The speaker was Alan Greenspan, then chief economic advisor to the President.

> If you extrapolate the strains that we now already see as a consequence of what we have for an extended period of time, the institutions—economical, financial, structural—begin to break down because they are essentially constructed or have been developed over the decades in the context of low, single-digit inflation, and it's by no means clear or had not been clear, I should say, how significant this element was until we actually have tested it, and having tested it, we found that it does not respond terribly well.
>
> Clearly, we see—I don't have to go through examples, I'm sure that all of you are most familiar with all of the various problems that each and every institution is having, but that clearly the savings and loans are under extraordinary pressure; insurance companies, banks, business—especially smaller business—were having difficulty getting financing.
>
> The system clearly does not work well under those conditions.

In the likely event that all of the above is not as clear as Mr. Greenspan appears to think it is, columnist James Kilpatrick commented on the passage:

Some years ago, Rudolf Flesch propounded a formula for determining ease in reading. The formula provides a fog index: 85 is easy, 65 is standard, 40 is difficult, and 15 is impenetrable. To judge from this passage from Greenspan, the gentleman scores 13.6.

Now, granted, the subject does not lend itself to baby talk. Flesch's famous fog index has limited application. All the same, the people have a right to expect some reasonable level of clarity in public discussion of the fix we are in.

And for those who would rush to Mr. Greenspan's defense on the basis that these lines are from a speech—probably extemporaneous—and were not really meant to be read, we would point out (1) that sloppy speaking is no more acceptable than sloppy writing, and (2) politicians, especially those in Washington, D.C., are prone to "extend and revise" their remarks as a matter of course. In other words, Greenspan or a member of his staff would have had ample opportunities to clean up the mess before it was printed in transcript form—*if* anyone really cared. As Jim Kilpatrick put it, "the people have a right to expect some reasonable clarity in public discussion" from their elected and appointed officials.

THE AIRMAN WAY

Airman is the official magazine of the U.S. Air Force. Major John T. Correll, a former editor of *Airman*, put together a lengthy guide on writing "Articles the Airman Way," from which the following pertinent excerpts are taken.

Do you honestly believe that Shakespeare wrote in iambic pentameter without making a conscious effort to do so? List your story elements—use an outline.

You should write with three books beside you: a dictionary, a Thesaurus, and *The Elements of Style* [written by William Strunk, Jr., and E. B. White and published by the Macmillan Co.—$1.25 in paperback].

You need the dictionary to check your spelling and to make sure that you are using words correctly. There are few instances in the English language when two words mean exactly the same thing. A motor is not always an engine. There is a difference in a bulwark and a rampart. One contributor wrote about a young lady who, upon hearing good news, was "esthetic." Perhaps so, but the writer meant "ecstatic."

The Thesaurus serves you up a selection of words and phrases that relate in some way to a central concept. It can suggest a sharper, more colorful way to say something.

The Elements of Style, in 78 pages, hits nearly every blunder in construction and expression that a writer is likely to commit. Even if you've read it, you ought to page through every few months. It's that good.

If you wish to write professionally, it is not enough to say *almost* what you mean. You must say it exactly.

Beware of word patterns that occur too often in your writing. If you cannot seem to get through a paragraph without using a dash, then you are relying too much on parenthetic thoughts. In my writing, I tend to begin too many sentences with adverb phrases. I must also be careful not to overuse "but" to begin sentences.

One of the reference works Major Correll counsels writers to keep always in reach—the Thesaurus—may cause as many problems as it resolves, if improperly or unwisely used. David Kinsler, writing in *Modern Office Procedures* (March 1974), covered that situation:

> The greatest danger to a writer, next to strong drink and evil companions, may be *Roget's Thesaurus*. That book ought to carry on its cover a label reading: "WARNING! Use of this book may be dangerous to your writing." Oh how cunningly the thesaurus tempts the writer to select a word that strikes him as vivid or suitable. But brother, the road to hell always beckons the unwary. Unless you look up the word you take a fearsome chance. The word may not mean what you think it means. "Fulsome" is a splendid example of one that doesn't mean anything you'd guess. Also "livid" and plenty of others.
>
> Words out of one's head can be wrong too, but the danger is much greater with words pulled from the thesaurus. One reason is that the ranks of thesaurus addicts swarm with people who search for words, however artificial, to make their work a shade classier than it might be otherwise. These pretenders seldom bother to use the dictionary to assay their new-found treasure. But, you may well ask, if the words in Roget are synonyms they must mean the same thing so why the need to look up meanings? Answer: Because the words in Roget are not synonyms. The point is a little technical, but it is not really difficult. Bear with me.
>
> No language needs two words of identical meaning, but all languages have words that come pretty close in meaning. These words are the true synonyms, and the purpose of a dictionary of synonyms is to discriminate between words that mean almost but not quite the same thing. A careful writer should own the Merriam-Webster *Webster's Dictionary of Synonyms*. Now back to Dr. Peter Mark Roget (1799–1869).
>
> He knew his business, and he said plainly that he was not writing a dictionary of synonyms. Even to call his work a dictionary of synonyms perverts his intent. His object was to produce a compendium of wordlists that would help a floundering writer to put an idea into words or to help him find a word that was eluding him. Next he invented an elaborate guide to lead the seeker—once he doped out how to work the guide—to the list of words that would help him.
>
> So remember, Roget's aim was to help a writer to put ideas into words. Toward this end he packed his lists with words of all sorts, some only vaguely connected with the central idea, some antiquated, some curious, some slang of the day (the 1850's), some learned words. His purpose was useful and legitimate, but every user should see the hazard of assuming that he is selecting from a list of synonyms.[7]

MORE EXPERT ADVICE

Here are seven more tips for faster, better writing, as gathered from professional writers by the newsletter *Chronolog:*

• Writing is actually two separate jobs. Each has its own pace and it can slow things down to try to mix them. The first job is the research and organization of ideas. The second job is putting the words on paper. The second job comes easiest when lots of data have been absorbed and the ideas have been thought out in detail. It pays to use socializing time to talk about the ideas. Once you can say them clearly, you'll be able to write them rapidly.

- When putting words down and you're stuck for a particular term or detail of thought, *don't stop to work it out.* Just type in three dots, or if dictating, just say "blank space." The missing element will usually come to mind the second time around without having to spend time hunting for it.

- Whenever possible, edit the rough draft by reading it aloud. Better yet,

Figure 9-1. Most comic strips are lessons in saying a lot with the fewest words. Mort Walker, in one of his popular *Beetle Bailey* strips, also makes several points about those who go out of their way to obfuscate in written communications. (© King Features Syndicate, 1975)

read it aloud to someone. Ambiguities, redundancies, miswordings are almost always more obvious when vocalized.

- One of the very best techniques of all: ask yourself a question as you write each sentence. Say out loud, or write in parentheses: "Who says?" "What's the proof of that?" "What does that mean?" Just ask the natural questions that pop into your head. These are the questions your writing will raise in the minds of others. Good writing anticipates questions, gives answers. After a little practice, the process will become a subconscious habit, and writing flow will come smoother and faster.

- Whenever making an abstract point, rephrase it afterwards with a concrete example. It's a great clarifier. And if you can't think of any examples, it's a clue that the abstraction may not be valid and may have to be eliminated.

- At some points writing will fizzle out. Where to go next will be unclear. The questioning system mentioned above may get things moving again. Or it may be that there's a trouble spot earlier in the writing. Try rewording the first sentence in the paragraph. Or reword any preceding sentence that deals with the subject you're currently stuck on. That will usually unclog the process.

- Try rereading your writing when fatigued. Watch for the places where your attention fades out. Mark these for later revision or elimination.[8]

WORDS, WORDS, WORDS

English speakers and writers are not plagued by a shortage of available words with which to express any main theme or nuance of thought. The situation is quite the opposite, and we are beset by a flood, rather than a drought, of words. An unabridged English dictionary contains more than 600,000 words, plus some 150,000 more technical terms. That communication *is* possible by using something less than three-tenths of 1 percent of the three-quarters of a million words in an unabridged dictionary is proved on a daily basis by Voice of America (VOA) Special English broadcasts. The VOA's *Special English Word Book*, listing about 2,000 words, is used as a guide by writers for the Special English programs. These include news broadcasts and feature programs such as "Science in the News," "Space and Man," and "People in America."

For the 500 most-used English words, the *Oxford English Dictionary* lists 14,070 separate *meanings*—or an average of twenty-eight meanings per word. One hundred of the most popular proverbs use only 650 words out of the more than 750,000 possibilities; less than one-tenth of 1 percent of the potential.

HOW TO GET IT ACROSS

Earlier in this chapter we suggested that ideas are more easily sold by the use of short paragraphs, short sentences, and short words. Let's now take a more detailed look at how to get across the facts in a brochure.

Unfortunately, there is no known way to cram a meaningful course in expository and creative writing into a few pages. Those readers with an interest in developing and sharpening their writing skills will find that many good books are available on the subject.

Use a sentence to express one idea, or one related range of ideas. When sentences get overly complex, then writing (and reading) becomes difficult. The same goes for complex words. Use the simplest, best-known word and the simplest word form that will get your meaning across.

The best short sentence is a simple declarative sentence containing a subject, verb, and object. Some writers believe more impact is obtained by varying sentence pattern and length with an average of seventeen to nineteen words per sentence.

Mark Twain, in his advice to beginning authors, demonstrated how long sentences can be made easy to read when they are built around one idea or a related range of ideas. "As a rule, write in short sentences. At times you may indulge yourself with a long sentence; but be sure there are no folds in it, no vaguenesses, no parenthetical interruptions of its view as a whole; when you have done with it, it won't be a seaserpent with half of its arches under water; it will be a torchlight procession."

Twain packaged the last fifty-four words into four independent units; really four sentences separated by semicolons. The sentence flows well, is easy to read, and the overall effect is dramatic.

Personal words and personal sentences are also to be desired in most writing. Questions, quotations, exclamations—even incomplete sentences and sentences beginning with a verb—help to personalize writing when used with judgment.

We have all had experience with trying to read sentences that are grammatically correct but cause problems of interpretation. A few examples:

I saw the General Motors Building flying over New York City.
They are designing architects.
Visiting clients can be boring.
They are working students.
He passed the Kennedy Center swimming down the Potomac River.

Such aberrations usually can be made understandable by recasting the word order, but in some cases the only solution is to back away and write a completely different sentence.

WRITING TOOLS

Words and punctuation marks are everyone's basic writing tools. Eight kinds of words, known as parts of speech, are the basis for all writing and speaking. Consider that Aristotle's division of words into parts of speech happened more than twenty-three centuries ago.

If a mental jogging is indicated, all words may be classified under at least one of these eight parts of speech—nouns, pronouns, verbs, adjectives, adverbs, prepositions, conjunctions, and interjections. How a word is used determines its classification.

While there are some rules for the use and placement of punctuation marks, the writer's eye, ear, and common sense often are the best guides. If clarity demands a pause (comma, semicolon, colon, parentheses, or dash) or a stop (period, question mark, or exclamation point) in the thought, insert a punctuation mark.

Paragraphing also is punctuating. Separate thoughts and ideas by proper paragraph packaging. Strive for short paragraphs.

AVOID REDUNDANCIES

English is about one-half redundant. The careful writer will weed out redundant words in editing his copy.

For	Say
very latest	latest
same identical	same
many in number	many
factual information	facts
ask the question	ask
few in number	few
basic fundamentals	fundamentals
necessary requirements	requirements
absolutely complete	complete
for a period of three months	for three months
cooperate together	cooperate
consensus of opinion is	consensus is

HOW MANY DRAFTS?

Few writers achieve perfection in their first drafts. "There is no such thing as good writing," someone once said. "There is only good rewriting."

Since no one writes exactly like anyone else, rules of thumb about how many drafts are necessary, and in what form, are essentially meaningless.

Some authors (not this one) are able to compose on a typewriter. Others must laboriously scrawl out the first effort in pencil. Ernest Hemingway reportedly wrote in pencil while standing at a specially constructed high desk.

At least two preliminary drafts are probably the average, before committing the effort to final typewritten form. Author Rudolf Flesch, of readability formula fame, advises: "Learn to cut. The most common fault of writing is wordiness . . ." Samuel Johnson said it more colorfully: "Read over your compositions, and wherever you meet with a passage which you think is particularly fine, strike it out."

After the final rewrite, read the copy aloud to yourself, to pick up any fine grammatical errors that your eyes may have missed.

When a piece of writing, done for whatever purpose, does not go through the two-way editing process of pruning and polishing, the results can be humorous *and* embarrassing. This was illustrated in a speech by the federal railroad administrator John W. Ingram in a speech to the

Association of Railroad Editors. Discussing some of the thornier problems of America's railroads, Ingram called the group's attention to a classified ad in *Railway Age*.

> On page 100 of that issue [in the classified ad section], there is a help wanted ad taking up one-sixth of the page, which is not cheap. The position this anonymous company is trying to fill is headlined across the top of the box: "Derailment Supervisor." What a title! It's as if United Airlines wanted a "crash coordinator," or Seatrain was looking for a "shipwreck superintendent!" Have we sunk so low in the railroad industry that we advertise for Derailment Supervisors the way we look for civil engineers? And the kicker in this ad is that it goes on to say (quote) "plenty of room for advancement!"

To recapitulate the writing guidelines, first

Plan. Know your readers, your purpose, and your subject. Select, sift, sort, and sell the facts. Then

Write. Tell the message simply, in short words, short sentences, and short paragraphs. Use personal words and sentences. Tie in with readers' interests—help them relate to your subject and your approach. Third,

Edit. Delete deadwood, such as redundancies. Prune unnecessary words and sentences; trim everything but the essentials; polish right up to and including the final rewrite. And, finally,

Check. Is the finished copy readable for average readers, but not obviously written down for any reader? As a general guide, strive for sentences of 17 to 19 words and 150 to 155 syllables per 100 words. Pearl Buck noted that it is easier to criticize than to create. Be your own best critic.

One irony of the English language is the word to describe a person who abhors the use of long words—ultra-antihypersyllabicsesquepedalianist.

QUOTATIONS

Occasionally, one searches for just the right quotation to set the mood or emphasize a point in a speech or brochure. Used sparingly, and with thought, quotations have their place. No one, to my knowledge, has ever published a list of quotations related to the design profession. The following quotes have been compiled over a period of many years, from a variety of sources, and are given here in the hope that readers may find them of use.

> Architecture is an art for all men to learn, because all are concerned with it.
> John Ruskin

> No house should ever be *on* any hill or on anything. It should be *of* the hill, belonging to it, so hill and house could live together each the happier for the other.
> Frank Lloyd Wright

> During the first 6000 years of the world, from the immemorial pagoda of Hindustan to the Cathedral of Cologne, architecture was the great handwrit-

ing of the human race. . . . The human race has had no important idea that was not written in stone.

> Victor Hugo

There is a magic in beautiful buildings which exercises an irresistible influence over the mind of man.

> Benjamin Disraeli

The need for beauty and the creation which embodies it is inseparable from man, and without it man, perhaps, would not want to live in the world. . . . But when the ideal, or tension toward the ideal, vanishes from man's life, man loses his equilibrium. . . . Man in these moments excites in himself alien tastes, unhealthy, sharp, inharmonic, sometimes monstrous ones, losing measure and esthetic feeling for healthy beauty and demanding instead of it exceptions.

> Fyodor Dostoyevsky

For an architect ought not to be and cannot be such a philologian as was Aristarchus, although not illiterate; nor a musician like Aristoxenus, though not absolutely ignorant of music; nor a painter like Appeles, though not unskillful in drawing; nor a sculptor such as was Myron or Polyclitus, though not unacquainted with the plastic art; nor again a physician like Hippocrates, though not ignorant of medicine; nor in the other sciences need he excel in each, though he should not be unskillful in them. For, in the midst of all this great variety of subjects, an individual cannot attain to perfection in each, because it is scarcely in his power to take in and comprehend the general theories of them.

> Vitruvius

That far land we dream about,
Where every man is his own architect.

> Robert Browning

Three things are to be looked to in a building: that it stand on the right spot; that it be securely founded; that it be successfully executed.

> Johann Wolfgang von Goethe

The fate of the architect is the strangest of all. How often he expends his whole soul, his whole heart and passion, to produce buildings into which he himself may never enter.

> Johann Wolfgang von Goethe

Mediocrity has no greater consolation than in the thought that genius is not immortal.

> Johann Wolfgang von Goethe

The artist may be well advised to keep his work to himself till it is completed, because no one can readily help him or advise him with it . . .

> Johann Wolfgang von Goethe

A lawyer without history or literature is a mechanic, a mere working mason; if he possesses some knowledge of these, he may venture to call himself an architect.

> Sir Walter Scott

The art of dancing stands at the source of all the arts that express themselves first in the human person. The art of building, or architecture, is the beginning of all the arts that lie outside the person; and in the end they unite.
Havelock Ellis

In the architectural structure, man's pride, man's triumph over gravitation, man's will to power, assume a visible form. Architecture is a sort of oratory power by means of forms.
Friedrich Wilhelm Nietzche

Since it [architecture] is music in space, as it were a frozen music . . .
Friedrich von Schelling

To mimic in slow structures, stone by stone,
Built in an age, the mad wind's nightwork,
The frolic architecture of the snow.
Ralph Waldo Emerson

Art is a jealous mistress, and, if a man have a genius for painting, poetry, music, architecture, or philosophy, he makes a bad husband, and an ill-provider.
Ralph Waldo Emerson

Architecture, sculpture, painting, music and poetry, may truly be called the efflorescence of civilized life.
Herbert Spencer

A man that has a taste of music, painting, or architecture, is like one that has another sense, when compared with such as have no relish of those arts.
Joseph Addison

The surest test of the civilization of a people—at least, as sure as any—afforded by mechanical art is to be found in their architecture, which presents so noble a field for the display of the grand and the beautiful, and which, at the same time, is so intimately connected with the essential comforts of life.
Herbert H. Prescott

All art is but imitation of nature.
Seneca

Why build these cities glorious
   If man unbuilded goes?
In vain we build the world, unless
   The builder also grows.
Edward Markham

When we mean to build,
We first survey the plot, then draw the model;
And when we see the figure of the house,
Then must we rate the cost of the erection.
William Shakespeare

Which of you, intending to build a tower, sitteth not down first, and counteth the cost, whether he have sufficient to finish it?

Luke 14:9

The hand that rounded Peter's dome,
And groined the aisles of Christian Rome,
Wrought in a sad sincerity;
Himself from God he could not free;
He builded better than he knew;—
The conscious stone to beauty grew.

Ralph Waldo Emerson

Record it for the grandson of your son—
A city is not builded in a day:
Our little town cannot complete her soul
Till countless generations pass away.

Vachel Lindsay

In building, rather believe any man than an Artificer for matter of charges. Should they tell thee all the cost at the first, it would blast a young Builder in the budding.

Thomas Fuller

Light, God's eldest daughter, is a principal beauty in a building.

Thomas Fuller

A man and what he loves and builds have but a day and disappear; nature cares not—and renews the annual round untired. It is the old law, sad but not bitter. Only when man destroys the life and beauty of nature, there is the outrage.

George Macaulay Trevelyan

I have built me a monument more lasting than stone.

Horace

Rome was not built in one day.

John Heywood

He couldn't design a cathedral without it looking like the First Supernatural Bank!

Eugene O'Neill

Sir Christopher Wren
Said, 'I am going to dine with some men.
If anybody calls
Say I am designing St. Paul's.'

Edmund Clerihew Bentley

A building is an act.

Louis Henri Sullivan

REFERENCES

[1]Sheridan Baker, *The Complete Stylist*, © Thomas Y. Crowell Company, New York, 1966, p. 5.

[2]Ibid., p. 9.

[3]From *Strictly Speaking*, © 1974 by Edwin H. Newman, reprinted by permission of the publisher, The Bobbs-Merrill Company, Inc., New York, p. 18.

[4]Ibid., p. 10.

[5]*Writing Words That Work*, USDA, Washington, D.C., 1970, p. 4.

[6]Gerre L. Jones, *How to Market Professional Design Services*, McGraw-Hill Book Company, New York, 1973, p. 28.

[7]David Kinsler, "Ban the Thesaurus?" Reprinted from the March 1974 issue of *Modern Office Procedures*, p. 8. © 1974 by Industrial Publishing Co., Division Pittway Corp.

[8]*Chronolog:* The Time Management Newsletter Guidelines Publications, Orinda, Calif. 94563, January 1975, p. 3.

Chapter 10

ILLUSTRATIONS

IN 1826 A FRENCHMAN, Nicéphore Niépce, made the first known photograph—a grainy representation of his garden at Gras. Today, Americans are taking an average of 17 million pictures *a day*—over 6 billion exposures a year!

The technology has been stretched to both extremes in an effort to satisfy our voracious appetite for a fairly permanent record of what we see. For the unashamed amateur, cameras have become simpler to load and handle. A really bad photograph is rather difficult to make, and to create a deliberate double exposure in many nonprofessional cameras, one must go to a lot of trouble to override the built-in double-exposure prevention devices.

At the same time, the ever-increasing mechanical intricacy of cameras available to the professional or commercial photographer makes them difficult to comprehend. What Disney and the National Geographic Society did for time-lapse photography is reflected in what other, more anonymous scientists did for extreme high-altitude photography for intelligence purposes (the U-2, the SR-71), photographs in and from space, infrared photography, and, as we will see in later pages, 360-degree photography.

THE SPACE PICTURE

A prime example of how far the development of specialized cameras has progressed is the equipment on board Pioneer 11, the 570-pound, $100 million robot spacecraft that photographed the planet Jupiter and is now headed for Saturn. Pioneer 11 reached Jupiter in December 1974 following a 620-million-mile, 607-day journey from Earth.

A type of camera called the Imaging Photopolarimeter (IPP), weighing 9.5 pounds, sent back more than fifty color and black-and-white pictures of Jupiter during the spacecraft's closest approach to the planet. The IPP provides data in a number of areas, using photometry (measurement of light intensity), polarimetry (photometry measurements of the linear polarization of light), and imaging.

A full explanation of the IPP's operation would be far too technical in these pages—particularly since the camera's specialized uses are not really pertinent to architectural photography, nor are they apt to be in the foreseeable future. Briefly, incoming light to the IPP is split by a prism into two separate beams. Each of these beams is further split by being passed through red and blue filters. Channeltron detectors turn the light into electrical impulses, which are telemetered in digital form to receiving stations on Earth. Computer rectification improves the incoming images. Black-and-white pictures require an average of three days rectification; color photograph rectification averages four days. The main task of rectification, or image buildup, is to sort out scan paths whose curvature changed steadily with Pioneer 11's movement, and to compensate for smear caused by high-speed rotation of the planet and the motion of the spacecraft.

LASER EVOLUTION

Lasers, which have been called "solutions looking for problems," are playing an increasingly important role in the graphics industry. The recent applications of lasers are more properly described as "evolutionary," rather than "revolutionary," since they are primarily based on existing technologies in laser, facsimile, microfilm, and printing.

The Associated Press has introduced Laserphoto to improve its photo-facsimile system. This involves the application of laser technology to obtain precise control of the scanning beam, resulting in a resolution of 100 lines per inch at the receiving end. A dry-silver paper developed by 3M enhances the speed and quality advantages of Laserphoto by making the transmitted image immediately available in the form of a crisp contrast print, without wet chemicals or other development methods.

In a lengthy survey article on photography in late 1974, *Newsweek* magazine stated:

> Once the mere recorder of reality, the camera is now a part of life itself, present at Everyman's birth, marriage, death and most significant occasions in between. Most important of all, the photograph—in all its guises, from simple snapshot to instant color—is at last the handmaiden of art as well as journalism, advancing in the hands of the present generation of photographer-artists into new realms of perception and expression.[1]

PHOTOGRAPHS AS COMMUNICATION

Confucius didn't say it, but he might have: Good photography, just as good writing, does not simply happen. It is the result of discipline and planning.

Why are pictures important, and why should all design professionals have at least a rudimentary knowledge of photography? Because pictures have the advantage of instant communication; they overcome language and other communication barriers; and they are attention-getters because of their prominence on the printed page or screen.

"Communication is the prime function of pictures . . . [it is] best achieved when pictures and words reinforce each other, when they can be made to work in concert."[2]

All too often, not enough effort goes into making a layout "read." Formula picture editing results in predictability, such as a lack of emphasis, a sameness of picture size, and too little openness (white space). As a rule, when page elements—whether they be photographs, type blocks or both—are floated in white space, the resulting emphasis imparted by the white surround increases readers' understanding of the layout and their interest in its message.

"The photographer's role is to comprehend the subject, to put his perceptions in visual form. The [picture] editor's job is to hone the photographer's material, to shape the message for his specific audience. The designer's task is to enhance readability by bringing refinements and esthetics to the picture-and-word presentation. From such collaboration and common purpose come effective communications."[3]

ELEMENTS OF A GOOD PHOTOGRAPH

All too often a considerable investment in fine design, copywriting, composition, plates, presswork, paper, and binding is handicapped because of poor photography. Experts are in general agreement that the difference between taking pictures and making photographs is composition.

Every photograph has three elements: the center of interest, the foreground, and the background. As we saw in the chapter on layout, the center of interest is not necessarily—or even desirably—the center of the picture. But whatever its location, the center of interest is the major object or point of the photo. How the eye is drawn to the focal point is up to the photographer.

An article in *Military Media Review* (1974:3) explained three methods by which a photographer can direct a reviewer's eye to the center of interest.

> One way is through *linear perspective*. This technique creatively uses the foreground of a picture to make the eye focus on, and follow a line. Stair bannisters, walls, clumps of trees, fences or furrows can all function as lines to lead the eye. The most obvious method of using these is to sight directly down one of them. As you become more aware of using your surroundings, you'll begin to see other possibilities.
> Linear perspective is also the term for the effect whereby parallel lines seem to converge as they recede into the distance. You can make this illusion work for you by composing your photo so the center of interest falls near where the lines converge.
> Another method of using the foreground is *framing*. With this technique,

the photographer surrounds the center of interest with a natural frame by using any available objects in the foreground. Interesting frames require imagination and an eye for composition. Some of the most common frames involve shooting over, around, or through furniture or natural foliage.

A four-sided frame is not necessary. Anything bordering even one side of the center of interest qualifies. Directing the eye to that point is the only requirement. This is most effective when the frame is out of focus, thus not drawing attention to the technique itself.

Throwing the foreground or background out of focus involves *selective focusing.* This is based on the optical phenomenon called "depth of field."

Simply put, the area in focus decreases as the lens aperture (f/stop) gets wider. Conversely, as the lens aperture gets narrower, the area in focus increases. What this means is that the more you open up the lens (stopping up to numerically lower f/stops), the amount of space in focus at any given distance from the lens narrows, or grows shallower. The opposite effect occurs as you begin to close the lens opening (stopping down to numerically higher f/stops).

EIGHT HINTS FROM THE PROS

Poor pictures, according to one picture editor, are caused by either bad ideas or good ideas executed by incompetent photographers. It is more difficult to make a good picture from a bad idea than it is to make a bad picture from a good idea. Hints from the pros include:

1. Strive to establish a point of view every time you aim the camera.
2. Don't think only in terms of a single photograph. The subject may be better covered by a photo series.
3. Be alert to distracting backgrounds, crooked horizons, fuzzy foregrounds (unless planned that way), and leaning buildings.
4. Don't shoot a hand-held camera at a slower speed than the fraction of 1 over the focal length of the lens. To avoid camera shake, don't use a 50-mm lens at shutter speeds slower than 1/50 of a second.
5. Explore effects from sidelighting and backlighting the subject. Use a lens hood and an increase of one to two f-stops over the light meter indication.
6. Compose photos in the smallest possible space. Don't take a group shot of ten people when two or three of them will tell the story. Avoid groups of more than four people as much as possible.
7. Put light subjects against dark backgrounds and vice versa.
8. Film is cheap. Photographers are expensive. Shoot as many pictures as possible on any assignment. Then pick the best negatives for printing. In most large picture publications, such as the *National Geographic* and the old *Life*, shooting ratios of 200 up to 500 for 1 are commonplace. It is not unusual for a staff photographer to shoot ten 36-exposure rolls of film of a subject, and have one frame from the group selected for the final layout.

STAGED PHOTOS

A brochure is a firm's opportunity to describe itself in the best possible light. In that sense, it's a biased presentation, but biased, it is to be hoped, in a positive and productive way.

Because we live in a visual age and are acclimated to absorbing information almost instantaneously from television, ads, movies, and news photos, pictures can be grasped immediately. One designer points out that photographs have the power to convince—that they can, and usually are, viewed as fact. "When they are staged, they should be done so well that they look real, like the famous set-up news photo of the Marines raising the flag on Iwo Jima," he adds.

Ira Shapiro, a frequent writer on brochure and annual report photography, suggests that a photograph's inherent potential is to document reality.

> But most annual report (and brochure) photos are badly staged and static, conveying phoniness and dullness. Boring photos are direct contradictions to words like "exciting growth" and "dynamic leaders." It's no wonder corporate pictures often generate skepticism about business.
>
> A recent annual report, for example, states "People make the difference" on the cover and then practically ignores them inside, highlighting equipment and buildings instead. Where are all the people? Another report has a section called "The Year of the Consumer" illustrated with a giant picture of its consumer research executives in a laboratory. Where are the consumers?
>
> Think about executive photos. Business magazines usually show dynamic people in action and use informal and punchy candids. Most annual reports (and design firm brochures) portray top brass in unsmiling mug shots or studio-type poses.[4]

If the aim is to portray principals and staff as highly conservative, then formality and stiffness are appropriate in photographs. But if that is not what you want to say about your firm's executives, then their photographs should show real people, unposed and in natural settings.

Shapiro cites the International Flavors & Fragrances 1972 annual report, which showed the company's two top executives in a sauna, wearing towels. That may be a little too open, honest, and down-to-earth for most principals of design firms.

EXAMPLES FROM ANNUAL REPORTS

The annual reports for the Xerox Corporation have featured people (clients, executives, employees) for several years. Many of the photographs in corporate annual reports would be equally at home in brochures for architects, engineers, and planners. Refer to Figures 4-7 and 4-8 for examples.

Ira Shapiro, quoted earlier, suggests a quick test for determining how well your photographs communicate.

"Just as you can judge an ad's visual effectiveness on TV by turning off the sound, try reading your organization's latest . . . brochure by looking only at the pictures. Does it communicate at all? Are you satisfied with the message?"[5]

COVERS

With possibly 50,000 professional design firms in business in the United States—architects, engineers, planners, and designers, plus various specialty consultants such as space planners, systems consultants, construction managers, and the like—the average client is apt to receive a number of brochures as soon as his project surfaces.

Those involved with designing, writing, producing, and distributing general capability and special purpose brochures should realize that the competition for the attention of potential clients is tough. It is worth an additional effort or two to try to give your brochure the something extra to make it stand out from other publications.

An obvious point of concentration is the cover. A study of corporate annual report covers by the Cleveland, Ohio, public relations firm of Selvage, Lee and Howard, Inc. turned up these statistics:

Percent Usage According to Company Size

Format	Sales to $500 million	$500 million to $1 billion	$1 billion and over	Average for all companies
Type only	21	23	18	21
Type and design*	17	11	21	17
Single photo	33	32	35	33
Group of photos	14	16	17	15
Embossed	9	13	8	10
Die cut	5	5	0.5	3.5
Other**	1	1	0.5	0.5

*"Design" used here to denote a graphic device other than a photo or drawing, such as a pattern or symbol.

**Including various combinations of the above formats.

COVER GUIDELINES

The Selvage, Lee and Howard, Inc., study, "Anatomy of the Corporate Annual Report," contained these guidelines for out-of-the-ordinary covers (read "brochure" for "annual report"):

The cover should capture attention immediately, promote a favorable first impression, and establish the theme of the annual report, the identity of the company making the report, and the period covered.

The cover should help make even a casual viewer want to open and read the report. It should convey the impression or "image" the company wishes to present: dignified, progressive, ultra-modern, or whatever.

An imaginative selection of cover paper suited to the graphics on that cover can suggest the nature of the product or service and the company that produces it. A metallic ink on a highly-coated gloss stock might suggest machinery or steel production, soft pastel colors on a matte or dull-coated cover paper might suggest paints, cosmetics, etc. The very feel and texture of the paper can suggest the quality of the product or symbolize the quiet dignity and efficient organization of the company.

Since a cover's purpose is to gain attention and establish the theme of the report, it is often one of the last and most thoughtfully designed pages in the report, or it may be designed in the early stages and serve as a design inspiration for all subsequent pages.

Our own advice is to give thoughtful attention to the brochure cover in the early stages of design. We have already commented on the importance of careful coordination of message and design, along with the establishment of an overall theme, all in the interests of achieving the preestablished objectives with the preselected publics.

Acetate overlays on the first cover—an expensive technique—can effectively give you two front covers. Corporations have used this approach to help illustrate such themes as "Meeting the Challenge of Change," where the overlay updates the information on the regular cover, or vice versa.

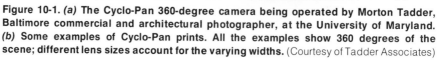

(a)   (b)

Figure 10-1. *(a)* **The Cyclo-Pan 360-degree camera being operated by Morton Tadder, Baltimore commercial and architectural photographer, at the University of Maryland.** *(b)* **Some examples of Cyclo-Pan prints. All the examples show 360 degrees of the scene; different lens sizes account for the varying widths.** (Courtesy of Tadder Associates)

THE 360-DEGREE PICTURE

Morton Tadder, president of the Baltimore commercial photographic firm of Tadder Associates, has developed some exciting refinements on the old 360-degree photograph technique. His camera makes a full-circle negative, in black and white or color, on 70-mm film. (See Figure 10-1).

A finished contact print is approximately 2½ inches high and, depending on the lens used, from 24 to more than 30 inches long. Enlargements to eleven or twelve times the negative size can be made by special enlargers.

What do Tadder's pictures have to do with brochure covers? For starters, consider the effect of wrapping such a picture around all four covers. For a vertical 8½ x 11 inch brochure format this would mean about a 150-percent enlargement of the negative, giving enough photo surface to cover 34 inches in width (8½ inches x 4 covers). That much enlargement would result in an untrimmed picture height of about 3½ inches. Figure 10-2 illustrates the application.

If the brochure has a horizontal format (11 x 8½ inches), then a 360-

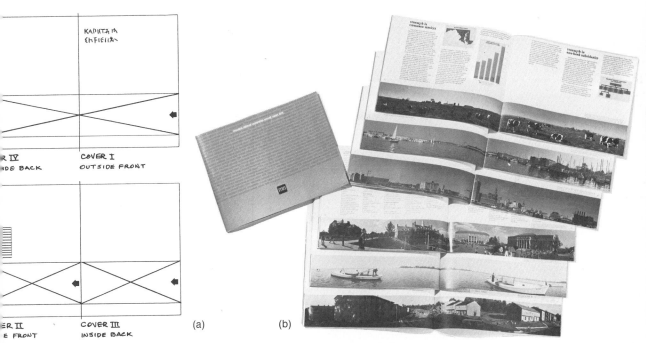

(a)   (b)

Figure 10-2. *(a)* **One method of spreading a 360-degree photograph across all four covers of a brochure. The picture starts on the inside cover, carries across both outside covers, and finishes up at the gutter of the inside back cover.** *(b)* **The second photo shows representative spreads from the 1974 annual report of the Maryland National Corporation. Each double-page unit has a Cyclo-Pan view running across the bottom of both pages.**

degree picture could be enlarged to approximately 180 percent of the original to span the 44-inch total width of the four covers. This would give an uncropped picture height of a little more than 4½ inches, or some 56 percent of the page's short dimension.

There obviously is no requirement that the elongated photo run over all four covers; a three-cover spread should also be effective. Depending upon how detailed the original subject was, even a two-cover span might be effective.

Nor must such a photo be restricted to covers. In an inside section on housing, shopping centers, educational complexes—any project that might benefit from the full-circle presentation—the picture could be run across two, four, or even six pages. It also lends itself to the foldout-page treatment.

THE NEGATIVE STRETCHER

The research department of Case-Hoyt Printers, Rochester, New York, has developed several fascinating new tools for designers. One of the most unusual aids is an electronic method of squeezing or stretching transparency images to fit a layout, without losing any detail of the original negative. This procedure can solve many cropping problems— to make a horizontal picture fit a vertical layout, or vice versa. The photographs in Figure 10-3 illustrate the Case-Hoyt technique.

Another Case-Hoyt innovation is the four-color continuous-tone lithograph, which must be seen in the original to be believed. Some of the finest printing reproduction of color photography I have seen is carried in Case-Hoyt's high-quality publication, *Response*. Any designer lucky enough to have files of the back issues of *Response* will know how high printing standards can be.

OTHER COVER TECHNIQUES

Eventually, of course, almost every new technique becomes a cliché, as designers pick up and improve upon or adapt innovative ideas in their own work. About twenty years ago I used a Flexwood cover on an architectural magazine I was then publishing. (Flexwood is not the easiest material for a printer to work with, incidentally. In addition to tearing up the rubber rollers as it goes through an offset press, it is tricky to print on and difficult to fold without splintering.) Thanks to a dedicated, patient printer, our results were outstanding, and the exercise was written up in several trade magazines. Within a year I saw at least a half-dozen other publications, including several architects' and engineers' brochures, with Flexwood covers. Presumably this flurry of Flexwood covers accounted for a brief sales spurt in replacement rollers.

An effective approach to covers, particularly when the designer wants to illustrate contrast between two ideas or objects, is to use a full-color photograph over a one-color phantomed illustration. Some years ago the New England Merchants Bank used this technique to depict a modern

Figure 10-3. Case-Hoyt made all three of these reproductions from the same 2¼ × 2¼ inch negative by using its electronic process for squeezing and stretching transparencies to fit predetermined formats. (Courtesy of Case-Hoyt Printers)

sailboat in a four-color photograph, laid over a drawing of a Viking ship. In printing, the older vessel was held back, or phantomed, to make the contrast even more direct. A long-established design firm might consider this for one of its early projects, overlaid with a color photo of a recent structure. If the two buildings could be related—office buildings or medical facilities, for example—the effect would be even better.

SCREEN PATTERNS

Moire (pronounced maw-RAY) patterns in printed illustrations are a technical problem that may occur when the printer or platemaker is making color separations or rescreening a black-and-white halftone. While the correction for moire is a production responsibility, it is well that the brochure designer be familiar with the causes and corrections of the disturbing patterns. (See Figure 10-4.)

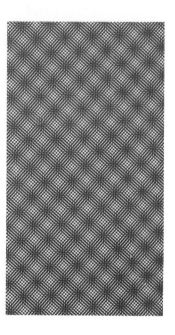

Figure 10-4. Two examples of moire patterns, caused when screens overlap improperly.

Moire patterns are formed when two or more screened images overlap because of almost identical angles of the screens. Five suggested methods for avoiding moire patterns in one-color printing are given by John Cogoli in *Photo-Offset Fundamentals:*

1.   A halftone screen which has a ruling either 50 lines finer or 50 lines coarser than the screening on the original (at its new size) may be used.
2.   When a screen is used, the copy or screen should be angled so the result is 30 degrees more than the original angle. This angle must be accurate to minimize the pattern. If the original angle was 45 degrees, the new print angle should be 75 degrees.
3.   The printed halftone may be enlarged, airbrushed, and then shot as an original photograph.
4.   The original may be reduced greatly (to less than 40 percent), causing the original screen to drop out.
5.   A clean piece of glass or clear film may be held before the lens and tilted back and forth during exposure.[6]

Caprock Developments, Inc., of Morris Plains, New Jersey, sells a rescreener to mechanically compensate for moire. It permits one-step rescreening of black-and-white as well as color halftone copy, using any desired enlargement, reduction, or halftone screen. The essential parts of the Caprock Re-Screener are a set of glass filters slightly over 2 inches in diameter, an adjustable filter holder, and a dial computer to use in selecting the proper filter.

According to Caprock's literature: "Shifting the camera out of focus, waving a piece of acetate in front of the lens during exposure, rocking the camera back and forth, rolling a clear glass in front of the lens, or using any other single filter device may do the trick occasionally, but the Caprock Re-Screener will always do it right the first time."

Sometimes a black-and-white halftone print can be shot as straight line work (no second screen involved) for acceptable results.

Avoidance of moire in four-color work is more complicated, and involves angling the halftone screen between each of the several images in the same set of full-color negatives. The classic screen-angle relationship is:

black	45 degrees
magenta	75 degrees
yellow	90 degrees
cyan	105 degrees

PHOTOMECHANICAL TECHNIQUES

Photomechanical variations to brochure illustrations may add just the right touch of seasoning. When used indiscriminately, the overall result may be very bad. Any photo or continuous-tone art, black and white or color, may be converted into sparkling art that will reproduce well under practically all printing processes.

One of the most familiar photomechanical processes is "line tone conversion," wherein a photograph is mechanically converted into poster-type line art. Line tone conversions may be reproduced in two or more colors.

A number of examples of photomechanical techniques are shown in Figure 10-5.

Special-effect photographs may be created initially in the enlarger, rather than by the printing house, by the use of special texture screens. Specially prepared 35-mm negatives of texture patterns, placed in contact with a regular 35-mm negative in the enlarger carrier, produce a print of the subject combined with a texture image. Patterson Products, Ltd., London, England, makes eight different texture screens in the 35-mm size—Old Master, Reticulated Grain, Tweed, Rough Linen, Drawn Cotton, Dot Screen, Gravel, and Tapestry. All eight screens retail for about $15 and can be used with either color or black-and-white negatives. See Figure 10-6 for an illustration of the effect of such screens.

Other special photographic effects are obtained through drop-out halftones, double-dot halftones, duotones, retouching, using the negative as

Figure 10-5. Illustrations of some of the photomechanical techniques available to the photographer and designer. (Top) The construction shot might be appropriate in almost any general capability brochure. Any photo or continuous-tone art, in black-and-white or color, can be converted into sparkling line art. Middle tones drop out, as these examples show, creating photomechanical variations of high contrast.

   (Opposite) The small photos, all from the Nekoosa Repro Papers library booklet *Photomechanical Techniques,* illustrate, from left to right, top row, one-stage tone drop, two-stage posterization, wavy line, and etching; center row, parallel line, mezzotint, concentric circle, and contour; bottom row, sonar, pebble, steel engraving, and cross line. (Courtesy of Nekoosa Edwards Paper Co., Port Edwards, Wisc.)

Figure 10-6. An example of the use of texture screens in printing or enlarging photographs. Left, the original photo, printed in the usual manner; center, the same photo printed with a reticulated-grain texture screen; right, the photo printed with a rough-linen texture screen.

a positive, and by the use of fisheye (180-degree coverage) and other special camera lenses.

DOUBLE DOTS AND DUOTONES

Double-dot halftones, normally reserved for black-and-white reproduction, result in more pleasing, deeper blacks, more apparent depth, and a greater range on the gray scale than is generally possible from the conventional single-dot plate-making process.

In the double-dot process, two halftone film positives are made with, say, a 150-line screen, with the screen angled between exposures. A composite film positive is then made of the two and a plate is made from the composite. In other words, double-dot halftones result from two films but are printed from a single plate.

A refinement of the double dot is when a plate is made from each of the two film positives and is used as a one-color duotone—that is, from two black impressions in two press runs.

If that last paragraph didn't drive you up the wall (don't worry, a lot of designers, plate makers, and printers are confused by the fine differences between double-dot halftones and a duotone black pressrun), let's turn to true duotones.

"A duotone is a two-color halftone image made from a single piece of continuous-tone, black-and-white copy with both printed images recording the approximate tonal relations of the original. The image printed with the darkest color emphasizes the shadow end of the illustration, while the image printed with the lightest color emphasizes the highlight end."[7]

Duotones have a depth and richness difficult to duplicate or improve upon by anything other than the four-color process. A duotone effect may be obtained by printing a simple image (usually black) over a continuous-tone tinted background.

MARKING AND SIZING PHOTOS

Never, *never* write on the back of a photograph, drawing, or any piece of original art. No matter how soft the lead, or how lightly you write, the marks may show through and ruin the art. Avoid the use of paper clips as well.

Instructions to the printer may be written in soft pencil on a tissue overlay of the photograph, but always be sure to have something between the tissue and the picture when you write. Instructions should include page number, position of the photo on the page, size, and special information such as outline, vignette, duotone, color-tint background, or mezzo-tint screen. To avoid unfamiliar subjects' being printed sideways or upside down, it's a good idea to indicate the top of the illustration by an arrow pointing to the word "top."

The desired degree of enlargement or reduction of original copy should also be shown on the overlay or in the margins. Show for either width or height—not both—in inches, percentage, picas, a fraction, or a decimal.

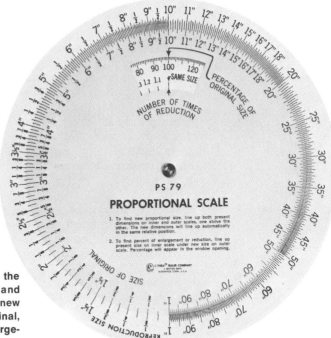

Figure 10-7. A proportional scale made by the C-Thru® Ruler Company of Bloomfield, Conn., and used to scale photographs and artwork to new dimensions in the same proportion as the original, as well as to calculate percentages of enlargements or reductions.

My preference is for a percentage, as "at 75%," which means the reproduction will appear at three-fourths the size of the original. "At 150%" means a one-and-a-half-times enlargement. Same-size copy is designated as "100%." Because it is possible to cause confusion with percentage resizing instructions, some designers prefer to specify enlargements or reductions by actual pica or inch measurements.

Instructions for color transparencies can be marked on the acetate sleeve in grease pencil.

Assembling all materials in an orderly manner will save time and trouble with the printer—which, in turn, means a fair chance to maintain schedules, to avoid mistakes, and to save your own time as production gets under way. Use large envelopes to hold all material for spreads or single pages. Identify the contents on the front of each envelope.

Some of the art, if not all, will have to be reduced or enlarged to fit into the spaces left for it in the layout. This change in size of the original is achieved by scaling or cropping or both. Scaling changes the size of the original, but not the dimension ratios; that is, the depth changes in direct ratio to the width. Cropping means to leave out areas.

In cropping, the unwanted sections of the illustration are indicated by crop marks at the corners. For several reasons, you should *never* actually trim a photograph or drawing to the exact area to be reduced or enlarged. Cutting off the unwanted portions means the art is ruined for future use, but, more important, the platemaker should always be given some leeway. If the designer has misfigured the area to be printed by a half-or quarter-inch, and the illustration is too small, problems may arise. Crop marks are best made in soft pencil on the overlay, but can be made in grease pencil on a photograph.

If an illustration is to be both reduced and cropped, it is safer to get a photostat of the artwork (reduced to the proper size). The photostat is then trimmed (cropped) and given to the platemaker as a guide for his work.

Scaling may be done by use of the diagonal line method, a proportional scale, a proportional rule, or the formula method. A proportional scale is illustrated in Figure 10-7. Always give the width first in scaling.

Enlargements or reductions may be sized by using the formula $W/H = w/h$, where

> W = width of the original
> w = width of enlargement or reduction in inches
> H = height of the original in inches
> h = height of enlargement or reduction in inches

Say the designer wants an illustration to fill a vertical space 6 x 9 inches. The artist makes the original 10 inches wide; how high must it be?

$$\frac{W}{H} = \frac{w}{h}$$
$$\frac{6}{9} = \frac{10}{h}$$
$$6h = 90$$
$$h = 15 \text{ inches}$$

Or, the designer has a vertical space 6 x 8 inches to fill. If the photograph he plans to use is 12 inches high, how wide should it be?

$$\frac{W}{H} = \frac{w}{h}$$
$$\frac{6}{8} = \frac{w}{12}$$
$$8w = 72$$
$$w = 9 \text{ inches}$$

ILLUSTRATION SOURCES

Obviously, your own photo files will be the primary source of illustrations for a brochure. Check with past associates, joint venturers, and consultants for project photos which may not be in your files. Client public relations departments can be a source of additional photographs. And don't overlook newspaper files; press photographers who cover ground-breakings, topping-out ceremonies, and building dedications, may have unpublished, but usuable, pictures.

Occasionally the brochure designer will feel a need to use a slightly offbeat illustration—something not apt to be found in his firm's own files. Perhaps it's a dusk shot of the Eiffel Tower, or a photograph of President Lincoln, or even a turn-of-the-century view of your city.

Newspapers were mentioned above. Their files usually go back as far as the paper's founding and they should be considered a primary source for local scenes.

STOCK PHOTOS

Stock photo houses make their inventory of pictures available to one and all. They have catalogs listing hundreds of subjects (adults, sports, children, buildings, and so on), all conveniently classified. Costs are much less than for custom photos. The wire services (UPI, AP) have large libraries of stock photos which may be purchased for one-time use.

Roloc Color Slides, P.O. Box 1715, Washington, D.C. 20013, has thousands of views available from all over the world. Roloc (color spelled backwards) slides are produced by a widely traveled, retired army lieutenant colonel, M. W. Arps, Jr., who converted his lifelong hobby into a business. Colonel Arps lists more than 6,000 slides in his U.S. catalog and well over 1,000 each for such countries as England and Germany.

Old-time photographs may be obtained from specialists such as the Bettmann Archive in New York City. If your interest is in Civil War scenes, for example, Dr. Bettmann will send an assortment on approval for your selection.

In exchange for a credit line, the public relations departments of most large companies will furnish photographs from their files. Chambers of commerce, state and local development commissions, and city and state recreational or tourist bureaus should not be overlooked as sources for certain types of photographs. The same holds true for most federal agencies in Washington, D.C.

CHARTS

Design professionals, by and large, are inclined to minimize or ignore the advantages of using graphs, charts, and tables to convey fairly large masses of statistics or other information in a reasonably simple and understandable manner. This applies to slide presentations as well as brochures.

The *Graphic Arts Encyclopedia* defines a graph as the "diagrammatic representation of changes in a variable quantity in comparison with those of other variables. The term is used in preference to 'chart' in scientific and technical work."[8]

"Chart," on the other hand, is defined as a "graphical representation showing values and quantities by means of bars, curves, columns and symbols."[9]

The *Encyclopedia* breaks chart nomenclature down into five types; bar, column, curve, pie, and surface. Those definitions:

> Bar Chart: Graphic representation comparing numerical values by means of rectangles of equal width. The bars extend horizontally on the chart and usually represent quantity. . . . Time, distance, or some other value is shown on the other dimension of the chart. Shaded patterns may be used to construct a chart with parallel double bars, divided bars, and symbols. A bar chart may also have a vertical baseline that divides the bars. Distances to the left of the baseline should show negative results, while those to the right should show favorable results. [10]

> Column Chart (also called Vertical Column Chart): Graphic representation having juxtaposed vertical columns that usually denote a quantity, with the horizontal dimension representing time or some other value. An additional value can be represented by using double or divided columns or symbols such as a pig, cow, and sheep, interpreted to indicate pork, beef, and mutton. [11]

> Curve Chart: Graphical representation that uses curves to reflect values such as time, distance, or any other condition desired. For example, the base of a chart may show a time value in years, months, weeks, or days, and the vertical dimension may reflect quantities. The curve chart is probably the most popular type of chart. [12]

> Pie Chart: Circular chart divided into wedges resembling the cuts of a pie. Each wedge represents a percentage of the whole "pie." This type of chart is easy to understand, but its use is limited because only one quantity can be compared with the whole. [13]

> Surface Chart: Graphical representation with plotted points moving across it from left to right in a logical sequence. The pattern thus reflected is extended to the base of the chart by shading or crosshatching. The shaded area is the predominant feature of the chart. The vertical scale may indicate quantities, while the base may reflect periods of time, expressed in hours, days, weeks, months or years. [14]

The relationship between a curve chart and a surface chart should be apparent.

In its 1974 annual report, the Campbell Soup Company used four of the five types of charts on one page. (See Figure 10-8.)

At the upper left a column chart shows the company's net sales from 1965 to 1974. To the right of the net sales chart is a pie chart showing the distribution of the 1974 sales dollar. In the lower left corner a surface chart compared the distribution of income from 1965 to 1974. The final chart, at lower right, is a bar chart representation of the annual rate of increase of consumer prices in ten selected countries, between July 1972 and July 1974.

These are the only charts used in this particular annual report, and the designer gave them emphasis by placing them on page 3, facing the president's message to Campbell stockholders.

Sea Pines Plantation, in its *1974 Vacation Guide*, used a symbol bar chart to show availability of tennis courts at different times of the year. (See Figure 10-9.) Each tennis racket stands for 1,000 players.

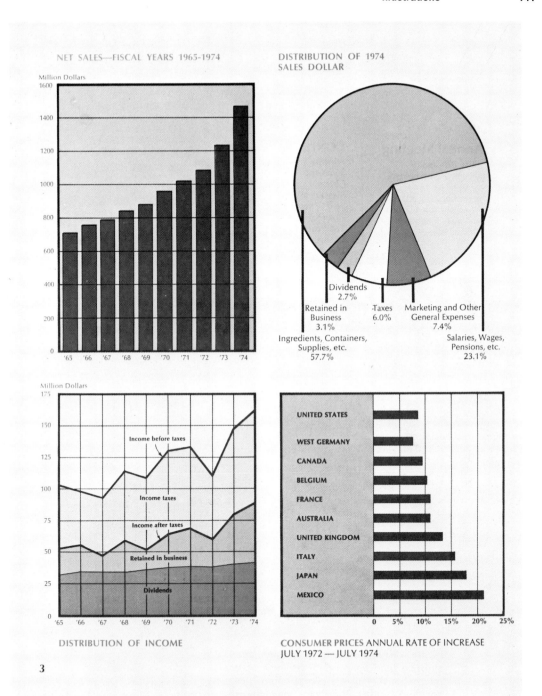

NET SALES—FISCAL YEARS 1965-1974

Million Dollars

DISTRIBUTION OF 1974
SALES DOLLAR

Dividends
2.7%

Retained in
Business
3.1%

Taxes
6.0%

Marketing and Other
General Expenses
7.4%

Ingredients, Containers,
Supplies, etc.
57.7%

Salaries, Wages,
Pensions, etc.
23.1%

Million Dollars

Income before taxes

Income taxes

Income after taxes

Retained in business

Dividends

DISTRIBUTION OF INCOME

UNITED STATES

WEST GERMANY

CANADA

BELGIUM

FRANCE

AUSTRALIA

UNITED KINGDOM

ITALY

JAPAN

MEXICO

CONSUMER PRICES ANNUAL RATE OF INCREASE
JULY 1972 — JULY 1974

3

Figure 10-8. A page from the 1974 Campbell Soup Company annual report. Four of the
five basic chart types are illustrated.

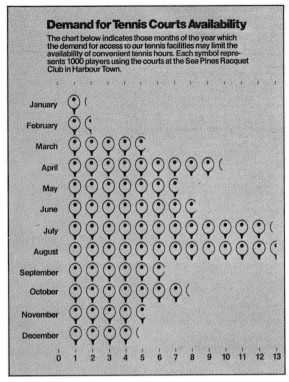

Demand for Tennis Courts Availability

The chart below indicates those months of the year which the demand for access to our tennis facilities may limit the availability of convenient tennis hours. Each symbol represents 1000 players using the courts at the Sea Pines Racquet Club in Harbour Town.

January
February
March
April
May
June
July
August
September
October
November
December

0 1 2 3 4 5 6 7 8 9 10 11 12 13

Figure 10-9. A symbol bar chart from the Sea Pines 1974 vacation guide to show tennis court availability. Each tennis racket and ball symbol stands for 1,000 players. Note that well over 12,000 players use the courts in July and August.

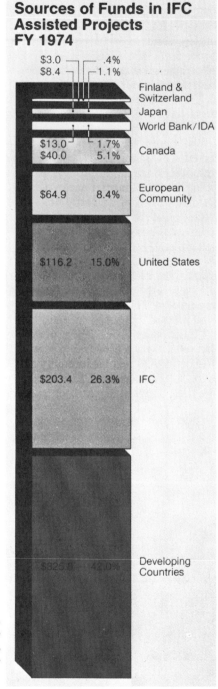

Sources of Funds in IFC Assisted Projects FY 1974

$3.0 — .4%	
$8.4 — 1.1%	Finland & Switzerland
	Japan
	World Bank/IDA
$13.0 — 1.7%	Canada
$40.0 — 5.1%	
$64.9 8.4%	European Community
$116.2 15.0%	United States
$203.4 26.3%	IFC
$325.0 42.0%	Developing Countries

Figure 10-10. This divided column chart, showing fund sources for projects of the International Finance Corporation (IFC), becomes a little cluttered for easy interpretation.

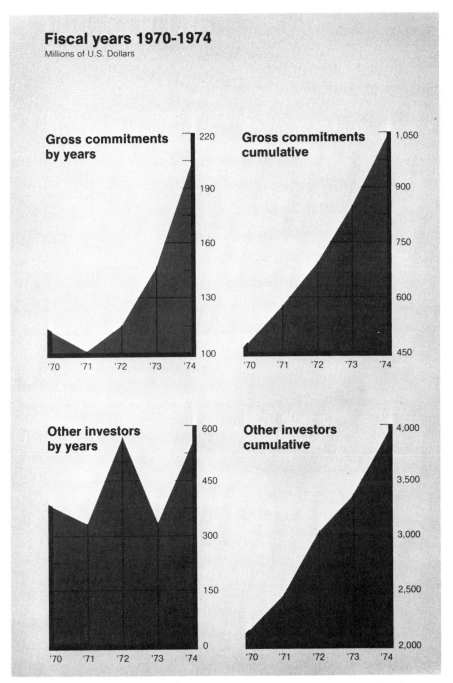

Fiscal years 1970-1974
Millions of U.S. Dollars

Gross commitments by years
220 / 190 / 160 / 130 / 100
'70 '71 '72 '73 '74

Gross commitments cumulative
1,050 / 900 / 750 / 600 / 450
'70 '71 '72 '73 '74

Other investors by years
600 / 450 / 300 / 150 / 0
'70 '71 '72 '73 '74

Other investors cumulative
4,000 / 3,500 / 3,000 / 2,500 / 2,000
'70 '71 '72 '73 '74

Figure 10-11. The information in these modified surface charts—on IFC's four-year gross commitments—is easily grasped by most readers.

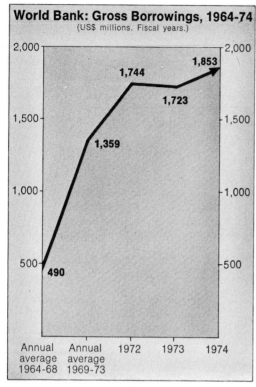

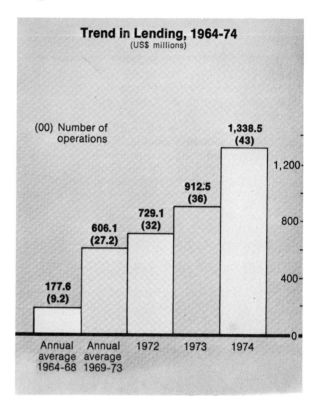

Figure 10-12. Classic examples of surface and bar charts, from the 1974 annual report of the World Bank.

1972 Distribution per dollar of sales and other income ($20,301.8 million)

Suppliers: 56.9¢   Employes: 28.2¢   Depreciation &   Taxes: 6¢
                                              Amortization: 4.5¢

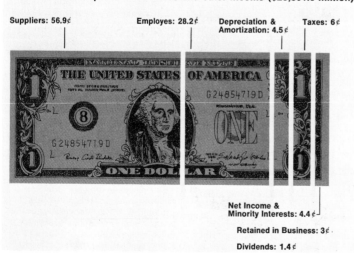

Net Income &
Minority Interests: 4.4¢

Retained in Business: 3¢

Dividends: 1.4¢

Figure 10-13. Pie charts come in many forms. This dollar-bill pie chart is from the Ford Motor Company's 1972 annual report.

The International Finance Corporation (IFC), a quasi-official arm of the World Bank, used a divided column chart in its 1974 report to show the various fund sources for IFC-assisted projects. (See Figure 10-10.) It is possible to cram so much information into a single chart that its basic purpose and simplicity are lost. The IFC column chart could be somewhat confusing to lay readers.

On another page of the IFC 1974 report a series of four modified surface charts show gross commitments and other investors for a four-year period. (See Figure 10-11.)

The World Bank's annual report for 1974 used a variety of column, double column, and surface charts to illustrate its activities. (See Figure 10-12.)

In its 1972 annual report, the Ford Motor Company used a dollar-bill pie chart to graphically represent 1972 distribution per dollar of sales and other income. (See Figure 10-13.)

KEEP CHARTS SIMPLE

Columnist David Kinsler, writing about the use of charts, pointed out a few of the problems and pitfalls to be avoided.

> Those who can stand charts usually like them straight. Multicolor work often only confuses. Black and white usually suffices, and the simpler the better. Executives should expect the studio to keep the proportions pleasing, the drafting excellent, the placement on the page felicitous, and the lettering legible. Executives should not tolerate a studio's blowing up what should be a neat little bar chart into a half-page monster with fat, misshapen, multicolored bars in order to produce what studio people call visual excitement. Those charts usually backfire. They repel the graphically literate while failing to attract the graphically illiterate.
>
> Executives should also insist on restraint in the studio in the treatment of tables. They should look like what they are expected to look like and not like typographical playthings. Good paper, comely proportions, and fine typesetting all help to make tables attractive. Funny type, zany folds, wild colors, and sideways printing can readily induce doubt about sanity in the executive suite. . . . One need not always be conventional, but when dealing with an orthodox subject, a little heresy goes a long way.[15]

If there is a desire to experiment in-house with the design and production of charts, a wide variety of graphic art aids are available from such suppliers as Avery Products Corporation (Chartpak), in Leeds, Massachusetts, and the Graphic Products Corporation (Formatt), of Rolling Meadows, Illinois. A review of the catalogs of these and similar companies should engender all kinds of ideas and approaches to charting.

A few of the charts that might be incorporated into general capability brochures are those showing territory maps and development, the growth of foreign business, the development of special building types within your firm over a five-, ten-, or twenty-five-year period, growth of total billings and/or staff, a pie chart showing where the building dollar goes, and surface charts showing construction-cost increases on an area or countrywide basis.

ARTWORK ILLUSTRATIONS

So far, this chapter has mostly discussed photographs. In brochures for design professionals, photographs are the dominant type of illustration, but the brochure designer must be familiar with other graphic possibilities.

The execution of the art can be in a variety of techniques or media. For black-and-white line reproduction one might choose from pen and ink, dry brush, brush and ink, wood engravings, linoleum blocks, or scratch board. Pencil, charcoal, and wash drawings are also used for black-and-white reproduction but require halftone screening like a photograph. Combining photographic material with pen-and-ink drawings can be an effective technique in the hands of an expert: This medium must be reproduced by a combination of the line and halftone processes, however, and is known as a "combination halftone."

Other fairly common artwork techniques, all of which are reproduced as halftones, are full-color paintings, photograms, photomontages, and three-dimensional art.

Line illustrations have no tonal changes or gray areas, such as are found in photographs. Line work is the easiest and cheapest kind of illustration to reproduce, but it must be carefully prepared for optimum results.

A photoengravers' handbook cautions: "The lines of the drawing should be clean and firm, neither too fine nor too close together. In the case of cross-hatching, the white spaces between the lines should be quite definite. The lines should not intersect at any angle of less than thirty degrees."

For consistently good results, the artist should use a brilliant white paper and waterproof, dead-black india ink for all pen-and-ink and brush artwork. Other hints for achieving first class results are as follows:

> All of the lines should be clean and all the edges sharp. The lens of a camera is more sensitive than the human eye. Blemishes and holes that may seem insignificant will actually reproduce on the negative and consequently on the final [offset plate or letterpress] engraving. Also, lines which fade away, rather than ending sharply, generally reproduce poorly.
>
> Instructions should never be written on the art. Instead, all marks should be made with pencil on a piece of tissue paper, and the paper then placed over the art. Be most careful not to write on the tissue while it is over the art. The depressions caused by the pressure of your pencil will be picked up by the lens and transferred to the negative.
>
> It is most economical to provide your engraver with artwork identical to the finished size. But, in some cases it is preferable to prepare the artwork larger and reduce it photographically. The process of reduction will diminish any imperfections and the result will be a sharper line. By the same token, if the artwork is to be enlarged, these imperfections (many of which might be imperceptible) will be magnified.
>
> One word of caution. If the artwork is to be prepared for reduction, take care that all fine lines and delicate shadings are kept in proportion to the smaller size. Extreme reductions eliminate fine lines and blend cross-hatchings into a solid.[16]

HANDLE WITH CARE

Most illustrations represent a fair investment on the part of the client. Even if that were not the case, the time lost in getting duplicate photographs or having a sketch or painting redone can mutilate schedules and result in higher costs. Prohibitions against writing on the front or back of photographs have already been set forth, but there are a few other basic precautions to observe with artwork.

1. Never trim a photograph to the final size.
2. Protect photographs and other artwork by mounting them on stiff boards and covering them with a paper flap.
3. Never roll photographs. Bends and creases can seldom be hidden from the camera. Cracks in the emulsion destroy the photograph for both present and future use.
4. Write all instructions on an overlay, but protect the artwork underneath when doing so.
5. Keep all liquids away from all types of artwork.

CAPTION TECHNIQUES

In addition to the usual method of placing an all-type caption in reasonably close proximity to the picture it describes, there are other acceptable ways of identifying illustrations in a brochure.

Figure 10-14 illustrates one of the alternatives, where the spread consists of practically all photographs and a bare minimum of text. The photo layout is duplicated in miniature at the bottom of the page, below the caption text. Each photograph location on the key is numbered to correspond with its caption above.

The same figure also shows another spread layout, with the caption key at the lower left corner. (These examples are from *Carte Blanche* magazine, May/June 1974.)

When it is absolutely necessary to use a picture of a large group, and to identify all the individuals shown, some designers add a simple line drawing of the picture. Individual positions in the sketch are numbered and names and titles are then listed by number in the accompanying caption. (See Figure 10-15.)

The ethical codes of most professional societies contain prohibitions against using testimonial statements in general capability brochures. There is a fairly effective captioning technique that seems to evade the ban on testimonials while nonetheless making full use of them.

For an office that had accumulated a long and impressive list of design awards, a brochure was designed in which all photograph captions were excerpts from award citations.

A municipal building, for example, was captioned: "A forthright statement of its municipal function. The lower level handles the city's business. It is sympathetic to its surroundings and is sensitively detailed with its traditional neighbors. A proud and dignified building. (Jury Comment, AIA Honor Awards Program.)"

Figure 10-14. Two versions of the numbered-box identification of photos.
(See also Figure 17-4.)

The News Center team: 1. Lee McCarthy 2. Al Johnson 3. Dan Daniels 4. Jim Upshaw 5. Dave Sheehan 6. Willard Scott 7. Janie Taylor 8. Bob Endicott 9. Mary Ann Maskery 10. Arch Campbell 11. Jim Vance 12. Marian Burros 13. Cathy McCampbell 14. Lea Thompson 15. Glenn Rinker 16. Stan Bernard 17. Angela Owens

Not shown: Marilyn Robinson, Fred Thomas, Bill Sternoff and Bob Kur.

Figure 10-15. Large groups become somewhat cumbersome to identify. When it is absolutely necessary to show many persons or objects in a picture, the line outline ID is about the simplest method of identifying everyone or everything. (See also Figure 7-6.)

An embassy in a South American country is described as "a well conceived and graceful expression of spacious contemporary architecture which has contributed to the beautification of the Capitol. (Diploma of Honor accompanying the Gold Medal of the City Council of Quito .)"

Obviously, this particular caption treatment is restricted to firms with enough citation winners among their major projects to fill a brochure. The firm in question has averaged some eight awards annually for its more than twenty-five years of operation, so its backlog of caption material might be described as adequate.

REFERENCES

[1]"Photography," copyright *Newsweek*, Inc., October 21, 1974, p. 64. Reprinted by permission.

[2]Gerald D. Hurley and Angus McDougall, *Visual Impact in Print*, Visual Impact, Inc., Chicago, 1971, p. 6.

[3]Ibid.

[4]Ira Shapiro, "Let Your Photos Do More Talking," *Public Relations Journal*, New York, September 1974, p. 12.

[5]Ira Shapiro, "Photography: The Blind Spot of Public Relations," *Public Relations Journal*, New York, April 1974, p. 59.

[6]John E. Cogoli, *Photo-Offset Fundamentals*, McKnight & McKnight Publishing Company, Bloomington, Ill., 1973, pp. 165–166.

[7]Erwin Jaffe, *Halftone Photograph for Offset Lithography*, Graphic Arts Technical Foundation, Pittsburgh, 1960, p. 184.

[8]George A. Stevenson, *Graphic Arts Encyclopedia*, McGraw-Hill Book Company, New York, 1968, p. 164.

[9]Ibid., p. 63.

[10]Ibid., p. 19.

[11]Ibid., pp. 75–76.

[12]Ibid., p. 105.

[13]Ibid., pp. 288–289.

[14]Ibid., p. 366.

[15]David Kinsler, "Sanity in Charts and Tables." Reprinted from the December 1973 issue of *Modern Office Procedures*, p. 8. ©1973 by Industrial Publishing Co., Division Pittway Corp.

[16]Leonard F. Bahr, *ATA Advertising Production Handbook*, 4th ed., Advertising Typographers Association of America, Inc., New York, 1969, p. 111.

Chapter 11
MECHANICALS: THE FINAL PASTE-UP

U SED MOSTLY IN OFFSET, "Mechanical" is a term for ". . . a camera-ready pasteup of artwork. It includes type, photos, line art, etc., all on one piece of artboard";[1] ". . . a combination of the type, drawings, illustrations, and all its other elements placed in position to be copied photographically and reproduced as a printed page or job. It is the completion of the final layout pasted up into a single unit ready for the camera."[2]

"Photomechanical" refers to any printing process (by mechanical means) from printing plates prepared photographically, including letterpress and direct and offset lithography. Mechanicals of pages and spreads are usually made up in the same size as the final product to be delivered by the printer.

CAMERA-READY COPY

Any printing job to be run on an offset press will have its art and copy elements prepared (pasted up) and ready for the camera, or "camera-ready." The carefully assembled camera-ready material is usually referred to as a "keyline paste-up"—a page-by-page assemblage of type proofs, line illustrations, rules, and sizing, cropping, position, and other instructions for illustration and color work.

Art for the camera is divided into three groups; line, continuous tone, and full color. Line and continuous-tone art are usually (but not always) carried on the same mechanical. The mechanical, therefore, has an important secondary function, in acting as a blueprint for illustration reproduction and printing production.

The preparation of mechanicals calls for precision work and close measurements. Some of the tools and other equipment used in making mechanicals include:

Drawing board and T square
Triangles (clear plastic)
Opaque: black and white
Cutting tools: scissors, razor-blade knife, and so forth.
Blue lead pencils
Grease pencils
Steel ruler with both inch and pica rules
Masking tape
Pens and india ink
Rubber cement

At its simplest, the mechanical is a piece of artist's illustration board, somewhat larger than the final size of the printed piece. To this board are attached, by cementing or pasting (hence the word "paste-up"), a number of line images, all in the same focus and, of course, of inspected quality. This board bears, furthermore, all notations that will enable it to serve as the blueprint of the job. The nature of these notations depends on the job.

Things are relatively simple if art-and-copy is to be reproduced in single color and if it consists of line images exclusively. As soon as line images must be combined with continuous-tone images, and particularly if they must be reproduced in more than one color, the assembly of art-and-copy becomes more complex.[3]

All instructions, notations, and other information on a mechanical are written in nonreproducible blue pencil (other colors will be picked up as black).

ALL-LINE PAGES

After type has been set, proofed, and approved, a set of reproduction proofs ("repros") are pulled and used by the artist or designer in the keyline assembly for offset printing work. Repros, because they will be part of the camera-ready copy, must be handled with the same care given any other piece of original artwork. The best rule is not to roll repro proofs, and to avoid creasing them by mounting them on heavy board. Protect them with tissue overlays.

Keylines are assembled as they will be seen in the finished brochure—as exact black-and-white copies of the spread. Every element is securely pasted to a board in its exact position. A final check can then be made of balance, contrast, sizes, lineup, and the like. The printer will assemble the individual pages into flats for proper press position. A flat is the carrier sheet, of opaque goldenrod enamel paper, for all negatives to be exposed onto a lithographic plate. (See Figure 11-1.)

If the spread is all line art (type, rules, line illustrations, screens, tints, and so on) the keyline will be complete and ready for the camera. If half-tones are included in the spread, the photographs or other continuous-tone illustrations usually are omitted from the keyline, and the areas they will occupy are outlined in blue pencil. Unscreened photos are mounted

Figure 11-1. Negative flats (offset). Blueline or brownline (vandykes) proofs will be made from the flat for customer approval before the offset plate is made from the negative. Minor corrections may be made on the negative.

separately. In such line/halftone combinations, the material to be screened is usually mounted on the board and line images are pasted in their exact positions on a transparent plastic overlay sheet hinged to the board. Each unit of board and overlays is shot separately and then stripped together into one flat.

In situations where halftone quality is not too critical, there is an alternative technique to shooting halftones separately from line art. Continuous-tone material is coverted into halftones before the mechanical is pasted up, by means of a Velox print. A Velox, as a screened reproduction of the continuous-tone image, is generally the equivalent of any other line image and can be placed on the mechanical with other line material. Veloxes have the additional advantage of eliminating windows on the mechanical and overlays on the film negative.

HALFTONE WINDOWS

When Veloxes are not used and continuous-tone art is to be screened by the printer, windows of Rubylith or Zip-A-Tone are cut to size and affixed to the mechanical. When the mechanical is photographed by the plate maker, the resulting negative will have a clear window in the blocked-off area. This simplifies the stripper's job of positioning and attaching halftone negatives on the line negative in making up the flat. The halftone can be mounted with tape or rubber cement, or the window can be cut out and the halftone spliced in.

PASTING UP THE MECHANICAL

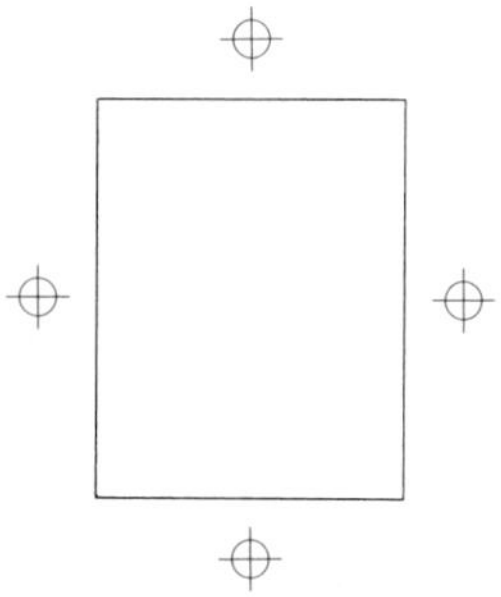

Brochure pages are always pasted up in pairs, with even-numbered pages on the left.

To position the individual elements on the mechanical, according to the layout, blue lines may be drawn in appropriate locations to indicate the size of each element. Put all materials on the mechanical for a last check of size and position before pasting them down. If your elements are supplied with waxed backs, then the next step is to press them down lightly until any final-minute changes have been made. Rubber cement also is commonly used to apply elements to a mechanical.

If there are color separations from the artist, mount each separation on an overlay. Multiple overlays are alternately hinged to the top, left side, right side, and bottom of the mechanical. To ensure precise placement and color registration, use register marks. (See Figure 11-2.) At least three register marks should be used: one at each side and one in the center of either the top or bottom of the layout.

Figure 11-2. Register marks are important in keying overlays to the pasted-up copy and art. At least three marks should be used for precise registration.

MECHANICALS CHECKLIST

The following checklist was compiled from several sources, including the *Handbook for Graphic Communications* and Cabibi's *Copy Preparation for Printing*.

1. Carefully proofread all copy.
2. Prepare mechanicals the same size as the completed job.
3. Paste up mechanicals on clean white board or heavy paper.
4. Square all elements in a paste-up to absolute accuracy. Line up type elements against square edges.
5. Measure off exact dimensions on the mechanical, allowing for proper page size, folding, and trimming.
6. For bleed photos, don't forget to allow at least ⅛ inch beyond trim lines.
7. Use only solid black, sharp line copy. Be certain that all line drawings are clearly inked in.
8. Carefully burnish down all elements in the paste-up.
9. Check that all markings on the mechanical that are *not* meant to

print are either in nonreproducing blue pencil or fall well outside the edges of the printed sheet.

10. Indicate tint areas on an overlay by solid black areas or with the proper benday screen.

11. See that halftone copy has well-defined tonal areas; touch up where needed. Do not over-retouch.

12. Replace broken type and smudged type areas with new repros.

13. Remove all unwanted marking on the mechanical with eraser or white opaque.

14. See that all windows for halftones are the correct size and in the proper position.

15. Be sure there is accurate register of all overlays and that sufficient register marks appear on each overlay and on the base mechanical board.

16. Key separate artwork for fast, positive identification of its placement in the flat. Delineate its position through use of photostats or precisely ruled lines.

17. Carefully mark screened and solid areas on the overlay, giving the percentage of screen required. Attach color swatches to the mechanical art.

18. Cover the mechanical and all overlays with a protective sheet of acetate or tissue.

REFERENCES

[1]*Pocket Pal*, 11th ed., © International Paper Co., New York, 1974, p. 178. Used by permission.

[2]John F. J. Cabibi, *Copy Preparation for Printing*, McGraw-Hill Book Company, New York, p. 121.

[3]Victor Strauss, *The Printing Industry*, Printing Industries of America, Inc., Washington, D. C., 1967, p. 744.

Chapter 12
MECHANICAL REQUIREMENTS

MECHANICAL REQUIREMENTS ARE PRIMARILY CONCERNED with the production aspects of a brochure, and include such considerations as the following:

- Paper stock requirements and selection: finish, weight, size, color, and the like
- Binding and inserting machine requirements
- Point-of-use requirements
- Color

PAPER

Because paper has such an important influence on the appearance, printability, and cost of any job (on long-run jobs the paper usually represents well over half the total cost of publication), we will discuss it first and in some detail.

History. The first paper makers were not people, but wasps. Since wasps could not be expected to keep up with even the minimal demands of early civilizations, people soon took over the task. Luckily, the invention of paper in second-century China slightly preceded the invention of any form of printing.

The Egyptians made a tissuelike writing material from papyrus plants some 3,000 years before Christ. Fragments of papyrus sheets, made of individual pieces of the white cellulose layers, glued together, exist today. Our word "paper" comes from the Latin "papyrus."

Several centuries later calligraphers and illuminators were using parchment and vellum sheets, both of which were much more durable materials for preserving valuable writings and records. Parchment was usually made from sheepskin and vellum was made from calfskin.

Historians generally agree that the Chinese invented paper about the time of Christ, or certainly no later than A.D. 100. The raw material for paper as we know it today must first be separated into individual fibers in some manner, a process called *pulping*. The Chinese, in their early efforts in pulp preparation, soaked bamboo in a lime-and-water solution. Fibers of the bamboo shoots were then separated by beating them with stones. The pulp was pressed against a flat surface, such as a large rock, and sun-dried.

These early techniques of paper making probably were transmitted along Central Asian caravan routes to Samarkand, where the Arabs encountered them early in the eighth century. According to the *Encyclopaedia Britannica*, Chinese prisoners taken at the Battle of Talas (near Samarkand) in 751 gave the secret to the Arabs. The Moors introduced the art into Spain before A.D. 1200. Paper mills were established in Italy, Germany, and France by 1400. The first mill in England was built about 100 years later, and parchment began to be replaced by rag papers. Germantown, Pennsylvania, near Philadelphia, had the first paper mill in North America—in 1690.

Until around 1860 linen and cotton rags and cotton clippings were the only significant source of paper-making fiber. Today, due to their limited quantity and high cost, rags make up only a small part of paper raw materials. A 100-percent rag-content bond can cost five times more than a No. 4 bond.

The early handmade papers had two outstanding characteristics: texture and permanence. Books up to 500 years old are still in existence today—and, with care, should last indefinitely.

A few years ago I spent an interesting several weeks in the National Archives in Washington, D.C., reading the original logs of such historic United States ships as the frigate *Essex*. The *Essex* log for 1801, for example, is in excellent condition, considering its age, and every entry penned by the ship's commander in chief, William Bainbridge, is clear and readable.

Until the invention of a machine that made paper in a continuous roll (web), all paper had been made in crude, hand-operated devices. The quality and uniformity of handmade paper depended altogether on the paper maker's skill. The basic paper machine was invented in 1800 by Louis Robert, a Frenchman. Robert's machine was financed and developed by others, including the Fourdrinier brothers of London, who built the first machine in 1803 after purchasing the patent rights. Today, paper-making machines are still called "Fourdriniers." (See Figure 12-1.)

Modern Paper Manufacture. Cellulose fiber is the basic ingredient of paper, and wood is the main source of commercial cellulose. The Nekoosa Edwards Paper Company publishes a booklet called *What Goes Into a Ton of Paper?* Since there are many grades and types of paper, Nekoosa's figures are representative of the process:

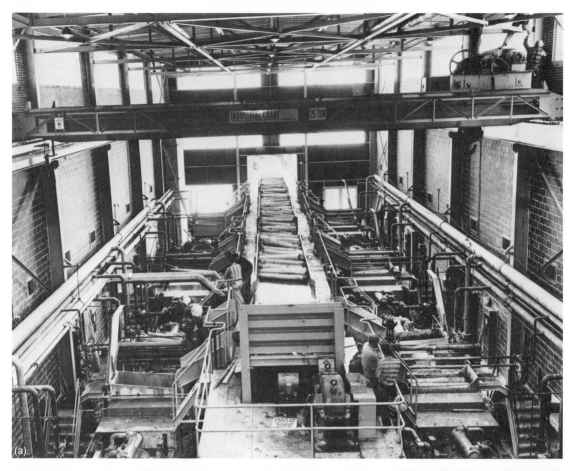

Figure 12-1. The paper-making process in brief. *(a)* **Where it all starts: a view of International Paper's groundwood mill in Mobile, Ala., where logs are reduced to pulp by grinders, on their way to becoming newsprint.** *(b)* **The wet end of a #2 pulp-paper machine, and** *(c)* **the dry end of the same machine as the finished paper is wound off on rolls.** *(d)* **The Paper Merchant, a machine longer than a football field, is capable of turning out up to 2,000 feet of fine paper per minute—or some 23 miles of paper per hour.** *(e)* **A supercalender stack puts a final high-gloss finish on publication papers.** (Figure 12-1d courtesy of Nekoosa Edwards Paper Company; remaining photos courtesy of International Paper Company)

Water	55,000	gallons
Sulfur	102	pounds
Magnesium hydroxide	94	pounds
Lime	350	pounds
Salt cake	80	pounds
Caustic	66	pounds
Chlorine	109	pounds
Starch	108	pounds
Wood	2	cords
Power	112	kilowatt-hours
Coal	1.2	tons
Alum	61	pounds
Clay	289	pounds
Rosin	16	pounds
Dye and pigment	20	pounds
Labor	20	work hours

Although these figures do not directly relate to the production of newsprint, for further comparison, a ton of newsprint will make about 7,000 copies of a twenty-eight-page newspaper. The combined annual requirement for two of the country's largest consumers of newsprint—the New York *Times* and the Los Angeles *Times*—is more than 660,000 tons. At 1975 prices that much newsprint cost over $185 million. One reason your newspaper no longer costs a nickel is the continuing escalation of newsprint prices—from $134 a ton in 1965 to more than $280 a ton in early 1975. Costs of fine printing papers have risen in proportion.

One of the best, relatively brief, and understandable explanations of the overall paper manufacturing process is found in the *Graphic Arts Encyclopedia:*

> Paper may be manufactured from wood, rags, straw, rope, jute butts, esparto grass, or other materials. Such woods as hemlock, poplar, birch, gum, spruce, and fir are commonly used for paper pulp. Wood may be transformed to pulp by mechanical or chemical means. Mechanical pulp is manufactured by grinding the wood into a fibrous condition. Newsprint, some wrapping papers, and paper bags are made from mechanical pulp. Sulfite, soda, and draft processes are chemical methods of making pulp from wood. The wood is reduced to fine chips, which are conveyed to a huge digester. There they are pressure-cooked with chemicals until the material has been reduced to a fibrous mass called cellulose, the chemicals having removed such unwanted elements as resin, sap, and lignin. The cooking mixture is drained from the cellulose by continued washing and separation. The pulp is then bleached, washed, drained, and sent to a beating machine. Here begins the actual process of papermaking, in which such additives as clay, rags, various stocks, coloring, and sizing are put in the pulp to give it its special quality and character. At this stage the pulp has the appearance and consistency of milk.
>
> In the sulfite process, the chips are cooked under pressure in a solution of calcium bisulfite. This method produces high-quality fibers for fine book papers. When wood such as gum, birch, or poplar is cooked under pressure with a caustic soda solution, the fibers are soft and short and form a more compact surface than sulfite fibers. Soda fibers are desirable for book

papers. The sulfate and draft processes are used, for the most part, in making wrapping papers and papers for bags.

When the pulp has been reduced to a fine milklike substance, it is piped along to the Fourdrinier papermaking machine. The pulp is conveyed along a traveling belt of fine cloth meshed with wire on the underside. The weight of stock to be produced determines the speed of the belt: a speed of 1 inch per second ultimately produces heavier stock than a speed of 10 feet or more per second. The belt vibrates as it moves to set the fibers. At the same time, the liquid content of the pulp either passes through the bottom of the mesh or is sucked off.

After the paper has been dried by heated iron rollers, it is passed through additional rollers, or calenders, where it is finished to the desired quality. Rag pulp is treated in much the same manner as wood pulp. Although the processes of cleaning, sorting, thrashing, bleaching, and digesting differ, the end result is the same when the pulp is ready for the beating process. Rag pulp may be added in various quantities to wood pulp during beating, or paper called "100 percent rag" may be manufactured from rag alone. Rag content, of course, lends a highly desirable quality to paper.[1]

Paper Characteristics.   Paper, and its proper selection, are important in every printing assignment, whether the job consists of fifty business cards printed one-up on a hand-operated platen press or 100,000 copies of an expensive four-color brochure on cast-coated book paper printed on the largest web offset presses. Several selection criteria for paper stock were listed at the beginning of this chapter, but a more complete list would include:

Grade	Durability (strength)
Finish	Tearing strength
Weight	Erasure qualities
Size	Bulk
Gloss	Foldability
Color	Surface treatment
Brightness	Ink receptivity (absorbency)
Opacity (show-through)	Performance on press
Smoothness	Pick resistance
Caliper	Dimensional stability (stretch)
"Feel"	Curl characteristics
Grain direction	Likesidedness
Refractiveness	Water resistance

Some of the above characteristics are technical and are problems more of the paper supplier and printer than of the designer. Since such considerations as finish, weight, opacity, foldability, and grain are important to the designer, however, we will discuss them briefly.

Paper Grades.   The main point to remember in paper selection is that there is no such thing as the perfect paper. Every sheet of paper represents a compromise among many properties and characteristics. Fibers are an example: long fibers give strength and tear resistance; short fibers impart smoothness, flat-lying qualities, and foldability. While both sets of properties might be desirable, it is not possible to achieve all of them in a single sheet. Only by understanding and acknowledging a paper's limitations can the designer deal with it effectively.

Printing papers are commonly classified under several grades or types, the purpose of which is suggested by the grade name:

Bible (25 x 38)	Newsprint (24 x 36)
Bond (17 x 22)	Offset (25 x 38)
Book (25 x 38)	Text (25 x 38)
Cover (20 x 36)	Wedding (17 x 22)
Gravure (25 x 38)	Writing (17 x 22)
Index (22½ x 35)	Label (20 x 25)
(25½ x 30½)	

Each paper classification has a predetermined basic sheet size, in inches, assigned to it. The figures in parentheses following each paper type give the basic size for the grade. Basis weight of a paper is the weight in pounds of one ream (500 sheets) cut to the standard (basic) size for that grade. Printing papers are referred to as "20-pound bond" or "60-pound offset." This simply means that 500 sheets of the basic size (25 x 38) of that particular offset paper will weigh 60 pounds. Standard weights of bond paper, in the basic 17 x 22 inch size, are 9, 13, 16, 20, and 24 pounds for 500 sheets. Note that the index grade of paper has two basic sizes, 22½ x 35 inches and 25½ x 30½ inches.

Caliper and bulk of a paper are not unrelated to its basis weight, and the relationship often is confusing to the layman. Caliper is the thickness of paper, usually expressed in thousandths of an inch. The instrument used to measure thickness is also known as a caliper, made especially for paper measurement. Bulk is a function of caliper and can refer to the number of sheets per inch or to the thickness of the total number of pages in a book or other publication. A 60-pound book paper, depending on its construction, may range from some 300 pages per inch (high bulking) to well over 700 pages per inch (low bulking). Thus, book publishers may issue a 720-page book that varies from 1 inch to more than 2 inches in thickness. High-bulking papers are sometimes aptly called "whipped-cream papers"; like whipped cream, they contain a lot of air.

Feel free to ask your printer or the paper house for samples of all papers you want to consider. Most paper suppliers have swatch books or folders available for this purpose. (See Figure 12-2.)

Opacity.   Printing papers, as we saw earlier in the recipe for a ton of paper, contain fiber, sizing materials, mineral fillers, and coloring. Mineral fillers, the most common of which are clay, calcium silicate, diatomaceous silica, talc, calcium carbonate, calcium sulfate, barium sulfate, zinc sulfide, and titanium dioxide, improve the paper's smoothness, ink receptivity, opacity, and color.

A lack of opacity, or excessive show-through of printed matter from the reverse side or the next sheet, reduces contrast and lowers print quality.

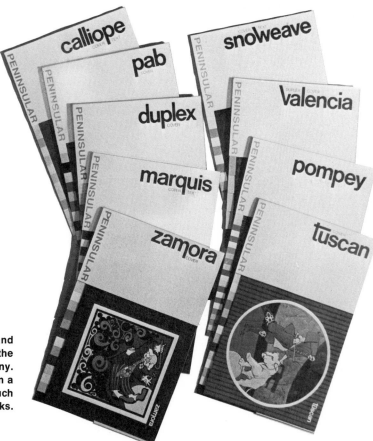

Figure 12-2. A selection of cover- and text-paper swatch books from the Peninsular Paper Company. Printing houses normally maintain a comprehensive library of such sample books.

Grain.   Grain is a characteristic of all machine-made paper and refers to the alignment of fibers in the paper. During paper making, fibers tend to be oriented with their length parallel to that of the paper machine. Grain direction, therefore, is synonymous with machine direction. The other dimension is called cross-direction or cross-grain.

Grain has three primary effects on paper properties:

• Paper folds smoothly with grain direction, but roughens or cracks when folded cross-grain. Tearing is easier with the grain.

• Paper is stiffer, has more tensile strength, in the grain direction.

• Paper contracts or expands more in the cross-grain direction than in the grain direction when moisture changes occur. Moisture often causes paper to creep and change shape.

A simple test to determine grain direction is to moisten the paper on one side. The paper will curl toward the dry side, with the axis of curl always parallel to the grain direction (with the grain).

Foldability.   Foldability, or folding endurance, is the number of double folds a paper will take before breaking, under test conditions. As a measure of durability, it is an important consideration in selecting paper or light board for envelopes or folders for brochure systems. Few things in a designer's life are more frustrating than to find out the hard way that his or her great brochure system does not travel well by mail because the carrier arrives looking like a Mack truck ran over it. In many such cases, it turns out that an unthinking printer folded the holder cross-grain and the designer did not catch the error.

A temperature-controlled vault in the research laboratory of the preservation department of the Library of Congress contains an array of paper-testing equipment able to simulate the worst fate a book or brochure could meet. One machine folds paper back and forth until it breaks. Newsprint can withstand about 25 folds; normal book paper, 250 to 300 folds; and 100 percent rag paper, 500 to 1,000 folds.

Tearing resistance is also a characteristic of durability in paper.

Paper Specification.   However much designers may be intrigued by the hundreds of available paper types, weights, and finishes, eventually they must choose the paper that they feel is right for their set of specifications.

Two *basic* considerations in stock selection are *objective* and *cost*. If the brochure is intended to reflect a high-quality, professional service operation, then the paper should project an image of solidity, prestige, dependability, and quality. As for cost, remember that on relatively short production runs, paper is one of the smallest cost factors. Occasionally a printer may even have sufficient quantities of leftover stock from previous jobs for your brochure. The cost of such surplus paper is usually negotiable.

Specific considerations for paper selection include brand, quantity, size and weight, grade and color, finish, grain, and any special requirements. The printing process to be used always is an important factor in stock choice; papers are especially made for letterpress, offset, and gravure presses. A few papers are considered multipurpose, but most are not.

Availability of a particular paper has become a key selection factor in recent years, as mills phase certain papers out of production. Do not lose sight of the fact that you may want to rerun the job at some future date, and it is preferable that the same stock be used in any future printings.

Fine printing papers should remain relatively easy to get. Since paper mills use the same machines to make the more expensive sheets as they do to make the inexpensive ones, mill and press time will usually be used for the former.

For cover paper, remember that the use of pockets will require a reasonably heavy stock, but not so heavy that it will crack or tear when folded.

Paper Math.   From the earliest layout, a brochure's page size should be planned so that it will cut out of a standard sheet with the least amount of

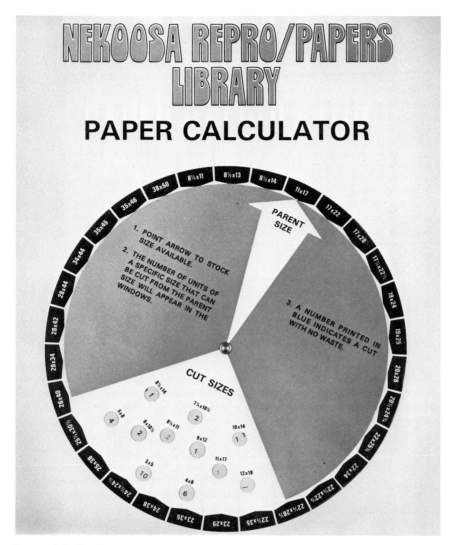

Figure 12-3. The Nekoosa paper calculator can help the designer figure page cutouts from standard sheet sizes. Wasting paper is to be avoided whenever possible. (Courtesy of Nekoosa Edwards Paper Company)

wastage, and with the grain running in the right direction. Paper calculators, such as the one distributed by Nekoosa (see Figure 12-3), are helpful in figuring the number of pages that can be cut from standard-size sheets.

To use the calculator, point the arrow at the parent sheet size shown in reverse on the outside ring of figures. From the 35 x 45 inch sheet size, for example, we have the following possibilities:

Page (cut) size	Number of pages from 35 x 45 inch sheet
3 x 5	105 (no wastage in this size)
4 x 6	62
5 x 8	36
7½ x 10½	18
8½ x 10½	16
8½ x 11	16
9 x 12	13
8½ x 14	12
10 x 14	9
11 x 17	8
12 x 18	4

There is also a formula method of figuring the number of pieces that will cut from a sheet. To find the number of 8½ x 14 pages in a 35 x 45 inch sheet, figure as shown, canceling up and down:

$$\text{(a)}\quad \frac{\overset{4}{\cancel{35}} \times \overset{3}{\cancel{45}}}{\cancel{8\frac{1}{2}} \times \cancel{14}} = 12 \qquad\qquad \text{(b)}\quad \frac{\overset{2}{\cancel{35}} \times \overset{5}{\cancel{45}}}{\cancel{14} \times \cancel{8\frac{1}{2}}} = 10$$

Method (a) obviously allows the most efficient use of the 35 x 45 sheet.

The chances of a brochure designer's having to get involved in "paper math" problems are minimal, but there may be some interest in seeing how total paper requirements for a job are figured.

In this practice problem we assume a need for 3,000 copies of an 11 x 8½ inch, thirty-two-page brochure, plus cover. An 80-pound cover stock, 20 x 26, is selected for the cover and a 70-pound coated book stock, 35 x 45, is to be used for the inside pages. The brochure will be saddle stitched on the 11-inch edge. Figure the following:

(a) How many sheets of the 20 x 26 cover stock are required?
(b) How many sheets of the 35 x 45 coated stock are required?
(c) What will the actual quantity be after adding 10 percent for spoilage to (a) and (b)?

1. *Cover.*   Two sheets 11 x 8½ are required—3,000 × 2 = 6,000 sheets 11 x 8½.

$$\frac{\overset{2}{\cancel{20}} \times \overset{2}{\cancel{26}}}{\cancel{8\frac{1}{2}} \times \cancel{11\frac{1}{2}}} = 4 \text{ out} = 1,500 \text{ sheets } 20 \times 26 \text{ required}$$

2. *Inside.*   Thirty-two pages. Sixteen sheets 11 x 8½ are required—3,000 × 16 = 48,000 sheets 11 x 8½.

$$\frac{\overset{4}{\cancel{35}} \times \overset{4}{\cancel{45}}}{\cancel{8\frac{1}{2}} \times \cancel{11}} = 16 \text{ out} = 3,000 \text{ sheets } 35 \times 45 \text{ are required}$$

3. *Allowing for spoilage of 10 percent.*
      Cover: 1,500 × 10% = 150
      Inside: 3,000 × 10% = 300
Thus, 1,650 sheets of the 20 x 26 cover stock and 3,500 sheets of the 35 x 45 book stock will be required.

It probably should be mentioned that at least a ⅛ inch extra margin is allowed for each edge of a page that will bleed. A margin of ¼ inch is safer. In the above example there is enough extra stock in each cut to allow for bleed edges and the subsequent trim, although it is a marginal situation.

BINDING

How the brochure will be given the finishing touch—the binding—is too important a consideration to leave to chance or printer's choice. The AIA recommends "a plastic spiral, presentation box, or other type of flexible binding." It might be well to point out here that a completely loose-leaf brochure, assembled in an attractive folder or box, actually involves no binding operation, as such. But if the systems approach to producing a brochure is taken, and the material sent to potential clients consists of a series of smaller booklets, or such booklets plus loose sheets, then there *are* binding considerations, of course.

Mechanical bindings—metal clasps, prongs, rings, screw posts, plastic rings or combs, or staples, as in saddle stitching or sidestitching—are distinguished from the standard, more permanent bookbinding methods. The latter include side-sewed, Symth-sewed, and perfect bindings.

Most brochures use the ubiquitous plastic spiral binding, of the type made by the General Binding Company (GBC). Admittedly, the plastic and metal mechanical bindings offer several advantages to the over-worked design professional:

- Flexibility in customizing and updating
- Pages that open and lie flat
- Page order that may be arranged in any way
- Pages that may be of varying paper weights, colors, and sizes
- Pages that need not be bound in even signatures; any number of pages may be used

A *signature* is the printed, folded, untrimmed sheet that makes up a section of the total brochure or book. Always made up in multiples of four, a signature usually contains at least sixteen pages. On a perfecting press, where both sides of the sheet are printed on one pass through, 128 pages, 9 x 6 inches in size, can be printed at a time.

Most graphic designers avoid using plastic or metal spiral bindings because they find them unattractive or unaesthetic. A few methods have been developed to camouflage these bindings so that the finished product resembles a hard-bound booklet. (See Figure 4-2.)

The binding alternatives, which are usually at least a little more expensive and often force some compromise with flexibility, include the standard bookbinding procedures. A relative newcomer to the binding scene is the method introduced by Velo-Bind, Inc., of Sunnyvale, California.

In the Velo-Bind system a comblike plastic binding unit is inserted through prepunched pages into a receptive strip at the back side of the pages. Brochures up to 3 inches thick may be bound by this method. (See Figure 12-4.)

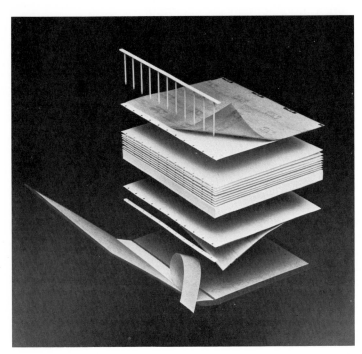

Figure 12-4. The Velo-Bind system for brochures, proposals, and booklets. Holes are punched in the material to be bound. A plastic binding strip (comb) is placed through the holes in both the pages and a bottom perforated strip. The binder then trims the excess and heat forms rivets on the bottom strip, providing a permanent binding. The hard or soft covers come in a variety of textures and colors. (Courtesy of Velo-Bind, Inc.)

The assembled booklet or brochure, with front and back soft covers in position, is inserted into a binding machine that holds the material under pressure while the extra lengths of the comb ends are sheared off automatically and rivet ends are heat-formed by the machine. By use of a simple accessory unit, the Velocaser, a hard cover may be added to the booklet. Cost of a complete Velo-Bind system is around $1,400. The equipment can also be leased. Some job printing shops have Velo-Bind units and will bind proposals, brochures, and special presentations in small quantities. Velo-Bind hard-cover booklets cost around $1.60 each in a print shop.

The disadvantages of the Velo-Bind process are two: Because the binding is similar to sidestitching, the booklet does not lie flat when opened, and changing or deleting pages usually requires a new set of plastic binders.

One brochure consultant suggests the GBC type of plastic spiral binding often is the best solution for smaller offices that produce their own brochures on limited budgets. But the consultant also advises client firms to buy a hand-operated binding machine for the plastic spirals, on the premise that if some binder is not readily available the firm will never get around to changing or updating its brochures. The desk-top GBC binder enables even the least-skilled employee to remove the plastic binders, punch holes in new and replacement pages, and reinsert the spiral binder.

POINT-OF-USE REQUIREMENTS

"Point-of-use requirements" is an elaborate term covering the expected end uses of a printed product. Such requirements vary, depending on whether the publication is intended for transient (throwaway) or lasting (filing and reference) use, and whether it is to be read by people or handled by machine. Appearance is usually a significant consideration. A professional brochure should not look like an advertising catalog, and vice versa. Point-of-use, for our purposes, probably is more directed to considerations of how and where a potential client may use and file the brochure.

Most clients, photographers, and printers are geared to handling the standard 8 x 10 inch and 8½ x 11 inch formats. Standard file drawers, photographic enlarging paper, bulk brochure paper sizes, presses, and envelopes all are generally keyed to an 8½ x 11 inch world. Put the shoe on your own foot—how much trouble and expense would you be willing to go to to accommodate oversized brochures and promotion booklets from materials suppliers?

Another reason for staying with standard sizes is the potential difficulty in marrying your brochure to those of other firms when preparing joint or common brochure presentations for associations and joint ventures.

Wastage in photographic paper and printing stock, and longer press runs to position plates with unusual or unfamiliar printing areas, are two of the probable additional costs an odd-size brochure may cause. This is not to discourage the use of nonstandard sizes and formats—sometimes they are particularly effective—but be prepared for more than the usual problems and some extra costs. Don't forget to check out wild-blue-yonder approaches with your mailing house and the postal service before the concept becomes too set; postal regulations and extra mailing charges have shot down their share of odd-size creations. Another point to keep in mind in this connection is that U.S. postal laws require that a book have at least twenty-four pages, including the cover, to qualify for the low book-mailing rate.

Before a design is too far along to be modified easily and economically, make up a full-size dummy of the brochure from samples of the cover and inside stock you plan to use. If it is a brochure system, to be carried in a folder or box, hand-make a carrier as well. Assemble the whole package, put it into the mailing envelope or box you expect to use, and mail it to a friend in a city at least 200 miles away. This is a fair test of a brochure's mailability. A better check is to make up three or four complete dummies and send them· to as many destinations in widely separated cities.

Jumbo formats of 16 x 20 inches or larger, for special proposals, capability brochures, and reports, have been rationalized by their designers as making the booklet too big to file and inconvenient to throw into the standard office wastebasket. In desperation, the reasoning goes, the recipient will leave it on his desk or a coffee table, where it will serve as a semipermanent promotion sign for the originating design office. It sometimes works out that way, and few things are more discouraging or distracting than to be making an impassioned pitch for *your* firm while a beautiful oversized booklet from a major competitor stares back at you from the corner of the potential client's desk. It's a form of psychological warfare in the design profession.

Color.   The effect of color is powerful:

> Color dominates most of what happens to us and what we experience in our lives. It exerts a decisive influence not only on our eyes, but on all our other senses. Its psychological effect, combined with our subconscious awareness of age-old symbolism attached to it, makes color an important factor in any visual appeal addressed to human beings. Every individual's well-being and state of mind are dependent on the quantity of light he encounters.[2]

Color has the ability to intensify and emphasize text and illustrations by endowing them with special characteristics. In its own right, color can make itself felt as a formative element; contrary to the intellectual appeal of text and line, color communicates basic emotional values. Human attitudes and reactions to colors and groups of colors are collective and unconscious—an unchangeable part of our culture. The more intense a color, the more sparing should be its use in general, and the more economic its use in combination with other colors. This is particularly true when a viewer or a reader is forced to tolerate intense color for any length of time. Note the absence of many popular colors in wall coverings, carpets, and furniture.

Printing papers and inks can be made in almost any color desired. The effect of paper color on ink colors must always be carefully considered. Pulp-dyed colored papers are the most satisfactory. The majority of printers feel that type is most easily read against soft white paper. Process colors look their best and most accurately reproduce the original image when printed on a neutral white paper.

Color, as most of us know, adds impact to printed materials by calling attention to a subject, permitting faster information retrieval, and helping to avoid confusion in information transfer. In a field experiment a few years back, researchers demonstrated that functional use of color leads to greater retention of information. In terms of effective information transfer, colors ranked in the following order: red (highest), blue, yellow, and black (lowest).

In another study of the effectiveness of color as an aid to faster communication, a series of tests was conducted with sample groups of business executives and university students. The test materials consisted of a package of charts, graphs, corporate reports, and other items. Subjects were asked to find certain information on a black-and-white page, then to find similar information on a four-color version of the same page. Both speed and accuracy were measured. The executives located information 70 percent faster on the color pages; the students located information 46 percent faster and made 39 percent fewer errors.

Strictly on the basis of legibility, psychological tests rank colors in the following order:

1. Black ink on yellow paper
2. Green ink on white paper
3. Blue ink on white paper
4. White ink on blue paper
5. Black ink on white paper
6. Yellow ink on black paper
7. White ink on red paper
8. White ink on orange paper
9. White ink on black paper
10. Red ink on yellow paper
11. Green ink on red paper
12. Red ink on green paper

Ten Tips on Color.   The Nekoosa Paper Company, in its colorful paper swatch book *Color It Nekoosa*, offers these tips on the use of color in brochure and booklet design.

1.   When colored inks are used on colored papers, best results will be obtained with a shade of the same color or of a complementary color. A green tint paper might be printed with a shade of green or a shade of red. Or it might be printed in green with initials and accents in red. Use of tint blocks is another way to help make the best use of color. In one press pass red can appear as a full deep hue and as the lightest pink, with all the variations in between.

2.   Black on yellow, orange on blue, and black on tangerine offer strong legibility. Least legible combinations are red on yellow, green on red, and red on green.

3.   The most exciting color is red. Violet and blue are the most subduing; green the most tranquil and neutral; yellow the most cheerful.

4.   The favorite color of most women is red; most men prefer blue.

5.   Red is the best impulse color, quickly attracting the eye and motivating the individual to action.

6.   Blue is also a favorite of older people, probably due to the fact that as we grow older the lens of the human eye grows yellower. (Yellow filters out blue light.) The lens of child's eye may absorb only 10 percent of the potential blue light, but the lens of an elderly person may absorb as much as 85 percent, an interesting fact to remember when selling to specific age groups.

7.   Colors of greatest appetite appeal, useful in food advertising (menus, direct mail, etc.), are orange, clear yellow, vermillion red, light green, tan, and brown.

8.   In the spring of the year tinted and pastel colors have great appeal,

while in autumn the public taste shifts to the richer shades of red, green, brown, or purple.

9.   Highly styled merchandise usually calls for unusual hues, while volume merchandise is moved with primitive colors like red, blue, green, and white.

10.   Dark colors tend to make objects look heavier and closer; lighter colors tend to make things look lighter and more distant.

REFERENCES

[1]George A. Stevenson, *Graphic Arts Encyclopedia*, McGraw-Hill Book Company, New York, 1968, pp. 270–271.

[2]F. H. Wills, *Fundamentals of Layout*, Dover Publications, Inc., New York, 1965, p. 46.

Chapter 13
DEALING WITH PRINTERS

SIR FRANCIS MEYNELL, A CREATOR of works of scholarship and beauty, once proclaimed: "Every well-designed book of advertisement or prospectus is the begetter of others, and good printing is one of the graces of life even where life is ungracious."

The early masters of the printing art combined a variety of talents—those of type founder, printer, editor, publisher, and bookseller. As presses proliferated and printed materials gained wider distribution, standards became lower and skills more specialized. Sir Francis, unfortunately, described an era of scholar-printers, when pride of craftmanship overshadowed commercial considerations. Equally unfortunate, in Sir Francis' time only the very wealthy could read and there was no reason to schedule press runs in the hundreds of thousands of copies.

STEPS IN PRODUCTION

Printing production may be divided into four major steps: (1) art and copy preparation, (2) conversion of art and copy into printing-image carriers, (3) presswork, and (4) binding and other finishing. We have dealt in some degree with each of these steps in the preceding chapters. The third step, presswork, provides the printed image—the ultimate goal of all printing production. Regardless of a job's purpose or manner of production, printing must always result in a visible image.

Some writers on printing production subdivide the four main steps into lesser ones to facilitate a comparison of various printing processes and methods. One such breakdown presents twelve stages of printing production:

1. Art and copy preparation
2. Composition
3. Graphic arts photography
4. Dot-etching, opaquing, and retouching
5. Planning of printing-image carriers
6. Stripping and gravure layout
7. Making of single-unit, or integral, image carriers
8. Producing of original materials for multiple-unit image carriers
9. Making of duplicate plates
10. Assembling of multiple-unit image carriers
11. Presswork
12. Binding and other methods of finishing

Not every printing job passes through all twelve stages, of course.

PRINTING PROCESSES

The various printing methods or processes may also be classified under four major divisions: letterpress (relief), gravure (intaglio), offset (planographic), and screen (porous). Printing-arts purists go to some trouble to differentiate between processes and methods, but since there is no apparent consensus as to which constitute "methods" and which "processes," we will avoid the semantic problems by taking no side in the matter.

A detailed explanation of the four main printing processes/methods will be found in Chapter 18.

Printing processes and methods may be evaluated for a particular job by applying the criteria of several appearance zones, or limitations. Victor Strauss calls the three primary zones those of (1) uniqueness, (2) interchangeability, and (3) disability. Under Zone 1 fall those effects and results unique or peculiar to a printing method, because of its intrinsic nature or existing equipment, and which cannot be duplicated by any other process or method. Under Zone 2 fall those effects and results which can be produced more or less equally well by at least two printing methods. Under Zone 3 fall those effects and tasks for which a given method is completely unsuited.

TYPES OF PRINTERS

Printers, just as architectural and engineering firms, come in different sizes and offer varying degrees of experience and expertise. Neighborhood shops may handle only the simplest work—small forms, calling cards, stationery, and announcements. Some commercial printers with eight to ten employees can handle color work. Medium- to large-sized lithographers can take on practically any type of commercial printing, but they are not usually interested in short-press-run work.

Before talking to a printer be sure you have established the broad objectives of the brochure, its physical details, and the contents. The determination of objectives and publics was discussed earlier. Physical details have to do with the size and number of pages, the quantity of brochures needed; the number of colors to be used; the type, weight, and grade of paper stock; folds; the type of cover; inserts; binding; and envelopes. Contents refers to the number of photographs, renderings, drawings, and charts (size and kind); the amount of copy; and the composition: display, text, machine, hand set, cold type, and so on.

After these details have been resolved, make up a comprehensive layout or dummy for the printer to use in bidding or estimating. The more complete the layout, the more accurate the estimate should be. Estimating printing costs today is practically a science and in better printing houses every operation is governed by job standards. The exact costs for all details are known, but if the printer is not furnished all information and specifications for a job, the estimate cannot be expected to be accurate.

Keep in mind that printing costs really represent the total of two subcosts—fixed costs and running costs. Whether the press run will be 100 or 100,000 copies, the fixed costs must be included in the price. They include design, typesetting, plates, and press makeready—basically labor and equipment depreciation. This is why 100 copies of a brochure might cost $1,000 and 500 copies cost little more than $1,500. On very long runs the fixed costs tend to average down in unit costs—a factor which does not always hold true in construction.

CHECKLIST

Instructions to the printer should cover all the following:

Quality: Highest, good, fair
Physical: Size, number of pages, colors, paper specifications
Delivery: Realistic dates for proofs, advance copies, and a schedule for shipping including final delivery
Type: Complete specifications
Illustrations: Complete instructions for all photos, art, charts, and the like
Proofs: Explicit type of proofs required
Finishing: Details of folding, trimming, imprinting, embossing, punching, die-cutting, binding, and so on
Packaging: Flat, banded, in cartons, envelopes, and so on[1]

There is, of course, no ideal printer (from a buyer's standpoint) and no ideal buyer (from a printer's viewpoint). But if such animals did exist, they might describe each other like this.

The buyer speaks:

> Ideal printers are pros. They know exactly how to get what I want, and they don't try to pawn off something inferior. They don't make up excuses or pass the buck when something goes wrong, and if there's a chance they can't make the delivery date they call me well before that date. If they think there's a better way to do the job than I've planned, they'll suggest it. They don't take advantage of me on pricing, and they keep me informed about new develop-

ments that I might apply to my jobs. They contact me regularly, and I appreciate their interest.

The printer speaks:

> Ideal customers are fair. They give me a reasonable delivery date, and stick to it. Their material is beautifully organized, with all instructions in writing. They don't hound me with changes every couple of hours. They know good printing, and expect it—but they don't nit-pick about things which are not my fault. They understand that certain things justify extra charges, and they accept them. They tell me when we've done a good job—and when we haven't. When I'm in trouble, I tell them, and whenever they possibly can, they bail me out. Finally, they pay their bills on time![2]

As we said, no such animal exists in either position, but a careful reading of the next few paragraphs might bring us to a kind of printing Camelot.

TAKE A PRINTER TO LUNCH

One way to eliminate many problems in the production of a brochure or any other printing job is to get acquainted with your printer and his or her equipment and operation. Follow a job through the whole process—copy camera, darkroom, making up negative flats, plate production and processing, and the press run.

Time is money to anyone in business, whether the business is engineering, architecture, or printing. The designer chalks up gains for everyone when the printer receives a clean, organized layout—no dirt, crooked copy, finger marks, and so forth. Printing a magazine, newspaper, or brochure requires detailed coordination and cooperation among client, designer, and printer. The easiest way of ensuring the best finished product is to give the printer the best input, in the form of layout and elements, that you are capable of. Remember the traditional comment of computer people when their machines goof, "Garbage in, garbage out." What you send the printer is what you get.

PRINTING COST CONTROL

In a graphic arts workshop of a few years ago, Seymour Sanders, president of the New York City–based Sanders Printing Corporation, gave these five methods of reducing or controlling printing costs:

1. Schedule your job for the day shift. Try to allow enough time in your own production schedule so the printer can produce your job on his day shift. That way you will generally get the benefit of his most skilled and efficient craftsmen.
2. The low bidder is not necessarily the most economical for you. In picking a printer, make sure you see examples of his work. Check to see if he keeps clients as repeat customers—and talk to those customers to confirm his qualifications. That way you avoid the printer who can't do your job properly, or the printer who "low balls" you on his estimate and then inflates his final price with unfair extras.

3. For long runs with process color, get a printer with a four-color press. If your run is 100,000 copies or over, and it prints in process color, significant savings can be realized by using a printer with a four-color press who sends a sheet through the press only once on each side. Below the 100,000 copy level, printers with two-color presses are able to give you superior quality at a competitive price on four-color jobs.

4. If your brochure will contain numerous illustrations, offset lithography is your best bet. Over 90 percent of all annual reports are printed by offset today because this method offers platemaking at a fraction of the cost involved in letterpress or gravure printing . . . the ability to make last-minute changes, by making over a plate quickly and economically . . . and presses that run faster than either letterpress or gravure equipment.

5. Give the printer four-color copy in final size or larger. Particularly when using four-color reflective copy, give the printer art that is clean and larger than the final printed size. For transparencies, have a color lab do the color balancing, the enlargements of duplicate transparencies to final reproduction size, and the required retouching. This way any color problems are corrected by pros who deal with such problems all the time—and at lower rates than most printers charge.

Joseph Verdone, of the IBM Office Products Division, offers a wealth of management and cost control tips to printers in his regular column, "Copy Corner." A few pertinent excerpts:

• Paste down black windows on artwork instead of cutting out windows on negative flats. Jobs can be stripped faster when patches of black paper, the size of the finished halftone, are pasted on the art. Then shoot the halftones and strip them in behind the clear windows in the negative, using rubber cement. If the halftone is to be reduced, mark the percentage of reduction on the edge of the illustration broad mounted glossy or on a protective overlay. If it is to be processed same size, label it "same size," or just "SS."

• Run lightest color ink first, then the darker colors. It is much easier and faster to wash up a press if a darker color is next. In most instances, only a quick wash up is sufficient to make the press ready. Work with yellows or light blues should be scheduled first, then red, blues, and finally black. Run transparent colors ahead of opaque colors.

• Reproduce halftones by the Velox method. Group glossy photographs and shoot a conventional halftone using a coarse screen such as 60, 70 or 80 lines. [This is called "ganging" photos.] Make a contact on Velox paper (contact paper). Cut the screened positive images apart and paste them down on the artwork. They can be positioned very close to line copy. Then shoot the entire flat. including the halftones, as a simple line job. This procedure eliminates stripping individual halftones in place, and allows you to paste halftones adjacent to line work, without the need for double burns.

• Use a "split-fountain" to create multi-color jobs in a single press run. Very colorful jobs can be created by simply dividing some press fountains and running several colors of ink at one time. Be careful on long runs since the inks tend to blend. [As clarification, the ink reservoir, or "fountain," is as wide as the press. By "splitting" or dividing the fountain with dams, up to four separate colors may be applied in the same press run. Obviously, the colors cannot be made to overprint each other in the process. The layout must be carefully done to take advantage of the several color spots.]

• Mark the perimeters of all screens, solids and reverses. Indicate the positions of all these elements in blue pencil on the artwork to facilitate late stripping. It is especially helpful to mark the tint percentage or label the areas "reverse," "solid," etc.

COPY EDITING AND PROOFREADING

There are two opportunities to catch errors in text material. The first is in the editing of original copy before it goes to the printer or typesetter. Copy is edited to correct bad grammar and misspelled words as well as to bring about consistency in such matters as capitalization, abbreviations, and spelling. This is also the last opportunity to rewrite the material for style or meaning at no cost to the client. Corrections on the manuscript are much less costly than corrections on the typeset proof. Author's alterations (AAs) are occasionally necessary, but usually they are not.

The *McGraw-Hill Author's Book* points out the following:

> Upon receiving proof, some authors suddenly decide to rewrite the book. Of course, if there are errors of fact or outdated materials, corrections must be made. But this is not the time to worry about the finer points of writing— polishing your writing at this stage can cost you money, and it will undoubtedly delay publication of the book.
>
> The costs of corrections always mount up much more rapidly than the inexperienced author expects. The original typesetting is done by machine. Corrections require hand work and minor corrections often result in the resetting of considerable material. The charge for altering 20 percent of the lines in a galley proof will amount to a good deal more than 20 percent of the original composition cost. And corrections made in page proof cost much more than those made in galley proof.
>
> You should therefore try to "justify" (compensate for) your corrections by adding the same number of letters that you delete or by striking out a word or words to make room for an addition. . . . Heavy resetting in page proof also leads to the risk of introducing new typographical errors, dropping lines of type, or requiring unexpected alterations in page makeup.[3]

A number of changes in a sixteen-page brochure could cause the type to exceed its allotted space and run over on an additional page. About the only solution to this kind of catastrophe is to make drastic cuts in the text or to have the entire job reset in smaller type.

The typesetter is charged with following the copy exactly as it comes to him in manuscript form. He follows copy-editing marks, alterations, and directions on the manuscript, but does not read for sense or style, of course.

Instructions to the printer and typesetter on the copy are called "marking up," and are very important to an accurate translation of the manuscript into print. Leonard Bahr, in the *ATA Advertising Production Handbook*, points out that correct markup eliminates guesses and facilitates production at every stage. Use of the conventional proofreader's marks saves time and prevents misunderstandings. If instructions can be interpreted in more than one way, they aren't marked properly. *A Manual of Style* explains the situation further.

Being human, [the typesetter] is almost certain, sooner or later, to make a mistake—to omit a letter, a word, sometimes a whole line, to misspell a word, or, worse, to substitute another word (country for county, for example). In the publishing business these errors are called *typos* (typographical errors). The printer's proofreader tries to catch any such slips and to correct them before proof goes to the author. Proofreaders, also being human, sometimes miss an error made by the typesetter. It is hoped that the author, though not a trained proofreader, will catch these residual errors. When an author or an editor spots and corrects a printer's error, he should point out that the matter was correct in the manuscript by circling "PE" (printer's error) or "as in copy" next to the correction in the margin. An alternative method of differentiation is to correct the printer's errors in one color and to make alterations in another; neither color should be that used by the proofreader.[4]

COPY EDITING

We will take up the two editing phases in their proper sequence; copy editing first, then proofreading. Obviously, copy is edited before it goes to the printer and typeset material is proofed considerably later in the process. As was mentioned in the chapter on typography, the safest procedure is to send the cleanest possible copy to the typesetter. After so many corrections are made on a manuscript, it can get terribly confusing to even the most expert typesetter.

Copy editors use some of the same marks as those found in proofreading, and some that are completely different. In copy editing, changes and corrections are in or next to the typewritten double-spaced copy. In proofreading, on the other hand, corrections are made in the left or right margins, next to the line of type in which the error appears. A mark in the type line—a caret for an insertion, a line through the word or letter to be removed—shows where the correction in the margin is to be made. An imaginary vertical line through the center of the proof tells the proofreader which margin to write the correction in, depending on which side of center the error occurs.

COPY-EDITING MARKS

∟   – Begin a paragraph, as⌊The old
                                                      town. . . .

TRⁿⁱ̂AⁱŜOⁱPᵉSE   – Transpose letters

Big ⁀wolf ⁀bad⌟   – Transpose words

. . . the last attempt.⌒   – No paragraph (run in)
⌒With this the. . . .

be here in⟨sixty⟩days   – Use figures

there were⟨9⟩in the   – Spell out

COPY-EDITING MARKS (cont'd)

in Ada, (Oklahoma)	– Abbreviate
The man from (Mo.)	– Spell out
king george	– Capitalize underscored letters
until The day	– Lowercase the slashed capital letter
sup pose	– Close up
untiltheday	– Space between words; separate
amog the may	– Insert missing letter
friend to the poor	– Insert a word or phrase
(X)	– Insert a period
Take a ~~long~~ word	– Delete lined-through word and close up
Takke a word	– Delete letter and close up

PROOFREADING MARKS

Proofreading marks are standardized and should be familiar to anyone who works with type and proofs in the English language—printing craftsmen, designers, writers, and editors. Proofreaders' marks are usually classified in one of two ways: (1) as operational signs, typographical signs, and punctuation marks, or (2) as signs covering the following points:

Size and style of type
Position
Spacing
Insertion and deletion
Signs and symbols
Paragraphing
Punctuation
Miscellaneous

For our purposes, the latter breakdown will be used, and the marks used for each category in the listing will be shown.

Size and Style of Type

lc –Set in lower case.

caps –Set in capitals.
(═══ under a letter or word means "caps.")

PROOFREADING MARKS (cont'd)

caps + lc —Set in lower case with initial caps.

sc —Set in small capitals.
(‗‗‗‗‗‗ under a letter or word means small caps.)

wf —Wrong font (refers to size or style of type).

ital —Set in italic type.
(_____ under a letter or word means ital.)

rom —Set in roman type.

bf —Set in boldface.

lf —Set in light face.
(〰〰〰 under a word or phrase means boldface.)

bf ital —Set in boldface italic.
(〰〰〰 under a word or phrase means boldface italic.)

⌄2 —Insert superior number.

⌃2 —Insert inferior number.

⌄a —Insert superior letter.

⌃a —Insert inferior letter.

Position

∧ —Caret; something to be inserted.

‖ —Straighten or align type vertically.

═ —Straighten the line horizontally.

⌊ —Move to the left (also, flush left margin).

⌋ —Move to the right (also, flush right margin).

⌐⌐ —Move letters or words up.

⌊⌋ —Move letters or words down.

⌋⌊ —Center word or material in line or page.

tr —Transpose marked letters or words.

⪌ —Set ragged margin.

Spacing

—Insert space.

⌣ —Leave less space between words.

PROOFREADING MARKS (cont'd)

eq # —Equalize space between words.

solid —Set solid, not leaded.

leaded —Set with additional space between lines.

⌒ —Close up; take out all spacing.

□ —Indent one em.

▭▭ —Insert number of em spaces shown.

l/s —Letterspace, as indicated.

↓ —Push down space that prints.

Insertion and Deletion

   —Take out; delete. The form of the delete sign varies among printing shops and among proofreaders. The main concern is that it is recognizable as an instruction to delete and will not be confused with any handwritten letter such as d, e, g, or l.

   —Take out character indicated and close up.

stet —Let it stand; retain crossed out word or letter. Dots (....) under the crossed-out material show what is to stay.

Signs and Symbols

use lig. —Use ligature.

/ —Virgule; stop mark.

⁂ —Insert asterisk.

(···) —Insert leaders (ellipsis).

Paragraphing

¶ —Begin a new paragraph.

fl ¶ —Flush paragraph, usually flush left.

no ¶ —No paragraph. Sometimes written "run in."

③ ¶ —Indent paragraph the number of em quads (spaces) shown.

hang in —Set as hanging indentation. Also called a lead-in, outrigger, or overhang.

PROOFREADING MARKS (cont'd)

Punctuation

⊙ –Insert period.

⋀ –Insert comma.

⊙ –Insert colon.

⋀ –Insert semicolon.

ꞌ/ –Insert apostrophe.

ꞌꞌ/ –Insert quotation marks.

=/ –Insert hyphen.

?/ –Insert question mark.

!/ –Insert exclamation point.

init. –Set as large initial.

/⅟ₘ / –Insert one-em dash.

/²⁄ₘ/ –Insert two-em dash.

/¹⁄ₙ/ –Insert one-en dash.

[/] –Enclose in brackets.

(/) –Enclose in parentheses.

Miscellaneous

X –Replace broken type.

9 –Turn over upside-down type or cut.

(?OK) –Query to author.

(sp) –Spell out abbreviated word or numbers.

see l/o –See layout.

OK w/c –O.K. with corrections.

OK a/c –O.K. as corrected.

Most publications that deal with typography and printing production show a simulated marked-up proof calculated to scare a neophite proof-reader silly. Such an example appears in the University of Chicago's *A Manual of Style* on page 73, reproduced below as Figure 13-1.

As some reassurance that galleys and page proofs usually come back in reasonably clean shape, a marked page proof from *How to Market Professional Design Services* is shown as Figure 13-2. Actually, the page proof in Figure 13-2 was one of the most heavily corrected pages for the book.

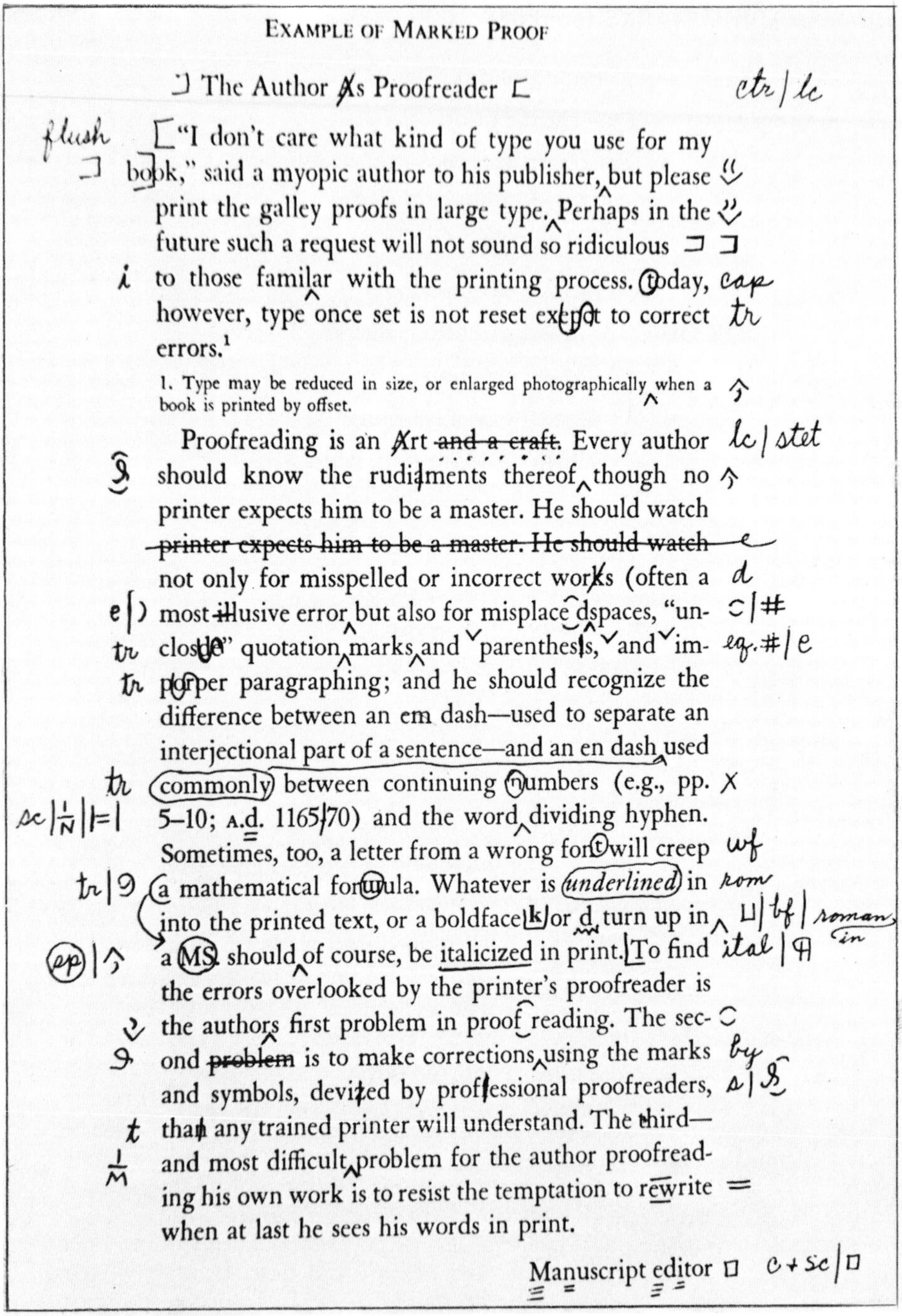

EXAMPLE OF MARKED PROOF

⌐ The Author As Proofreader ⌐   *ctr/lc*

flush ⌐"I don't care what kind of type you use for my
book," said a myopic author to his publisher, but please
print the galley proofs in large type. Perhaps in the
future such a request will not sound so ridiculous ⌐ ⌐

i to those familar with the printing process. Today, *cap*
however, type once set is not reset except to correct *tr*
errors.[1]

1. Type may be reduced in size, or enlarged photographically when a
book is printed by offset.

Proofreading is an Art and a craft. Every author *lc/stet*
should know the rudiments thereof, though no
printer expects him to be a master. He should watch
printer expects him to be a master. He should watch   *e*
not only for misspelled or incorrect works (often a   *d*
e most illusive error but also for misplaced spaces, "un- *c/#*
tr closed" quotation marks and parenthesis, and im- *eq.#/e*
tr proper paragraphing; and he should recognize the
difference between an em dash—used to separate an
interjectional part of a sentence—and an en dash used
tr commonly between continuing numbers (e.g., pp. *X*
sc|¹⁄ɴ||=| 5–10; A.D. 1165/70) and the word dividing hyphen.
Sometimes, too, a letter from a wrong font will creep *wf*
tr|9 a mathematical formula. Whatever is *underlined* in *rom*
into the printed text, or a boldface k or d, turn up in   *lⱼ/bf/roman*
a MS should, of course, be *italicized* in print. To find *ital/¶*
the errors overlooked by the printer's proofreader is
the authors first problem in proof reading. The second problem is to make corrections, using the marks *by*
and symbols, devized by proffessional proofreaders, *s/ş*
t than any trained printer will understand. The third—
⅟ᴍ and most difficult problem for the author proofreading his own work is to resist the temptation to rewrite =
when at last he sees his words in print.

Manuscript editor   *c + sc*

Figure 13-1. A marked proof "example," from the University of Chicago's *A Manual of Style*. See Figure 13-2 for a more realistic example of a marked proof.

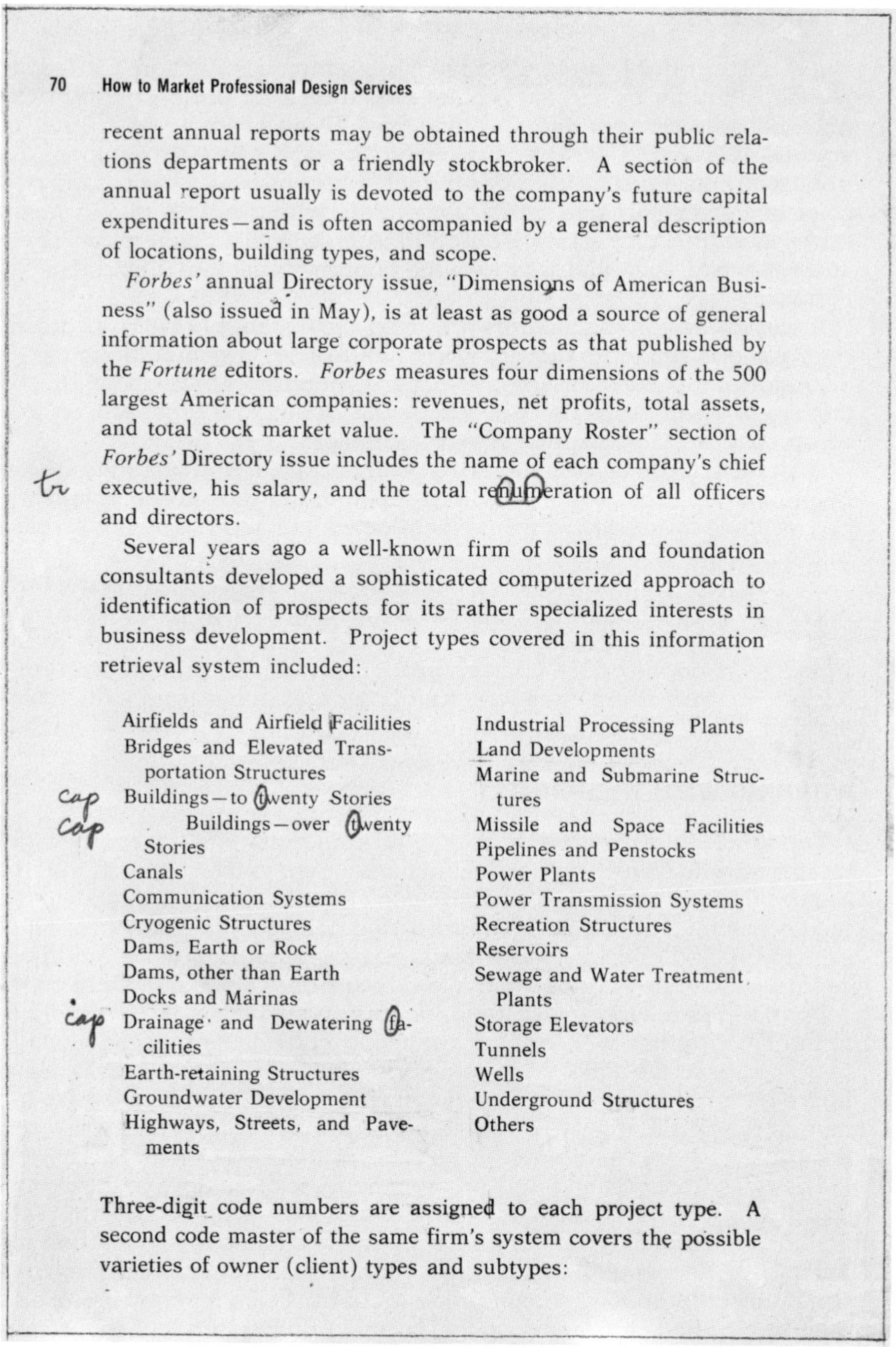

70 How to Market Professional Design Services

recent annual reports may be obtained through their public relations departments or a friendly stockbroker. A section of the annual report usually is devoted to the company's future capital expenditures—and is often accompanied by a general description of locations, building types, and scope.

Forbes' annual Directory issue, "Dimensions of American Business" (also issued in May), is at least as good a source of general information about large corporate prospects as that published by the *Fortune* editors. *Forbes* measures four dimensions of the 500 largest American companies: revenues, net profits, total assets, and total stock market value. The "Company Roster" section of *Forbes'* Directory issue includes the name of each company's chief executive, his salary, and the total remuneration of all officers and directors.

Several years ago a well-known firm of soils and foundation consultants developed a sophisticated computerized approach to identification of prospects for its rather specialized interests in business development. Project types covered in this information retrieval system included:

Airfields and Airfield Facilities
Bridges and Elevated Transportation Structures
Buildings—to Twenty Stories
Buildings—over Twenty Stories
Canals
Communication Systems
Cryogenic Structures
Dams, Earth or Rock
Dams, other than Earth
Docks and Marinas
Drainage and Dewatering Facilities
Earth-retaining Structures
Groundwater Development
Highways, Streets, and Pavements

Industrial Processing Plants
Land Developments
Marine and Submarine Structures
Missile and Space Facilities
Pipelines and Penstocks
Power Plants
Power Transmission Systems
Recreation Structures
Reservoirs
Sewage and Water Treatment Plants
Storage Elevators
Tunnels
Wells
Underground Structures
Others

Three-digit code numbers are assigned to each project type. A second code master of the same firm's system covers the possible varieties of owner (client) types and subtypes:

Figure 13-2. A marked-up page proof for page 70 of *How to Market Professional Design Services.* This was one of the most heavily marked pages in the book.

TAKING BIDS

If this is a firm's first experience with brochure production it is recommended that the design-team chief obtain at least three printing bids, each based exactly on the specifications. There are not very many "or equals" in printing and it is possible, through seemingly minor and apparently constructive changes in such things as type, paper stock, and color placement, for one printer to come in with a bid up to 30 percent lower than the competitors. You and the prospective client might never know the difference, but why take the chance? Insist that all bidders use identical specs.

If outside design consultants are used they probably will use a cost-analysis form similar to that shown in Figure 13-3. The form in Figure 13-3, designed by the Hammermill Paper Company, offers an organized method of assembling the pertinent details about your brochure, as well as an easy way to compare bids or estimates.

After all bids are in, samples have been reviewed, and assurances have been received that deadlines will be met and the proper equipment will be available for the job, a printer is selected—on the basis of both these and other factors.

As Seymour Sanders pointed out a few pages back, low bidders are not necessarily the most economical. By looking at samples of their work and checking with present clients on their qualifications (how much repeat work do they do?), one can probably avoid the printers who can't do the job right or the ones who sandbag on estimates and then inflate the final price with unwarranted extras.

WORKING WITH THE PRINTER

The ideal situation is to be able to turn all materials—properly organized and with clearly written instructions—over to the printer at the first session. The job rates a better-than-even chance of being printed without time-consuming and expensive errors and delays if the material is properly assembled and identified. Each page or spread may be put into a separate folder or envelope to avoid mix-ups and misunderstandings.

Provide clean, typed, proofread, double-spaced copy. If the copy goes to the typographer with a lot of confusing corrections and deletions, it only increases the time the typesetting-machine operator must take to figure out and set your job. It is usually much less expensive to take the time to retype dirty copy so that the typographer can set it quickly and accurately.

The rules about editing and proofing copy before it goes to the printer are broken all too often. Once the material is in type proof form, AAs (author's alterations) are charged back to the client over and above the bid price. AAs might be compared to change orders or extras in construction, subject to about the same amount of abuse by unknowing clients and by unprincipled contractors. As the printing production process proceeds through blue-line proofs and plate making, AAs become increasingly expensive.

COST ANALYSIS

PROJECT _____

CUSTOMER _____

1. Page size_____

2. Number of pages _____

3. Cover size and stock _____

4. Style of binding_____

5. Number of copies to be produced _____

6. Size of paper to be ordered _____

7. Number of sheets required for project _____

8. Paper costs:

	Substance_____	Substance_____	Substance_____
	(Grade)	(Grade)	
a. Number of M sheets	_____	_____	_____
b. Price per M sheets	_____	_____	_____
c. Total Cost of Paper (a x b)	_____	_____	_____

9. Mailing costs:

	Substance_____	Substance_____	Substance_____
	(Grade)	(Grade)	
a. Weight of dummy (include envelope)	_____	_____	_____
b. 1st class postage per unit	_____	_____	_____
c. Total 1st class postage (Line (b) x No. of copies mailed)	_____	_____	_____
d. 3rd class postage per unit	_____	_____	_____
e. Total 3rd class postage (Line (d) x No. of copies mailed)	_____	_____	_____

10. Cost Comparison:

	Substance_____	Substance_____	Substance_____
	(Grade)	(Grade)	
a. Paper cost	_____	_____	_____
b. Postage cost (1st class)	_____	_____	_____
c. Paper & 1st class postage	_____	_____	_____
d. Postage cost (3rd class)	_____	_____	_____
e. Paper & 3rd class postage	_____	_____	_____

Figure 13-3. A sample cost-analysis form, based on one developed by the Hammermill Paper Company.

If it is not possible to send the text to the printer in one package, send it in as few batches as possible. Typesetting machines must be set up each time and typesetters must refamiliarize themselves with the job—both of which tend to increase costs and fracture deadlines.

Copy fitting—making the text for the brochure come out even with the amount of space assigned to it in the layout—is an art. Nonprofessionals usually require crutches to help them write copy to fit. Some typeface sample books show the relation between pica or elite typewriter sizes and the width of characters in a given typeface. If the typist types to the proper, predetermined width on the page, each line of copy should closely correspond to the line width to be typeset.

Photographs should be sized and marked, and instructions given as to cropping, page number, position, and any special considerations such as COB (cut out background, where everything in a photograph behind a subject is opaqued out). Grease pencils should be used to mark photographs in the margins. Lengthy instructions are best done in soft pencil on a tissue overlay.

BE YOUR OWN ESTIMATOR

Various desk-top estimating catalogs for establishing printing estimates and bids are available to the printing trade. We mention them here in the unlikely event a design firm would want to dig that deeply into the mysterious world of printing estimating.

The Porte Publishing Company, of Salt Lake City, publishes three catalogs: the *Franklin Offset Catalog*, the *Franklin Printing Catalog* (for all commercial letterpress work), and the *Franklin Lettershop & Bindery Catalog*. The catalogs are leased for about $30 a year, with updating sections furnished periodically. Tables in the offset catalog are based on camera-ready copy.

By using the Franklin catalog tables one can come up with fairly accurate cost estimates for a great variety of printing jobs. The variable always would be whatever additional charge the printer believed the traffic would bear.

A good brief book on the subject is *Printing Estimating*, by Gerald A. Silver, published by the American Technical Society, Chicago. Figure 13-4, which shows an estimator's worksheet, is from the book, as is Figure 13-5, which shows a sample quotation sheet.

The sample job covered by the forms is for 2,000 copies of a two-color letterhead. Three columns are provided on the worksheet to enable the estimator to work out the cost of three different quantities of the same item at the same time. Many customers ask for prices on at least two quantities. For a brochure, the printer might be asked for quotes on 1,000 and 3,000 copies.

The quotation form is to briefly define the job and the sale terms, including the price. Normally, the customer is not furnished with a detailed manufacturing cost analysis, but there is no rule that says you cannot ask for a more detailed breakdown. Make certain the quotation includes an approximate delivery date.

Estimator's Worksheet

NAME _Steven's Manufacturing_ DATE _May 7, 19-_

ADDRESS _1234 Monlux Street_ PHONE _901-2231_

2000 8½ x 11, 25% rag bond letterheads
Reflex blue, job black
Composition 8 lines
Letterpress, both colors

		2 M	M	M
STOCK	$4.85 per M	9 70		
CUTTING				
COMPOSITION	8 lines	5 00		
MAKE-UP		3 00		
PASTE UP				
ART WORK				
REPRODUCTION PROOFS				
LINE NEGATIVES				
HALF TONE NEGATIVES				
STRIPPING				
PLATES				
MAKE-READY				
PRESS RUN	2 runs of 2 M $9.00 each	18 00		
WASH UPS	Reflex blue	2 50		
HOLD PLATES				
INK				
BINDERY				
TRIMMING				
FOLD				
GATHER				
STITCH				
SEWED				
WRAP				
BAND				
PUNCH				
PERFORATE				
PAD				
DELIVERY				
TOTAL PRINTING COST		38 20		
TOTAL PURCHASES	none			
TOTAL COST OF JOB		38 20		
MARKUP 35% (from mark-up summary)		12 37		
QUOTATION		50 57		

Figure 13-4. Estimator's worksheet, used to figure the cost of 2,000 two-color letterheads on 25-percent rag bond. (From _Printing Estimating,_ by Gerald A. Silver, p. 17. Reproduced courtesy of American Technical Society)

Quotation   YOUR COMPANY NAME

Customer: *Steven's Manufacturing*   Date: *May 7, 19—*
1234 Monlew Street

WE TAKE PLEASURE IN SUBMITTING THE FOLLOWING QUOTATION:

Quantity	Item	Unit Price	Amount
2 000	*Two – color letterheads*		
	Size 8½ X 11, 25% Rag Bond		
	Reflex blue ink and job black		
	ink		
	8 lines of composition	$25.28	$50.57
	Delivery: 4 working days		

Prices on this estimate are not final and seller reserves
the right to revise prices to reflect increases in labor or
material costs occuring between the dates of this estimate
and acceptance of order.
  A variation in quantity of ten percent over or under con-
stitutes filling this order. Price to be adjusted proportionately.
  We are not responsible when paper, plates, negatives or
type are furnished by customer.
  All negatives, plates, cuts and type remain the property
of _____ unless invoiced separately and noted
to the contrary.
  Quotation subject to acceptance within fifteen days.
  Quotation subject to change if there are any changes or
alterations from original instructions, layout or copy.

Richard Martin, Estimator

THANK YOU FOR ALLOWING US TO SUBMIT THIS ESTIMATE

Figure 13-5. The quotation sheet for the job estimated in Figure 13-4. This is all a customer normally sees of the estimator's computations. (From *Printing Estimating*, by Gerald A. Silver, p. 18. Reproduced courtesy of American Technical Society)

Many quotation forms include printing trade customs, usually on the back of the form. A list of accepted trade customs recommended by the Printing Industry of America, Inc., will be found at the end of this chapter. Keep in mind that the customs contractually bind both parties, unless written exception is taken and agreed to by both parties.

M WEIGHT

Basis weight, the standard comparison of paper weights, was discussed in Chapter 12. Remember that basis weight (or substance) is the weight in pounds of 500 sheets (one ream) of a given paper in the basic size. The basic size for bond paper is 17 x 22 inches, so one ream of 20-pound bond weighs 20 pounds.

Since printing today usually is ordered by the thousand sheets, most printers refer to paper weights in terms of 1,000 sheets rather than the traditional ream. The M weight (M meaning 1,000 in Roman numerals) is the weight of 1,000 sheets (two reams) of paper of a particular size—not necessarily the basic size. If the sheets are larger than the basic size, the M weight will be greater than the total weight of two basic-sized reams. A package of 17 x 22 inch bond paper labeled Sub. 20 (20 pounds per 500 sheets of the basic size) is the same as a package labeled 40M (40 pounds per 1,000 sheets). "Sub." is an abbreviation of "substance," which means the same as basis weight.

PRINTING TRADE CUSTOMS

Printing contract standards are similar to AIA contract standards, and any printing customer should be aware of them. As we said above, unless specific sections are exempted during the pricing stage, and agreed to in writing by both parties, the customer is subject to the trade customs. Printing industry associations in some large metropolitan areas, such as New York City, use slightly different versions of the trade customs, but those of the Printing Industries of America govern most of the country, and are shown below.

1. Orders regularly entered cannot be cancelled except upon terms that will compensate against loss.
2. Experimental work performed at customer's request, such as sketches, drawings, composition, plates (including lithographic plates), presswork and materials shall be charged for at current rates.
3. Sketches, copy, dummies, and all preparatory work created or furnished by the printer, shall remain his exclusive property and no use of same shall be made, nor may ideas obtained therefrom be used, except upon compensation to be determined by the owner.
4. Art work, type plates (including lithographic plates), engravings, electrotypes, negatives, positives and other items when supplied by the printer shall remain his exclusive property, unless otherwise agreed in writing.
5. Alterations: Proposals are only for work according to the original specifications. If through customer's error, or change of mind, work has to be done a second time or more, such extra work will carry an additional

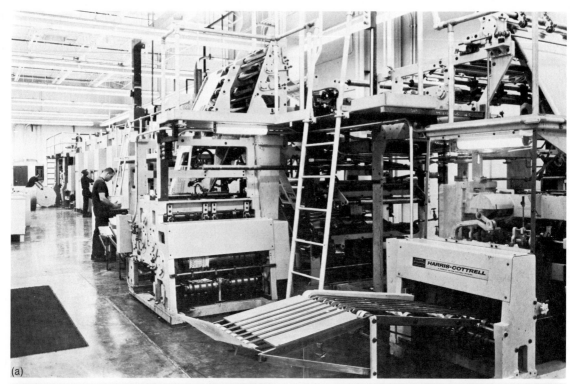

Figure 13-6. *(a)* **The Harris-Cottrell Model 1000 web offset press. Each perfecting unit on the Model 1000 simultaneously prints one color on each side of the paper web as it travels through the press at speeds of up to 1,000 feet per minute.** *(b)* **The Harris-Cottrell 43 × 64 inch web offset press. This press can handle an impression area more than three times that of the standard Model 1000 press, running at speeds of 1,200 feet per minute.** (Photos courtesy of Harris Corporation—Printing Press Division)

charge, at current rates for the work performed.

6. Standing type matter, plates (including lithographic plates), and negatives will not be held after completion of the order except by special agreement and charge therefor.

7. Proofs: Two proofs shall be submitted with original copy. Corrections, if any, to be made thereon and to be returned marked "O.K." or "O.K. with corrections" and signed with name or initials of person duly authorized to pass on same. If revised proofs are desired, request must be made when proof is returned. Printer is not responsible for errors if work is printed as per customer's O.K.

8. Press proofs: An extra charge will be made for press proofs, unless the customer is present when the form is made ready on the press, so that no press time is lost. Presses standing awaiting O.K. of customer will be charged at current rates for the time so consumed.

9. Over runs or under runs not to exceed 10% of the amount ordered shall constitute an acceptable delivery and the excess or deficiency shall be charged or credited to the customer proportionately.

10. Customer's property. The printer shall charge the customer, at current rates, for handling and storing customer's stock or customer's printed matter held more than thirty (30) days. All customer's property that is stored with a printer is at the customer's risk, and the printer is not liable for any loss or damage thereto caused by fire, water leakage, theft, negligence, insects, rodents, or any cause beyond the printer's control. It is understood that the gratuitous storage of customer's property is solely for the benefit of the customer.

11. Delivery: Unless otherwise specified the price quoted is for a single shipment, F.O.B. customer's local place of business. All proposals are based on continuous and uninterrupted delivery of complete order, unless specifications distinctly state otherwise.

12. Terms: Net cash thirty (30) days. All claims must be made within five days of receipt of goods.

13. Delays in delivery: All contracts are made contingent upon wars, strikes, fires, floods, accidents, or other contingencies beyond the printer's control.

14. Repairs, changes, trimming, mortising, anchoring, special proving, or similar work required on materials which are furnished by the customer, including but not limited to drawings, engravings, electrotypes, and negatives, shall be billed at current market rates.

15. Paper stock furnished by the customer shall be properly packed, free from dirt, grit, torn sheets, bad splices, etc., and of proper quality for printing requirements. Additional cost due to delays or impaired production on account of improper packing or quality shall be charged to the customer.

16. Color proofing: Because of the difference in equipment and conditions between the color proofing and the pressroom operations, a reasonable variation in color between color proofs and the completed job shall constitute an acceptable delivery.

REFERENCES

[1] Based on *The Printer and The Buyer*, by the Chillicothe Paper Company. As reprinted in *Delaware Valley Industry* magazine, March 1971.

[2] Ibid.

[3] *The McGraw-Hill Author's Book*, McGraw-Hill Book Company, New York, 1968, pp. 40–41.

[4] *A Manual of Style*, 12th ed., rev., The University of Chicago Press, Chicago, 1972, p. 76.

Chapter 14

BROCHURE SYSTEMS

$\mathbf{A}$ BRIEF DESCRIPTION OF THE MOST common types of brochures was given in Chapters 3 and 4. One type is the brochure system. The systems approach to brochure design may encompass the following:

1. A series of bound booklets
2. A collection of unbound single or multiple (foldout) sheets
   a. assembled into a single folder or box holder
   b. assembled by groups in carriers on the basis of building types or in-house specialties and services
3. A combination of (1) and (2), that is, loose-leaf (unbound) sheets plus booklets

There is some logic in also including under brochure systems a brochure in which part of the contents is bound into the cover and the remainder is carried in a pocket or pockets in the inside front or back cover. Examples of all these variations will be shown on following pages.

The most common form of a brochure system is the series of bound booklets. Such a system is based upon an umbrella booklet, which contains general information about the firm—a kind of compact general capability brochure. Seldom more than twelve pages long, the umbrella brochure *could* stand alone in its brief presentation of a firm's experience, staff, and capabilities. However, a true system of brochures will include companion booklets, graphically related, about in-house services offered and about various building or client types with which the firm has had significant and demonstrable experience.

For example, a complete system might consist of the following booklets:

1. Umbrella
2. Architecture
3. Interior design
4. Planning
5. Graphics
6. Landscape architecture
7. Mechanical and electrical engineering
8. Structural engineering
9. Civil engineering
10. Construction management
11. Value engineering
12. Design/build
13. Computer services
14. International operations

These would represent the in-house services of a fairly large organization. The second tier of booklets, on building or project types, could cover the following:

1. Religious buildings
2. Government buildings
3. Educational buildings
4. Residential areas
5. Highways and bridges
6. Dams
7. Office buildings
8. Airports
9. Transportation
10. Planning
11. Industrial
12. Commercial
13. Health facilities

A single important completed project could appear in several booklets. For example, a dormitory for a state university might be shown in the booklets covering government buildings, educational buildings, and residential work. An office building for the Federal Aviation Agency, located at a major airport, could be included in the booklets covering government buildings, office buildings, and airports.

The total number of different booklets (and subjects) included in a brochure system is up to a firm's imagination and bank balance. In most cases, a package of from two to four (always including the umbrella brochure) will cover the interests and requirements of a prospective client. Some examples of brochure systems are shown in Figure 14-1.

A primary requirement for any brochure is flexibility—its adaptability to different clients and projects. One obvious method of obtaining maximum correlation with individual client needs and interests is to custom-assemble each brochure, but this solution is hardly the answer for most firms.

(a)

(b)

We've mentioned flexibility. What are some of the other important considerations in designing a brochure? The list might include the following items:

- Outstanding design and graphics.
- Interesting, non-jargon-filled text.
- Excellent illustrations.
- All important points about a firm's experience, staff, services, cost controls, and the like.
- A reasonable cost per unit, to encourage effective distribution.
- Overall dimensions within 8½ x 11 inches, to meet filing requirements. This includes the 8½ x 8½ inch square format. Up to a 9 x 9 inch square is acceptable, but larger dimensions will only invite client resistance because of the filing problems involved.

Approaching the subject of what makes a good brochure from a slightly different angle, we could say that the basic ingredients include some nostalgia, some avant-garde touches, and a preponderance of contemporary elements.

Nostalgic, or historic, ingredients include a brief firm history and a few examples of the earliest firm projects. The latter is not too relevant, of course, if the firm is less than a year old. Since avant-garde means "in the vanguard," anything indicative of professional leadership and breakthrough design will satisfy this requirement. Finally, the brochure should project a contemporary image in all respects—layout, type, art, photographs, language, and projects shown.

Since total flexibility is impractical for most firms, the brochure system approach is one of the better compromises. In addition to the family of same-size booklets or individual pages, a smaller leaflet, usually keyed graphically to the rest of the system, is often produced. The leaflet, or folder, sized to fit in an inside coat pocket or a number 10 envelope, may be left with a potential client in preliminary meetings as a reminder of your firm. Some business development directors take a set of brochures to talk from, but leave only the small folder. Pertinent brochures are mailed to the client later, with a letter of transmittal reiterating the salient points covered in the meeting. This procedure gives two good contacts for one.

Designing and producing a complete system or family of brochures can be both time-consuming and costly. Fortunately, it is seldom necessary to produce all of them at once. Begin with the umbrella booklet and add others as convenient and necessary. If the system consists of bound brochures, a program for updating should be established. Ordinarily, no more than one of the booklets will be in revision at a time, so that costs

Figure 14-1. Two excellent brochure systems. *(a)* A seven-element system from Daniel, Mann, Johnson, & Mendenhall (DMJM). The DMJM umbrella brochure is at the top of the right column. *(b)* The other system is one formerly used by the Kling Partnership but which has now been replaced.

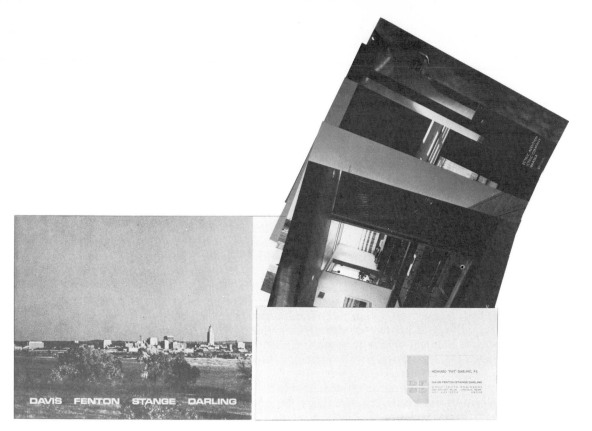

Figure 14-2. Combinations of bound booklets and loose-sheet inserts offer a lot of flexibility. The back cover of Davis/Fenton/Stange/Darling's booklet is extended into a folder to hold project photos. Anderson Associates' brochure uses a back flap to carry project descriptions.

for the total system can be spread over a long period. In effect, the system amortizes itself.

If the system is based on individual project sheets, revisions and updating are somewhat simpler but no less demanding of a scheduled procedure. As a job moves from concept through design and construction, so might the project sheet go through three or four versions, finishing with a sheet on the completed building. It is obviously much cheaper to replace one or several separate sheets than to reprint an entire booklet to show the current status of a job.

At least one architectural firm mails out single new project sheets as they become available. The project descriptions are designed as complete mailing pieces. No request is made to the receiver to add the new sheets to the firm's system on file, but many clients do just that. It's a type of good, professional, continuing contact with the firms and individuals

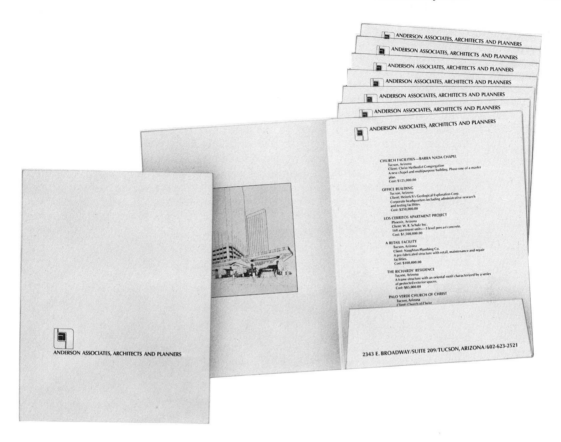

on your mailing list of past, present, and potential clients.

The combination bound booklet and loose sheets, as a variation on the brochure system, is perhaps of greater interest to small- to medium-size firms. Material that is apt to remain fairly constant—history, philosophy, principals, and so on—is put into several pages that are stapled or otherwise attached to the cover. Loose sheets on individual projects, lists of references, staff biographies, representative client lists, and representative project estimates, bids, and costs are placed into a pocket on the inside back cover. Properly designed and produced, this type of brochure can serve a firm well. (See Figure 14-2.)

The design of the carrier for a brochure system is just as important as the material to be transmitted. Too many systems are mailed in a flimsy box or other type of holder and arrive on the client's desk with all the charm of a wadded-up newspaper. The importance of testing the mailing container, before giving final approval to the printer, has been mentioned elsewhere. This step is particularly important with a brochure system, because of the combined weight of individual booklets or sheets. TAC protects its system with sturdy holders of different sizes to accommodate varying numbers of folders. While mailing costs are somewhat higher, the guarantee of the package's arriving in something approaching mint condition probably warrants the increased postage.

Before launching a brochure system, the designer should review a number of the systems now in use and select the best points of each to incorporate in one for his firm. No one has yet designed the *best* system for all potential clients. In the unlikely event that that ever happens, the lucky firm presumably will end up with all the work, since that is the ultimate test of the effectiveness of marketing efforts.

Chapter 15

MISCELLANEOUS TIPS AND SUGGESTIONS

IN THIS CHAPTER WE'LL TRY to set down a number of helpful tips, ideas, and suggestions which did not seem to fit logically into previous chapters. There may be small areas of duplication, but it is to be hoped that any overlapping will be minimal. Some of the material is based on an article, "Ways to Save Production Dollars," from an early issue of *Impact*, a monthly newsletter published by Robert L. Baker, Suite 903, 360 North Michigan Avenue, Chicago, Ill. 60601. Now well into its second decade of publication, *Impact* covers trends, techniques, ideas, and editorial tools in and for the communications field. As of this writing, a year's subscription costs $15.

PRINTERS

Pick your printer to fit the job. Don't go to a basement printer for 100,000 copies of a four-color brochure, or to a firm that prints 250-page catalogs in full color for 100 copies of a black-and-white leaflet. If printers can't or don't want to handle your job, there is nothing to prevent them from subcontracting it to another printer and charging a good commission for their trouble and your ignorance. Be logical. Would you take a $65 million industrial complex to a three-man design firm—or a $25,000 house to SOM?

Be certain that your designer has specified the correct method of reproduction for your job (offset, letterpress, gravure, and the like) if you want to obtain the desired results at the lowest cost and on time.

If your firm has a fair amount of printing done on a continuing basis, get competitive bids—perhaps every six months, and at least annually. It's a businesslike way to make sure that you're always getting the best job at the best price.

Consider all these factors in selecting a printer: general reputation, price range, quality of craftsmanship (based on samples of work similar to your job), expert proofreading, prompt invoicing, clear and accurate job tickets within the shop, ability to keep promises and meet deadlines, extra services, and good processing, packing, and delivery of the completed job.

ARTWORK

Be wary of such costly production procedures as surprinting, drop-out halftones, bendays, morticing, silhouettes, multiple-screen effects, reverses in process colors, art heads, and most other engraving extras and "gingerbread."

Always check finished art carefully. Any changes made later may require new plates. And don't deliver material piecemeal to the printer. Give art with copy. This avoids double handling and reduces the chances of error and the loss of important elements.

Where a drawing has been planned, ask yourself whether or not a photograph would do the job as well. Photography is usually cheaper than art.

PHOTOGRAPHS

Good photographs help reduce the cost of retouching.

In making a series of portraits or similar photos try to keep the camera angle, lighting, framing, and subject-to-camera distance the same. This allows the printer to group or "gang" the photos and shoot a number of halftones at one time.

It is advisable to get a signed release from *every* staff member whose picture appears in a brochure or any other promotional material for the firm. If minors are involved, permission must be obtained from their legal guardians. Failure to do so could be very costly if a disgruntled or former employee wanted to claim invasion of privacy. Employees have the right *not* to have their likenesses used for commercial or trade purposes. Make the release binding by paying a consideration (a dollar or two or a copy of the photo) for all rights to use the picture, including advertising and other forms of promotion.

A short-form model release, as used by a well-known East Coast commercial photographer, reads:

> For value received, I hereby grant to [*photographer's name*] and his assigns permission to use my photograph and/or statement for advertising, trade or similar purposes.

> Date_____   Name_____

> Date_____   Witness_____

There is a much longer form of release, normally used for commercial models, that covers practically every contingency known to humans. It is not recommended for general use with employees; most of them would be frightened off by the legalese in it.

PICTURE ABUSE

Endless and ingenious are the devices with which an editor can mutilate his pictures. He vandalizes by cutting pictures into tiny squares. He bastardizes by mixing art and photograph. The temptation to get cute and clever with pictures should be resolutely resisted. No editor would dream of instructing his compositor to pi his type. But he will often *pay* a layout artist to make a shambles of his photography! He won't play childish games with his prose. But he will permit picture nonsense to be perpetrated. He hasn't learned that chopped-up photographs are no better than scrambled sentences. . . . The best picture handlers are purists. The best approaches are simple and straightforward. The safest rules are these:

If a picture is bad, it shouldn't be used.
If a picture is good, it should be given unimpaired display.
There is no point, really, in messing around.[1]

STOCK PHOTO SOURCES

Stock photo houses were mentioned in Chapter 10, but complete information was given for only one source (Roloc Color Slides). A number of other excellent sources are available to the designer who wants a particular kind of shot but whose budget does not allow for extensive travel, costly location setups, and expensive commercial or architectural photography. Keep in mind that commerical photo libraries sell prints from their negatives for one-time reproduction only. Multiple usage, as in a brochure *and* a book, must be paid for each time.

These are some of the best-known stock photo sources:

Photo Library
Black Star Publishing Company
450 Park Avenue South
New York, N.Y. 10016

Black Star is an old-time photo house, with staff photographers or stringers in most major cities of the world. They do not publish a catalog, but inquiries on specific subjects will be answered with several prints on approval. Well over a million negatives (black and white and color) are in Black Star's library.

Bettmann Archive, Inc.
136 East 57th Street
New York, N.Y. 10022

Bettmann specializes in very old photographs; some half-million negatives of mainly historical figures and subjects are on file. There is no complete catalog, but a book, *Bettmann Portable Archive*, is available for around $20. Photos will be sent on approval.

Wide World Photos, Inc.
Associated Press
50 Rockefeller Plaza
New York, N.Y. 10020

Subject catalogs are issued from time to time on the "millions" of negatives in Wide World files. The primary clients of this photo library are magazines and book publishers, but they will sell to anyone. Unless credit has previously been established with Wide World it may be somewhat difficult for the average design firm outside New York City to get a selection of photographs on approval.

Photo Library
UPI
220 East 42d Street
New York, N.Y. 10017

UPI's commercial film library maintains more than 3 million negatives—color and black-and-white—on file. A catalog is available. Here photographs are filed by subjects (A to Z) and by personalities (A to Z). A selection of prints will be sent on approval.

Photo Research International (Photri)
P.O. Box 971
Alexandria, Va. 22313

Photri is operated by Jack Novak, a retired Air Force colonel. A subject catalog is available. The files here are not as extensive as some of the others listed, but Colonel Novak seemingly knows where to find any photo not in his files. Selections sent on approval.

H. Armstrong Roberts
4203 Locust Street
Philadelphia, Pa. 19104

All subjects are covered in Roberts' 1 million black-and-white and over a half-million color photos. Catalogs on various subjects will be sent on request. A selection of pictures will be sent on ten-day approval.

EROS Data Center
(Earth Resources Observation Systems)
Sioux Falls, S. Dak. 57198

EROS is part of the U.S. Department of the Interior's Geological Survey and is a rather specialized photo library. EROS's basic photo source is the NASA Earth Resources Technology Satellite (ERTS). ERTS travels in polar orbit around the earth at an altitude of 567 miles. Each of the photos taken by the satellite covers an area 115 x 115 statute miles. ERTS sends back new images of an area every eighteen days. The pictures are available in black and white or in simulated three-color form. (See Figure 15-1.)

The Data Center also processes and distributes high-altitude aircraft

Figure 15-1. An ERTS satellite photo covering the southern end of Florida. Lake Worth is at the top right of the land mass; below Lake Worth the cities of Fort Lauderdale, Hollywood, Miami Beach, Miami, and Coral Gables can be identified. Key Largo is just out of the picture to the lower right.

photos of many areas of the United States. Upon receiving an inquiry, the center sends an order kit, including a United States map keyed to all ERTS's coverage areas. A 14½-inch-square black-and-white photo (scale 1:500,000) costs $5. Color in the same size is $15.

Audiovisual Archives Division
National Archives and Records Service
General Services Administration (NNV)
Washington, D.C. 20408

If the picture wanted is in the National Archives, the price is hard to beat. An 8 x 10 inch black-and-white photo is less than $3 and is cleared for all types of use and for as many times as the buyer wants to use it. The basic files are from pictures made by service and government photographers. Explain your photo needs in a letter and

Audiovisual Archives will tell you what they have. No selections on approval here; it's really worth a trip to the National Archives to review their stock of more than 5 million still pictures, including 5,000 Matthew Brady–supervised shots and 223,000 photos from Nazi files. Some 1.5 million maps, 2.4 million aerial photos, and more than 82,000 reels of motion picture film are also in the archives.

LAYOUT

Deciding on the printing process to be used *before* layout and art are executed keeps costs down. Different preparations for these two steps are required for each printing process. Offset is usually best for complex layouts.

Consider carefully the position of bleed pages. Consult your printer on how many and where. Reduce the number of bleed pages if you can. They take longer to lock up and may require a larger sheet of paper—which could lead to unnecessary paper wastage.

Remember, changes and corrections are easier to make and are far less costly in the dummy stages, rather than later.

FORMAT

Always check early with the printer to be sure your format is proper for the equipment. It is sometimes possible to get a two-color effect by using a second color on only one side of the press sheet. In such cases the printer can make up a dummy showing which pages will be two-color pages.

Rely on the printer for dollar-stretching suggestions. If a second color is used for the front cover only (in a self-cover brochure), the designer may be passing up free color on fifteen or more additional pages.

PAPER

The growing paper shortage, with consequent reductions in allocations of at least some grades to distributors and printers, was alluded to in Chapter 12. The shortages had their roots in several concurrent events and developments. A number of obsolete mills closed down completely when they were unable to meet federal antipollution requirements. Accentuating the overall problem was a shortage of raw pulp, caused by both increasing domestic and foreign market demands. Price controls in this country caused manufacturers to accept the increasingly higher bids from a growing overseas clientele. A general cutback in new plant construction of pulp-processing plants and paper mills exacerbated the situation. Through at least 1976 the dismal outlook is for less production, growing demand, and predictably skyrocketing prices.

With all this in mind, select paper and a format carefully. Odd page sizes can cause high paper wastage. A premium-grade paper can add considerably to total costs; be certain the paper used is the best for the audience, budget, and purpose. We're not suggesting that brochures be printed on newsprint—but consider some of the kraft paper selections in early planning.

COLOR

Multiple-color effects can be had from only two colors of ink by using colored stock and overprinting screens of each color. All such effects should be carefully planned. Consider substituting tint blocks for true duotones in two-color halftones.

A cost and time saver in two-color work is to skip the color proof. But in complicated work or process color, *get* the proof.

On short-run, multicolor jobs, try to plan art work so that colors don't touch or overlap. Hairline registration of colors increases the job's cost because of the time required for accurate registration.

COPY

Get all necessary clearances and approvals in the manuscript stage. Do the tough or touchy items in the earliest possible stages of the brochure's development, and have some pertinent filler material as backup in the event that higher authority has insurmountable objections to the original treatment.

Cut the copy to its essentials before it goes to the typesetter. Eliminate all useless words and avoid overset (too much copy, too little space) by typing copy to fit. Send only clean, accurate copy. Remember, it costs money to set type and even a dozen useless words can run the typesetting bill up by several dollars.

Develop an internal style sheet and insist that everyone involved in copy preparation use it as the final reference. This will ensure consistency and encourage accuracy. Consistent style in spelling, capitalization, and punctuation is the mark of a good writer and editor. Always recheck all statistics, proper names, technical terms, foreign words, and unusual spellings.

Keep a record of the sources of data, illustrations, art, and any other material that may have to be verified or identified later.

Corrections may be handwritten (better yet, hand printed) in the body of the copy if they are few and clear. Otherwise, retype the pages involved—a typist's time is far less costly than a typesetter's or compositor's. Make sure that any deleted words or phrases are clearly deleted, and that the text reads smoothly on either side of the deleted matter. Not smoothing out the text around deletions and additions is an often-committed sin of the experienced as well as the inexperienced writer.

Include clear, explicit directions about size, leading, and style for each typeface. Key all typed copy to its exact position on the layout.

PLATES

Once the offset plate has been made, major changes cannot be made without going to the expense of making a whole new plate. This does not mean starting the job from scratch, of course, since any changes can be stripped into the flat and the new press plate made from the corrected negative.

Be careful on halftone screens, particularly in letterpress work. The coarser the screen, the cheaper its production cost, but the printer should be consulted as to the best screens for the paper to be used for the job. We've already mentioned the economies to be achieved by "same-focus" shooting and ganging of halftones, as opposed to making separate shots of each element. Usually there is some sacrifice of quality in these procedures, but it may not be evident to anyone less than an expert.

TYPESETTING

Use a colored pencil to indicate type size, typeface, line length, and other typographical instructions to make them easier to see and read.

In letterpress production have the printer hold all type and cuts if there is a chance the job may be reprinted. Some shops charge a fee when the storage period exceeds thirty days, but this can be far cheaper than redoing the entire job.

PRESS RUNS

If you want to see press proofs, check them at the printing plant and be there when they come off the press. Delays for delivery of proofs and waiting for their approval may be charged for at regular press time rates.

Avoid excessive overruns on a job. Trade customs allow the printer to bill for up to 10 percent overrun, but state your requirements as early as possible. This can prevent delays and extra expense in such items as paper stock. It might even allow the printer to get a better price for the paper by shopping around, although this edge is being dulled by paper shortages.

Avoid rush jobs and last-minute changes as the plague. They inevitably result in overtime work by high-priced employees. A printer is justified in adding a large markup to your bill for rush delivery. And remember, once the presses start to roll, the cost of stopping them for custom changes can be mind boggling.

FOLDING

If the job requires any unusual folds, check to see if the folding can be done by machine. Hand-folding is expensive, and it may be possible to modify the job slightly and adapt it to machine-folding.

Plan large-quantity jobs on the press sheet so that they can be gang-folded. A big machine can fold thousands more individual pieces per hour than a small, friction-type folder can.

Review all other processes, including cutting, punching, stitching, die-cutting, laminating, embossing, trimming, and collating, to make certain that they are handled as efficiently and economically as possible.

DISTRIBUTION

To cut mailing costs, keep the weight of the paper stock down and watch the size of the brochure. A reduction in size of as little as a quarter of an inch can save many dollars in postage charges.

Unless there is a compelling reason to go to the extra expense of a custom-designed mailer, make certain the job fits into a standard-size envelope. Standard sizes in inches for square envelopes include 7½ x 7½, 8½ x 8½, 8¾ x 8¾, 9½ x 9½, and 11 x 11. The largest standard-sized square envelope is 20½ x 20½ inches, but we hope that the previous discussions on optimum brochure formats will make any mention of envelope size exceeding 9½ x 9½ inches academic.

Booklet envelopes are available in these standard sizes:

No. 4½	5½ x 7½	No. 7¼	7 x 10
No. 5	5½ x 8⅛	No. 7½	7½ x 10½
No. 6	5¾ x 8⅞	No. 9	8¾ x 11½
No. 6½	6 x 9	No. 9½	9 x 12
No. 6¾	6½ x 9½	No. 10	9½ x 12⅝
No. 7	6¼ x 9⅝	No. 13	10 x 13

Certainly, in that range of sizes, a designer should be able to find an appropriate envelope for his brochure. Occasionally, a brochure can be designed as a self-mailer, wherein the address label is affixed to an area of the cover (usually the back), and an envelope or other type of mail cover is eliminated. Although this approach unquestionably saves money, the unprotected brochure is likely to arrive in something less than presentable condition. After seeing hard-bound books—mailed in heavy-duty, padded book-mailing carriers sold by the postal service—arrive in a condition that could only have been caused by repeated passes of a fully-loaded freight car, or by being thrown from a plane at 40,000 feet into holiday traffic on the Pennsylvania Turnpike, I am not an enthusiastic supporter of self-mailers.

SUPERVISION

Keep accurate, running accounts of printing expenditures. Watch particularly charges for author's corrections, overtime, overruns, paper charges, typesetting charges, and photo and art costs. Know in advance what nonchargeable services can be expected from the printer. Always get firm written estimates on all extras to be charged for.

SPRECHEN SIE DEUTSCH?

Some design and construction firms with growing overseas commitments might want to follow the lead of certain large U.S. corporations with foreign markets and production facilities and print sections of their brochure in one or more foreign languages. Corporations using the multilingual approach include General Motors, ITT, Rockwell, TRW, Litton, Burroughs, Gulf Oil, J. P. Morgan, Beatrice Foods, Singer, AMF, Continental Can, and Philip Morris.

Philip Morris, for example, operates and sells in many countries. The board of directors' "Review of the Year" for 1973 was translated into French, Spanish, German, Italian, and Dutch. The first few paragraphs of each foreign language section are reproduced in Figure 15-2.

Some corporations release complete foreign language versions of their

Review of the Year

Nineteen seventy-three marked the 20th consecutive year in which your company reported new records for operating revenues, profits, and earnings per share. Consolidated operating revenues reached $2.6 billion, an increase of 22.1%, and net income rose to $149 million, a gain of 19.4% above 1972. Fully diluted earnings per share were $5.21 and primary per share earnings were $5.42, representing annual increases of 19.2% and 16.1%, respectively.

We are pleased with the 1973 results, achieved in a most difficult year marked by price controls, materials shortages, major currency realignments, and the energy crisis.

Philip Morris further increased its share of the world cigarette market and strengthened its position as the second largest publicly-held cigarette producer in the world. In 1973, world-wide cigarette industry sales increased 4% to over 3.6 trillion units, and Philip Morris, including both United States and international sales, had a 6.7% share of the world cigarette market. On a world-wide basis, Marlboro continued to be the largest selling cigarette brand—a position it gained in 1972. Within the United States, Marlboro, the number two brand, moved very close to the top position.

Rètrospective de l'année

En 1973, pour la vingtième année consécutive, votre société a enregistré à nouveau des résultats sans précédent pour ce qui est du chiffre d'affaires, des bénéfices et du revenu par action. Le chiffre d'affaires consolidé a atteint 2,6 milliards de dollars, soit une augmentation de 22,1%, et le bénéfice net s'est élevé à 149 millions de dollars, soit une progression de 19,4% par rapport à 1972. Le rendement par action (en tenant compte des titres convertibles) s'établit à 5,21 dollars et le rendement effectif par action à 5,42 dollars, soit un accroissement annuel de 19,2% et de 16,1% respectivement.

Nous sommes satisfaits des résultats obtenus en 1973, une année rendue extrêmement difficile par suite du contrôle des prix, des pénuries d'approvisionnement, de réalignements importants des parités monétaires et de la crise de l'énergie.

Philip Morris a encore accru sa part du marché mondial des cigarettes et a renforcé sa position en tant que deuxième producteur de cigarettes du monde dont les actions sont cotées en bourse. En 1973, les ventes mondiales de l'industrie de la cigarette ont augmenté de 4% pour atteindre plus de 3600 milliards de cigarettes, et Philip Morris (en tenant compte des ventes aux Etats-Unis et à l'étranger) obtenait 6,7% du marché mondial de la cigarette. Marlboro demeurait la marque de cigarette la plus vendue dans le monde—position qu'elle avait acquise en 1972. Aux Etats-Unis, Marlboro, qui occupe le deuxième rang, s'est rapprochée très près de la première place.

Informe del año

En este ejercicio de 1973 conmemoramos los veinte años consecutivos durante los cuales vuestra Compañía ha venido reportando nuevos records de ingreso bruto operacional, de ganancias y de utilidades por acción. El ingreso bruto operacional consolidado se elevó a U.S.$2.600 millones, un aumento del 22,1%, y las ganancias netas ascendieron a U.S.$149 millones, un incremento del 19,4% sobre 1972. Las utilidades por acción, incluyendo bonos convertibles, fueron de U.S.$5,21 y las utilidades efectivas por acción fueron de U.S.$5,42, lo que representa aumentos sobre el año anterior del 19,2% y 16,1%, respectivamente.

Nos sentimos complacidos de los resultados obtenidos en 1973, sobre todo porque se lograron en un año sumamente difícil caracterizado por los controles de precios, la escasez de materiales, el reajuste de las paridades de las principales divisas y la crisis energética.

Philip Morris amplió en mayor grado su participación en el mercado mundial de cigarrillos y reforzó el segundo puesto que ocupa entre las mayores empresas cigarrilleras del mundo cuyas acciones se cotizan en la bolsa. En 1973, las ventas mundiales de la industria del cigarrillo aumentaron 4% hasta sobrepasar los 3.600 billones de unidades; la participación de Philip Morris en el mercado cigarrillero mundial, que abarca las ventas en Estados Unidos y en el extranjero, fue del 6,7%. A escala mundial, los cigarrillos Marlboro siguen siendo los de mayor venta —un puesto que ostentan desde 1972. En Estados Unidos, la marca Marlboro ocupa el segundo lugar pero redujo considerablemente la distancia que la separa de la primera.

Rassegna dell'anno

Anche per l'esercizio testè conclusosi, la Vostra Società ha incrementato il fatturato, gli utili e il reddito per azione; il 1973 rappresenta così il ventesimo anno di costante ascesa del livello di tali fondamentali dati finanziari. Rispetto al 1972, il fatturato consolidato e l'utile netto hanno registrato un incremento del 22,1% e del 19,4%, raggiungendo, rispettivamente, la cifra di $2,6 miliardi e di $149 milioni. Il reddito per azione (tenendo conto dei titoli convertibili) è dunque stato di $5,21, ed il reddito effettivo per azione è stato di $5,42, il che rappresenta un aumento rispettivamente del 19,2% e del 16,1%, per rapporto al 1972.

I risultati ottenuti nel 1973 sono tanto più soddisfacenti in quanto conseguiti in un anno particolarmente difficile, caratterizzato da controlli del livello dei prezzi, da difficoltà nell'approvvigionamento di materie prime, nonché da fondamentali variazioni delle parità monetarie e dalla crisi energetica.

La Philip Morris ha ulteriormente esteso la propria quota del mercato mondiale delle sigarette e rafforzato la propria posizione al secondo posto nella graduatoria mondiale delle società produttrici di sigarette quotate in borsa. Il fatturato totale nel mondo delle aziende del settore ha registrato nel 1973, un aumento del 4%, totalizzando la cifra globale di 3.600 miliardi di pezzi; la Philip Morris, tra il fatturato per gli Stati Uniti e quello estero, si è assicurata il 6,7% del mercato mondiale. Le Marlboro continuano ad essere la marca di sigarette più venduta nel mondo, mantenendo così la posizione raggiunta nel 1972; sul mercato interno degli Stati Uniti, esse sono al secondo posto, ormai molto vicine alla posizione di testa.

Geschäftsverlauf und Ausblick

Auch im Geschäftsjahr 1973 konnte Philip Morris Inc.—zum 20. Mal in ununterbrochener Folge—die Umsatzerlöse, den Jahresüberschuss und den Gewinn je Aktie gegenüber dem Vorjahr erhöhen.

Die konsolidierten Umsatzerlöse erreichten $ 2,6 Mrd. und lagen damit um 22,1% über dem Vorjahrswert. Der Jahresüberschuss stieg im Berichtsjahr um 19,4% auf $ 149 Mio. Der Gewinn je Stammaktie betrug $ 5,42, was einer Zunahme von 16.1% gegenüber dem Vorjahr entspricht. Unter voller Berücksichtigung aller Umtauschrechte ergibt sich ein Gewinn je Stammaktie von $ 5,21, was eine Verbesserung von 19,2% gegenüber dem Vorjahr bedeutet.

Diese Zahlen sind um so erfreulicher, wenn man bedenkt, dass das Geschäftsjahr 1973 durch Preiskontrollen, Rohmaterialienverknappung, beträchtliche Verschiebungen der internationalen Währungsrelationen sowie die Energiekrise gekennzeichnet war. Philip Morris konnte seinen Anteil am Welt-Zigarettenmarkt weiter steigern und unsere Position als zweitgrösste notierte Aktiengesellschaft unter allen Zigarettenherstellern der Welt festigen. Der weltweite Absatz der gesamten Zigarettenindustrie erhöhte sich 1973 um 4% auf über 3,6 Billionen Zigaretten. Unser Absatz in den Vereinigten Staaten und auf den Auslandsmärkten sicherte uns einen Anteil von 6,7% am Welt-Zigarettenmarkt. Unsere Marke Marlboro nimmt weiterhin den im Jahre 1972 erreichten ersten Platz auf dem weltweiten Zigarettenmarkt ein. In den Vereinigten Staaten kam diese Marke—derzeit auf dem zweiten Platz—der Spitzenposition sehr nahe.

Terugblik op het jaar

Negentien-drie-en-zeventig was het 20ste achtereenvolgende jaar waarin uw bedrijf nieuwe rekords boekte in omzet, winst en winst per aandeel. De gekonsolideerde omzet steeg tot $2,6 miljard, een toename van 22,1% en de nettowinst steeg tot $149 miljoen, een toename van 19,4% vergeleken met 1972. De winst per aandeel (rekening houdend met konverteerbare obligaties) bedroeg $5,21 en de winst per aandeel voor konversie bedroeg $5,42, hetgeen neerkomt op een stijging van respektievelijk 19,2% en 16,1% in vergelijking met 1972.

Wij zijn verheugd met de resultaten van 1973, die werden behaald in een uiterst moeilijk jaar, dat werd gekenmerkt door prijskontroles, tekorten aan grondstoffen, belangrijke valutaherwaarderingen en de energiekrisis.

Philip Morris vergrootte voorts zijn aandeel in de internationale sigarettenmarkt en verstevigde zijn positie als de op één na grootste sigarettenproducent ter wereld die op de beurs staat genoteerd. In 1973 steeg de verkoop van de sigarettenindustrie over de gehele wereld met 4% tot ruim 3,6 biljoen eenheden. Philip Morris bereikte op de internationale sigarettenmarkt een marktaandeel van 6,7%. Marlboro bleef het meest verkochte sigarettenmerk ter wereld. Deze positie werd in 1972 bereikt. Binnen de Verenigde Staten schoof Marlboro, het op één na meest verkochte merk, heel dicht op naar de eerste plaats.

Figure 15-2. From the Philip Morris 1973 annual report. The English version is followed by translations into French, Spanish, Italian, German, and Dutch.

annual reports. Gulf Oil, ITT, and Rockwell have issued a number of brochures, annual reports, and catalogs in Russian. It is advisable to use a professional translation service if a foreign language brochure seems appropriate. Most such services are located in New York City; All-Language Services, Inc., 545 Fifth Avenue, New York, N.Y. 10017, seems to be a leader in corporate translations. All-Language Services "guarantees" its work (who do you have on staff qualified to check the accuracy of a Dutch or Chinese translation?) and will send specimen translated corporate annual reports and prices on request.

COUPON CLIPPING

This idea may well be abhorrent to some readers, and impress others as silly, but it's worth at least minimal consideration. Include a reply card in the brochure, either as an insert or a tip-in, both to encourage and ease the job of response and to check on the general effectiveness of the brochure. The reply card should be addressed to a person in the firm—a principal or the one in charge of business development. And any resulting correspondence should be signed by the person to whom the card is addressed.

```
Mr. Smith:

      Please send me more information about Smith, Smith,

Danzowinski & Associates' experience with

      ☐ Office buildings          ☐ Laboratories

      ☐ Housing developments       ☐ Industrial buildings

      ☐ Hospitals                  ☐ Theaters

      ☐ Educational facilities     ☐ Other _____

I found the SSD&A brochure

      ☐ Interesting and helpful    ☐ Not pertinent to our

      ☐ Too long                      interests

      ☐ Not informative            ☐ Did not give enough

                                      details on _____

      Date _____    Name _____

                               Title _____

                               Company _____
```

Figure 15-3. A possible format for a reply card to be included in general capability brochures. At least one firm uses this method of asking readers to react.

As a start, the request card might ask what kind of additional information the receiver would like to have—more material on a specific building type (this could be a check-the-box approach), elaboration on one or more of the services offered by the firm, such as construction management services, or a list of references for a specific project shown in the brochure. Don't be afraid to ask for reader reaction. The reply card might look like the one in Figure 15-3.

While we're not even suggesting here that a firm carry a reply coupon on the last page of its brochure, consider the consternation to be caused by a coupon printed in reverse (see Figure 15-4).

Name _____
Address _____
City _____
State _____ Zip _____

Figure 15-4. This has to be one of the most frustrating graphic details ever dreamed up by a designer—a reverse reply coupon.

POP-UPS

Another gimmick, which might serve as an attention-getter because it has not—to our knowledge—been used before, is a strategically spotted pop-up. The cost of including an effective pop-up would probably be prohibitive in most cases.

Chris Crowell & Company, Inc., in Darien, Connecticut, is one source of a variety of pop-ups. Two of the Crowell items, including an elaborate one advertising Kodak Instamatic cameras, are shown in Figure 15-5.

(a)

(b)

Figure 15-5. Crowell & Company pop-ups. *(a)* The house *could* be used by a design firm. *(b)* The more elaborate pop-up for Kodak pops-up a full-size reproduction of an Instamatic camera. The text is in Spanish.

The text for the Kodak pop-up is in Spanish. The smaller, stock pop-ups, in quantities of up to 5,000, should run under 15 cents each applied to a brochure page in the Darien plant.

Hammermill Papers has a brochure, *Selling the 3rd Dimension,* which illustrates a number of simpler pop-up ideas. Your printer should have a copy or be able to get one for you. Some of the Hammermill examples are freestanding; others are true page pop-ups.

REFERENCE

[1]Gerald D. Hurley and Angus McDougall, *Visual Impact in Print,* Visual Impact, Inc., Chicago, 1971, p. 165.

Chapter 16

PROPOSALS AND SPECIAL BROCHURES

MANY DESIGN FIRMS ARE BORN, lead reasonably productive lives, and eventually sell out, merge, or die without ever responding to a request for proposal (RFP). In marketing workshops we still run across a few practitioners who have never even heard the term "RFP."

EXAMPLE OF AN RFP

In the interests of continuing education and expanding readers' horizons, we reprint in full a very detailed request for proposal issued a few years ago by Johns Hopkins Hospital, in Baltimore. Various methods of preparing proposals will then be discussed.

THE JOHNS HOPKINS HOSPITAL
REQUEST FOR PROPOSAL, INFORMATION AND QUESTIONS FOR
FINAL ARCHITECTURAL COMPETITION

The Johns Hopkins Medical Institutions, which is comprised of the University Schools of Medicine, Hygiene and Public Health and Health Services and The Johns Hopkins Hospital, have recently completed a phase of planning which defined the state of our physical plant here on the East Baltimore campus and has further helped to clarify broad objectives for rebuilding our facilities in order to support our immediate and long range programmatic objectives in education, research and patient care. (See attached Volume II JHMI Redevelopment Plan.)

The Hospital, in coordination with the School of Medicine, is now attempting to develop specific priorities for the first phase of this rebuilding. The Medical School has identified its first structure, an Oncology Center, which will be funded in part by the federal government and sited adjacent to existing Hospital structures. The Hospital's priorities, although somewhat less specific, have been identified as:

    A. Replacement and modernization of beds.
    B. Expansion of Radiology.
    C. Expansion of Clinical Laboratory.
    D. Replacement and expansion of Outpatient Facilities.
    E. Replacement of four Operating Rooms.
    F. Expansion of the Power Plant.
    G. Expansion of Parking. (Not specifically a part of Phase I.)

In addition to the above information, you should be aware of the following facts and assumptions:

    A. This will principally be a Hospital project since the Oncology Center will be considered as part of the Phase I Hospital construction. Architects have been identified for this structure, which will be proceeding at a very rapid schedule. It is emphasized, however, that this structure will be closely integrated into the overall redevelopment plan design.

    B. Several major programmatic decisions have not been made:

        1. The exact site of the construction has not been determined.
        2. The number of new replacement beds has not been determined.
        3. The size of the expansion of Radiology and Clinical Laboratory has not been determined.
        4. The size, location and operational characteristics of the Outpatient Facility have not been determined.

    C. The scope and gross program for the Oncology Center has been developed by the University and funding by the government is expected within a matter of weeks.

    D. Life cycle costing is as important as construction costs. The Hospital is interested in taking every precaution to insure that its new facilities are efficient in the use of all supporting personnel and physicial services in the best environment we can provide at the lowest possible cost.

    E. The major sources of funds for the Hospital will come from the sale of bonds through the Maryland Authority for Health and Higher Education. Additional funds will be derived from the University and Hospital Centennial Fund Campaign and the previously identified federal cancer construction grant. Total project costs, including the Oncology Center, are estimated to be in the range of 40–50 million.

The Hospital's Trustees have authorized the hiring of a construction management and an architectural firm in order that the Institutions may immediately proceed to establish specific priorities and undertake the construction of these facilities.

The Construction Manager selected for this assignment is Turner Construction Company. The attached copy of pertinent portions of the Turner Construction Company's proposal for services as a Construction Manager for this project is attached hereto. While it is emphasized that the Institutions have not yet negotiated a contract for these services and, therefore, not identified the specific functions contained therein which would be performed, we do believe that this proposal best represents the philosophies and level of services which the Hospital will require to achieve a successful project. In order to be sure that we develop the most compatible team, we would like your comments on the proposal.

It is anticipated that the selection of the architect will be made by March 30, 1973. In order to do this, the following schedule has been established:

A.	Request for Proposals issued	March 22, 1973
B.	References presented to Mr. Thomas E. Arrigo of Turner Construction Co., 1528 Walnut Street, Philadelphia, Pa. 19102, (215) KIngsley 5-2838, no later than the close of business (may be telephoned in and later confirmed).	March 23, 1973
C.	Firms desiring a site visit to the Institutions for the purpose of obtaining additional information may schedule visits on March 23, 24 or 25 by calling Mr. Richard W. Trompeter, the Johns Hopkins Hospital, (301) 955-5400, no later than 12:00 p.m., March 23.	March 23–25, 1973
D.	Proposals due in Mr. Trompeter's office, Room 428A of the Administration Building, 601 North Broadway, Baltimore, Maryland 21205, or at the first floor Information Desk of the Administration Building, no later than 8:00 a.m., March 28.	March 28, 1973
E.	Selection of final candidates	March 28–29, 1973
F.	Visits to final candidate's offices.	March 28–29, 1973
G.	Final interviews with presentation of fee schedules.	March 30, 1973

Final candidates will be advised of the composition of the visiting team as soon as possible. They will be advised at that time of the specific time the team would like to visit for no more than 3 or 4 hours in order to meet personnel and review facilities.

The final selection will be made by Mr. Henry J. Knott, Chairman of The Hospital's Building Committee; Mr. Robert Harvey, Mr. J. Crossan Cooper, Jr., Mr. Harrison Garrett, Mr. Jerold C. Hoffberger, Mr. Blanchard Randall and Mr. Oliver H. Reeder, Trustees of JHH; Mr. William McGuirk, Chairman of the Board of Trustees, JHH; Dr. Steven Muller, President, JHH and JHU; Dr. Robert Heyssel, Director of the Hospital; Mr. David Price, Executive Director, Medical Planning and Development Committee; Dr. Guy McKhann, Chairman of the Professional Committee; and Mr. Richard W. Trompeter, Project Director.

In order that the Institutions may better understand your organization and its methods of operation, it is requested that the following information be included in your qualification statement, in addition to any standard format you might have. Fifteen copies of your proposal should be provided to Mr. Trompeter. Each item should begin on a new page with double-spaced typing and tabbed for easy identification. Candidate firms selected for final interview will be required to submit their fee proposal at the time of interview.

A. *Firm Objectives*

1. Brief statement of firm's overall objectives.
2. Describe fields in which you feel your firm is eminently qualified or specialists.
3. Please indicate your fee philosophy, being as specific as you feel is appropriate at this time.

B. *Firm History*

1. Date of establishment.
2. Location.
   a) Principal office.
   b) Secondary offices.
      (Indicate office which would handle this project with an *)
   c) Subsidiaries.
3. List commissions for the past five years, giving the following pertinent information:
   a) Project name
   b) Location
   c) Brief description (including level of responsibility, scope, etc.)
   d) Year built
   e) Building area—New
      Building area—Alterations
   f) Consultants: Mechanical
      Electrical
      Hospital
      Elevators
   g) Structural System
   h) Contacts: *Address*   *Telephone*
      Owner
      General
      Contractor(s)
4. Indicate any project on which you have been involved where you did not complete the final design. Indicate the reason.
5. Construction Cost Volume of Work you designed for years:

	Total	*Hospital Work*
1958		
1963		
1968		
1969		
1970		
1971		
1972		
1973 (projection)		
1974 (projection)		

6. Describe the other commitments your company has, including location, size and your resources devoted to these projects.
7. Attach a copy of your latest certified financial statement from your accountant, as well as copies for the two previous fiscal years.
8. Is your firm a subsidiary of others: ——— ———
                                         Yes   No

   If "Yes," of what Corporation?

9. Describe, to the extent possible, future commitments you anticipate during the Hopkins' project.
10. Describe your organization's understanding and experience in
both federal and public (underwritten) financing.

C. *Firm Personnel*

1. Provide resumes of firm principals that will be involved in
project and advise *how they will relate to the project.* Resumes
should include date of birth, previous firms, education, professional registration by States, Professional memberships and
honors received.
2. Indicate usual "chain-of-command" for a project of this type,
including master planning, programming, design development and contract drawings.
3. Who in "chain-of-command"
   a) Makes client contacts and control.
   b) Makes project policy decisions and control.
   c) Makes day-to-day detail decisions.
   d) Assumes responsibility for "interaction" between designers, specification writers, planners, estimators, detailers,
   engineers (including consultants), etc.
4. Identify the principal who will be assigned full-time to this
project:
   a) Complete descriptions of education, training and experience and time in organization.
   b) Describe the individuals he will report to in your organization and any other responsibilities he will be assigned
   during the life of this project.
   c) State the level of authority he has in your organization.
   d) When will he be available?
5. Indicate consultants (name no more than three in each case)
one of which in each category you would employ for this
project. (If you suggest these functions are to be performed by
your own staff, merely indicate "in-house".)
   a) Hospital planning.
   b) Structural engineering.
   c) Mechanical engineering.
   d) Electrical engineering.
   e) Elevator consultant.
   f) Hospital equipment consultant.
   g) Soils consultant.
   h) (Others you may wish to note.)
   i) (Others you may wish to note.)
6. Describe the relationship your firm should have with the
mechanical and other engineering consultants.
7. Describe what problems may develop and your solutions to
"interfacing" with another architect on the development of the
Oncologic Facilities in an integrated Master Plan.
8. Identify consulting firms (i.e., engineering, hospital, etc.) with
which there has been repeated associations on past and current projects.
9. Professional Staff Size:

	No. of Personnel		
Categories	*Present*	*1968*	*1963*
Principals			
Project Architects			
Designers			
Job Captains			
Staff Architects			
Detailers			
Specification Writers			
Field Staff			
Estimators			
Graphic Designers			
Planners			
Structural Engineers			
Plumbing Engineers			
HVAC Engineers			
Electrical Engineers			
Landscape Architect			
Others you may wish to list _____	_____	_____	
Total			

Note by * any functions that have been added during periods above.

Note by ** should you propose to use a consultant rather than "in-house" staff on this project.

D. In frank terms, describe the weaknesses and value of The Johns Hopkins Medical Institutions' Redevelopment Plan as your firm sees its relationship to this construction project.

E. Identify the problems associated with this project as your organization understands the situation.

F. Specifically, critique the schedule contained in the Construction Manager's proposal from a planning and design standpoint. Indicate in bar chart form at least the following milestones:

    Master Plan
    Phase I Program Development
    Schematics
    Design
    Construction Start

G. Comment on the cost data presented by the Construction Manager and the Redevelopment Report.

H. 1. Describe your firm's ability and technique for cost estimating.
    2. Indicate your firm's ability to assist in life costing.
    3. Indicate in specific terms the services that you feel a hospital consultant/hospital management engineering firm should provide and how their input should be utilized by your firm.
    4. The Hospital has been talking to a number of hospital consultants and hospital management engineering firms. If your firm does not have this capacity or needs to have this function supplemented, please indicate the firm you would prefer to work with in this effort and indicate any other firms which you would consider appropriate for this task should your first choice not be appropriate for one reason or another.

    I. *Brochures*

        1. Attach any of your firm's brochures that you feel illustrate your capabilities.

        2. As in (1.) above, but pertaining to Hospital Work.

Note that the Johns Hopkins selection committee essentially dictated the order of the proposal response:

A. Firm's objectives, including fee philosophy.

B. Firm's history.

    1. Date established.

    2. Location of principal office, branch offices, and subsidiaries.

    3. Commissions for last five years.

    4. Projects where design uncompleted.

    5. Volume of work for nine years.

    6. Current work in-house.

    7. Certified financial statements for three years.

    8. Future commitments anticipated.

    9. Experience in public work.

C. Firm's personnel.

    1. Résumés of principals.

    2. Chain of command (organization chart). Explain in detail.

    3. Identify principal to be assigned to project full-time. Give complete biography, level of authority, availability, etc.

    4. Names of consultants in at least seven categories of specialization.

    5. Description of firm's relationship with all consultants and other architects who may be involved.

    6. A list of consulting firms previously worked with.

    7. Breakdown of professional staff.

D. Frank discussion of JHMI's Redevelopment Plan.

E. Identification of problems of the project, critique of the CM schedule, and comment on CM cost data.

F. Firm's knowledge of cost estimating, life-cycle costing, necessary consultants, etc.

G. General capability and special (hospital) brochures enclosures.

RFP GUIDELINES

The proposal must convince the prospective client that the proposing firm's methodology is sound and that the principals have a clear, thorough understanding of the client's requirements.

Proposal submission usually is at least a two-stage procedure. The client initially requests expressions of interest in a project, to which interested firms respond with general capability and qualifications material, plus letters of interest. Following the client's evaluation of the material received, RFPs go out to selected firms. Formal proposals are then prepared and sent to the client to assist him in making his final decision.

It goes without saying that interviews with selected firms often precede the client's final choice.

Some clients, like the Johns Hopkins Hospital selection committee, provide a detailed scope of work in the formal RFP. Other clients leave it up to the short list of consultants to outline and define their understanding of the project's scope and the best methodology to use.

Tony Mavis, then director of business development and public relations for Parsons, Brinckerhoff, Quade and Douglas, wrote on proposal preparation several years ago in *Consulting Engineer* magazine. Proposal contents, according to the article, usually consist of "cover, title page, table of contents, letter of transmittal, scope of services and work to be accomplished, methodology, organization, time schedule, and cost."[1]

> Properly prepared proposals also should include a one-page or two-page summary up front to tell the client what is covered in the proposal, the understanding of his requirements, how long the project will take, and how much it will cost. The individual sections can then go into as much detail as necessary to describe and justify the scope of work and the proposed cost. The proposal cover should contain the client's name; city and state; project title; whether the proposal is for architectural, planning, or engineering services and whether it is for design or for study; the date; and the name of the consulting firm, or firms if it is a joint venture. The cover ought to be by a graphic designer, if one is on the staff, or by a freelance artist retained to design a standard format for use with all proposals.[2]

TRANSMITTAL LETTERS

Letters of transmittal for proposals range from very short to very detailed. Properly composed, the latter might substitute for the recommended one- or two-page summary.

Here is an example of a brief letter of transmittal, patterned after an actual joint-venture submission to the Navy Facilities Engineering Command for the Travis Air Force Base New Generation Military Hospital Project. On special joint-venture stationery, the letter read:

Department of the Navy
Naval Facilities Engineering Command
Washington, D.C. 20390

Attention: R. E. Dunnells
                Captain, CEC, USN
                Deputy Commander for Facilities Acquisition

Gentlemen:

The Joint Venture of Jones, Smith & Brown (JSB) and the John Doe Partnership (JDP) is pleased to submit its response to your questionnaire of 19 January 1973 for the New Generation Military Hospital Project.

For easy reference the material presented herein contains a section for each of the items in the questionnaire.

Key personnel of JSB, as sponsor firm of the Joint Venture, key personnel of JDP, and project designees of the Joint Venture consultants are available for personal interview, should you so desire.

We welcome this further opportunity to assure you of our continued interest in the project and to present our combined qualifications. We look forward to your favorable actions.

Yours very truly,

JONES, SMITH & BROWN
/s/ Raymond A. Smith, AIA
THE JOHN DOE PARTNERSHIP
/s/ John B. Doe, P.E.

The 100-page proposal following consisted of nine tab-indexed sections, each covering a specific item in the Navy's questionnaire:
    Joint-venture responsibilities
    Experience as joint venturers
    Hospital design efforts and awards
    Role of special consultants
    Existing and projected workloads
    Joint-venture organization and personnel
    New generation construction methodology
    Seismic design considerations
    U.S. government project experience
This joint venture consisted of the two primes plus six consultants—for food service, health-care planning, light-care facilities, cost control, data systems, and landscaping.

COVER GIMMICKS

A proposal cover does not often lend itself to unusual touches, but something different occasionally suggests itself. We once advised a client, who was submitting a proposal on a large expansion project to a major paper maker, to bind his material in a cover stock made by the paper house. Obtaining a sheet of the appropriate cover stock turned out to be a little involved, but it was eventually found. Our client was awarded the job—and who can say the extra touch on the cover didn't help.

In New York City some years ago I sat in on a meeting called to plan the content of a joint-venture proposal for the New York Convention Center. The planning group consisted mostly of principals, and there was no one around the conference table whose client time-charges were less than $40 an hour; some undoubtedly went for well over $100 an hour.

During the day-long session it developed that one of the firms represented had done a concept study for a large facility on the identical site under consideration for the Convention Center—and one of the sketches *could* be read as a convention center. A decision was quickly made to get a low aerial photo of the site, use it for the proposal cover, and overlay it with the providential sketch.

Since speed was of the essence, the talk turned to the practicalities of getting the aerial photo in time, and at a reasonable cost. One of the conferees recalled that tourists could take a $5 helicopter flight over Manhattan, and that the route generally covered the riverfront site.

Accordingly, a draftsman from our host office (who was also a pretty fair amateur photographer) was called in, briefed on the site, the photo angle, and the necessity for fast work, and given $100 from petty cash to cover camera rental, film, cab fare, and one helicopter ticket.

About two hours later he called from the heliport to report that everything had gone well, except that the helicopter had not come anywhere near the site. The pilot overheard the conversation and agreed, upon payment of another fare, to take off immediately and fly anywhere the draftsman/photographer directed. The desired photograph was thus obtained for a total outlay of less that $50. It made an outstanding cover for a proposal that probably cost in the neighborhood of $20,000—considering the total value of the time of the individuals involved in its preparation.

PROPOSAL CONFERENCES

In the Mavis article, cited earlier, the proposal conference is mentioned as the usual method of preparing a basic outline for the proposal's sections and for developing a scope of service. Mavis covers the assignments to individual conference participants and the establishment of deadlines.

> One should not wait until all the writing is completed before reviewing and editing the copy for reproduction. For example, decisions regarding the exact wording on the proposal cover and the title page can be made at the proposal conference. They can then be processed through the graphics section, the plates obtained, and the necessary quantity printed. Immediate attention to long lead items, such as organization and bar charts, maps, and CPM charts, will be appreciated as the proposal deadline approaches. An experienced coordinator familiar with various reproduction techniques can be extremely helpful in relieving the project manager of these details. The project manager then can devote what time he has to the preparation of the technical input for the proposal without concerning himself about the quantity, format, and reproduction of the contents.
>
> It is essential to remember that sloppy reproduction can ruin a proposal that otherwise might be superb. The benchmarks of a good proposal are: clean paper; clear, clean, and even typing with a modern typeface; adequate and correctly proportioned margins; careful spacing between paragraphs; logical and uniform positioning of centerheads and subheads; sharp illustrations prepared or traced in ink and carefully reproduced; and care in collating and binding. [3]

STANDARD FORMS 254 AND 255

Practically every design professional developed a familiarity with the U.S. Government Architect-Engineer Questionnaire Standard Form (SF) 251 during its fourteen-year lifespan. The author must admit to some part in putting SF 251 to rest. At the request of the editors of *Architectural*

Record I wrote a piece for the April 1973 issue of the magazine called "Whatever Happened to Standard Form 251?" The thrust of the article was that a proliferation of supplementary forms from major government agencies had turned an old friend into a *Non*standard Form 251—and that perhaps it was time to revise the form.

The article attracted immediate interest from the General Services Administration and the American Institute of Architects, among others, and remedial action was promised. An ad hoc committee of federal contracting officers and representatives of the design professions was empaneled to review SF 251.

Eighteen months later, in November 1974, the General Services Administration announced two proposed new forms (SF 254 and 255) to replace the old SF 251. Following publication in the *Federal Register*, the new forms became official on October 30, 1975. As of this writing practitioners have raised a number of questions about the replacement forms, concerning both format and content. Some of the federal procurement people have expressed themselves as less than enchanted with the new system.

The apparent central theme of the charge given to members of the SF 251 review committee was to keep any replacement to a single, standard system. Time will tell whether this approach was valid or not, and whether all federal agencies, including AID, really can base their entire selection procedure on a two-form, two-step system. Following a period for shakeout and refinement, perhaps the new forms will prove to be eminently practical and completely responsive to federal agency procurement needs. At this early stage one can be hopeful.

OTHER SPECIAL BROCHURES

Special or highly customized brochures for potential clients were discussed briefly in Chapter 4. It is safe to say that special brochures represent a very small percentage of all brochures used by architects, engineers, and others in the design and construction fields. One reason for this is their relatively high cost. Even if a firm has the equipment in-house to set copy in cold type, the use of original photographs (especially color) to illustrate a custom booklet can quickly drive the cost of one such brochure to well over $100.

There *are* potential clients and projects, of course, that warrant such treatment. When this is the case, and the decision is made to put together a special brochure, it's best not to dwell on the cost. An outstanding final product should be the only consideration.

REFERENCES

[1]Anthony N. Mavis, "Preparing Proposals That Sell," *Consulting Engineer*, August 1968, p. 87.
[2]Ibid.
[3]Ibid.

Chapter 17

PUTTING IT ALL TOGETHER

NO AMOUNT OF RESEARCH AND planning, plus consultants and in-house expertise, is to any avail unless a brochure results. We've seen all too many offices get bogged down at some intermediate point in the production of a new brochure. At best, several months are lost through foot dragging and inattention; at worst, the project gets shelved, gathers dust for a while, and is forgotten until a principal asks, "What about a new brochure?"

This chapter is a kind of exercise in putting together a general capability brochure for a fictitious design firm. We'll be drawing on the material in the preceding sixteen chapters, and by the time our make-believe booklet goes off to be printed we hope to have demonstrated that there are no secret ingredients and no mysteries in the process.

THE FIRM

Our client in this case is an eighteen-person firm of architects, engineers, and planners—Taylor, Underwood & Ingalls. TU&I, in business for fifteen years, has had two previous brochures for use in business development. The first was a poorly conceived, sloppily organized, and badly printed booklet, which everyone would rather forget. It was used for almost five years. The principals finally became too embarrassed to hand it out to prospective clients and the firm limped along for a couple of years without any real brochure. No apparent damage was done, since the economy was soaring and work seemed to come in through the windows as well as over the transom.

About eight years ago a consultant was brought in to design a new promotion booklet. That became an on-again, off-again, process and some eighteen months later TU&I at last had a decent general capability brochure. Simple arithmetic shows that they have been using it for about six years, probably at least three years too long.

The partners are Paul Taylor, architect, Jerry Underwood, architect and planner, and Jack Ingalls, engineer. The staff is made up of two secretaries, two senior draftsmen, three junior draftsmen, one spec writer, three engineers, and one field person. Annual billings have been running between $550,000 and $600,000. The firm's really big year, 1970, saw billings of $750,000. TU&I knows that its weekly new-construction work requirements average out to $200,000. With the economy in a downswing, and new work a little harder to come by, the partners have decided it is time to update and upgrade the firm's brochure.

A few other biographical and background items: TU&I is located in Columbus, Ohio; Taylor is a graduate of the University of Cincinnati; Underwood is from Harvard; and Ingalls is from Notre Dame. All three were born in Ohio, but only Paul Taylor is a native of Columbus. While most of the firm's work has been within a 50-mile radius of its home city, the practice could be termed regional. Several projects have been in Illinois, two in Missouri, and three in Indiana.

If TU&I has an identifiable specialty, it would be in school work—primarily high schools and junior colleges. Secondary specialties would be in residential developments and recreation facilities.

THE PLANNING

At a partners' meeting a few weeks ago Jack Ingalls again brought up the subject of a new brochure. It seems that more and more prospective clients, after flipping through the present brochure, were asking what the firm had done lately. There was no practical way to update the almost-six-year-old booklet. As would be expected, some of the firm's major and most significant projects had been completed in the last few years, and it was a source of continual frustration that they were not described in TU&I's only real promotion piece—the brochure.

Having just finished reading a great new McGraw-Hill book on planning and producing brochures, Ingalls pushed to get a decision from his partners to go ahead on a new brochure. He suggested that they retain a design consultant, draw up a schedule, and commit themselves to having a new brochure in no more than eight months. Agreement was reached, Ingalls was appointed project manager, and a design consultant was brought in from a local advertising agency. Fortunately, the consultant had had extensive experience with service accounts (as opposed to product promotion) and, even more fortunate for TU&I, she had recently worked on two other brochures for area design firms.

The next step, as Ingalls knew from his reading, was to define the objectives of the brochure and identify the publics it should reach and influence. The objectives, in this case, were pretty simple and straightforward. Ingalls outlined them in the following list.

1. Replace an outdated brochure.

2. Update project illustrations, descriptions, and lists.
3. Explain new services offered by TU&I.
4. Reflect staff changes and added capabilities.
5. Give TU&I a promotion piece at least equal to that of its competition.
6. Adequately reflect TU&I's understanding of and approach to good design, graphics, and clear exposition.
7. Have built-in flexibility.
8. Show that TU&I's development has matched or exceeded that of its competition and of the construction field in general.
9. Serve as a recruiting tool for TU&I staff.
10. Be an internal staff-morale builder.

Undoubtedly, other objectives and considerations of lesser importance could have been added to the list, but the above ten points were enough to get the production team into the next stage—defining the publics to be reached. The "team," as of now, consisted of Jack Ingalls and Susan Andrews, the consultant.

After considerable discussion among the principals, with input from consultant Andrews, the list of TU&I's most important publics, in order of importance, was reduced to six:

Potential clients
Actual clients, past and present
TU&I staff
Potential staff
News media
Contemporaries (peer group)

Jack and Susan were also getting a production schedule roughed out. The agreed-upon schedule, in flowchart form, resembled the example shown in Figure 5-1. Approximately one week's cushion was built into each of the five main elements of planning, design, and production: advance planning and research, writing, design layout, art and photography, and production. In the end, this proved to have been a wise move.

Copies of the firm's two previous brochures were pulled from the files and carefully reviewed for strengths and weaknesses. The score was lopsided in favor of weaknesses, as might have been predicted, and the team decided to start from scratch in planning the new booklet.

CENTRAL THEME

In earlier chapters the desirability of a central or running theme for the brochure was stressed. Ideally, a theme would encompass the main graphics, headlines, format, and text. Admittedly, the ideal seldom is achieved.

As a starting point for the TU&I theme a logo was developed. The firm had never had one before—which had not really proved to be a serious handicap to its design output. But now that an all-new image was within their grasp, the principals decreed that a logo be created. Logos of other

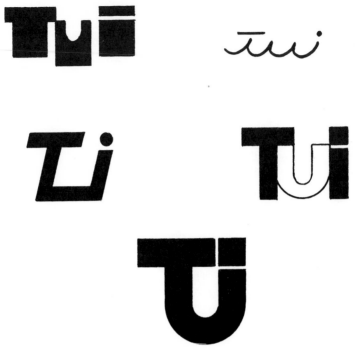

Figure 17-1. Some of the developmental sketches for the TU&I logo. The final version is at bottom center.

design firms and of various corporations were reviewed.

A lot of scratch paper bit the dust on the way to TU&I's logo. Some of the early sketches, along with the final design, are shown in Figure 17.1. The logo, once designed, could be applied to all office graphics, including stationery, business cards, report forms, statements, and drawings. It would lend itself to straight printing, embossing, and die-cutting.

During the early weeks of Jack and Susan's research, they studied around fifty brochures, annual reports, and similar graphic products. They decided to go for a combination of bound booklet, loose-leaf pages, and folder. The folder (see Figure 17-2) had left and right sections that opened back; the right section was a half-sheet. An integral flap in the center section was to hold loose-leaf supplemental brochure pages and reprints. Closed, the folder measured 10 x 9 inches and would fit into standard file drawers. Its 9-inch height would give it extra visibility in most files.

Keeping standard book-paper sizes in mind, dimensions of the internal booklet were set as 9¾ inches wide by 8½ inches high. The self-cover booklet thus nicely cut out eight pages (four spreads) from a 25 x 38 inch standard book-paper sheet:

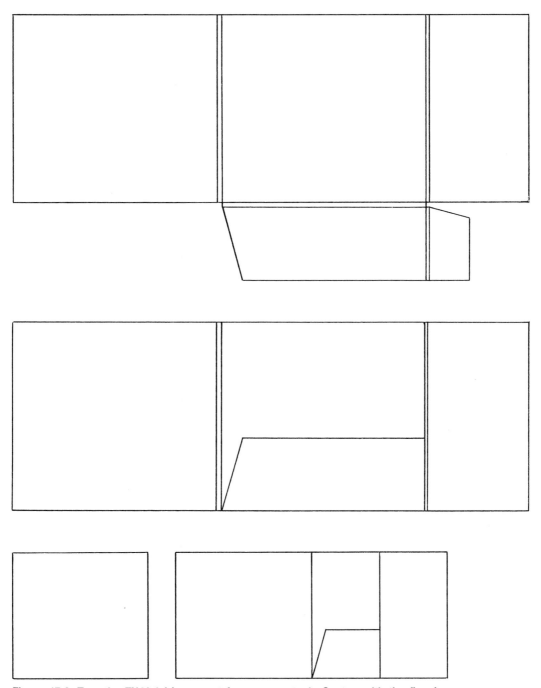

Figure 17-2. Top, the TU&I folder as cut from cover stock. Center, with the flap for loose-leaf sheets assembled. Bottom, showing how right and left sections fold over the center section.

$$\frac{\overset{2}{\cancel{25}} \times \overset{4}{\cancel{38}}}{\cancel{9\tfrac{3}{4}} \times \cancel{8\tfrac{1}{2}}} = 8 \text{ pages out}$$

We can verify that the spreads will work:

$$\frac{\overset{1}{\cancel{25}} \times \overset{4}{\cancel{38}}}{\cancel{19\tfrac{1}{2}} \times \cancel{8\tfrac{1}{2}}} = 4 \text{ spreads out}$$

These cuts will result in about 25-percent wastage of the total sheet size.

The booklet was planned for sixteen pages, including the self-cover. The page-by-page outline looked like this:

Cover I: Regular brochure cover, including firm's name, disciplines (architecture, engineering, and planning), and a portion of a 360-degree photo that will wrap around the outside folder and onto the cover.

Cover II: Part of a photograph that jumps the gutter onto page 1. (Thumbnail page layouts are shown in Figure 17-3.)

Figure 17-3. *(a)* **Blank thumbnail sketch sheet for the TU&I brochure.** *(b)* **Thumbnail sketches for the TU&I brochure. The brochure is an integral part of the folder. The outside back cover (Cover IV) is left blank so it can be glued to the center section of the wrap-around folder. The flap covers the lower part of page 13 (Cover III).**

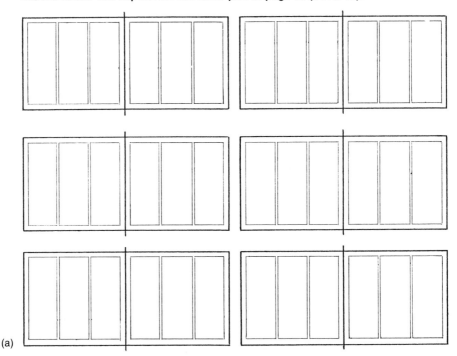

(a)

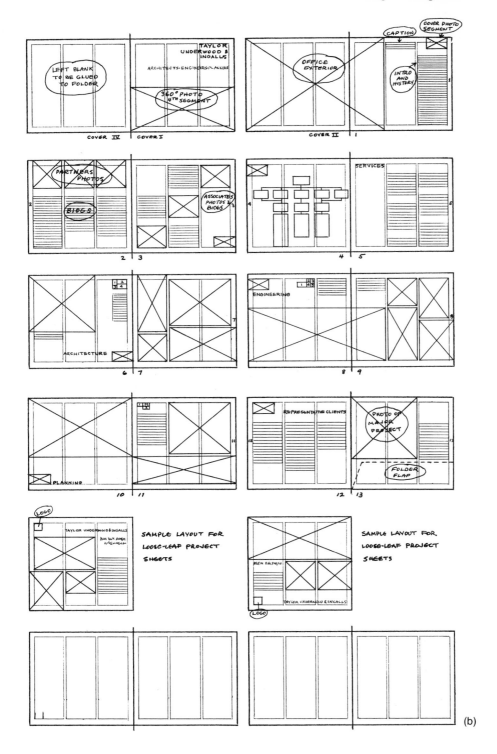

(b)

Page 1: Remainder of a large photo of the exterior of TU&I's office. Brief introduction and short history of the firm.

Page 2: Photos and biographies of the three partners.

Page 3: Photos and biographies of the firm's three associates.

Page 4: Organization chart.

Page 5: Description of services offered.

Pages 6–7: Spread on representative architectural projects.

Pages 8–9: Spread on representative engineering projects.

Pages 10–11: Spread on representative planning projects.

Page 12: Listing of representative clients.

Cover III: Photo of a major project. Also additional information about the office and about the partners' memberships in professional organizations.

Cover IV: Blank. To be glued to outside folder to hold booklet in place.

The covering folder (see Figure 17-2) has gross dimensions (before cutting) of 25⅝ inches wide by 12½ inches high. Standard cover-stock dimensions include 20 x 26, 23 x 35, 26 x 40, and 35 x 46. The 26 x 40 inch sheet is checked out:

$$\frac{\overset{1}{26} \times \overset{3}{40}}{25\frac{5}{8} \times 13\frac{1}{4}} = 3 \text{ out}$$

When quarter-inch trim margins are allowed for, there is less than 3 percent wastage from this sheet size.

FORMAT

From the 9¾ x 8½ inch dimensions outlined for the booklet, it is apparent that a basically horizontal page format will result. The designers debated the relative merits of vertical versus horizontal format before opting for the latter. Part of the rationale for a horizontal format was that most building photographs are shot in those dimensions. As in many of the early choices and decisions, this one was at least a little subjective— the consultant preferred the horizontal format.

The point was made in Chapter 3 that optimum brochure dimensions seem to be 8½ x 11 inches, based on standard file-drawer capacities and client preferences. Yet the external folder for the TU&I brochure measured 9 x 10 inches—that is, the shorter dimension was ½ inch more than the optimum 8½ inches. Since this is the vertical dimension there should be no filing problem. The extra ½ inch in height was a deliberate design detail to make the filed TU&I folder/brochure more noticeable among its 8½-inch-high competition.

The 360-degree photograph to be wrapped around the outside folder, and continued on the cover of the bound-in brochure, was to show one of TU&I's award-winning recreational developments outside Columbus.

Note in the thumbnails (see Figure 17-3) that the folios (page numbers) are located at the optical center (see Figure 6-4) of the outside page margins. It was decided to set folios in 16-point Galaxy Demibold Italic.

The folder was to be of ivory cover stock, the internal brochure of ivory

54. Custom fabricated aluminum
sign structure with multicolor
graphics are utilized throughout
"Scope," a sports complex and
performing arts center in Norfolk.

55. Internally illuminated aluminum
sign with translucent Fiberlite sign
face for strength and durability.

56. Any letterform may be
reproduced in the Fiberlite process
and protected by embedment of
graphics.

57. Twelve-foot-long Fibergraphic
Monolith with applied
Spectralegends is representative of
size flexibility available with this
technique.

58. Wooden sign with applied acrylic
precision-cut graphics enhance a
residential environment.

12

**Figure 17-4. An example of numbered-box captions for multiple photographs on a page.
This illustration is from the brochure of Architectural Graphics Incorporated.**

text stock, and the separate inserts for the folder flap of colored text stock to harmonize with the folder color. Black ink was to be used throughout.

Note that a theme of sorts was carried through the brochure by repeating, in smaller scale, an important detail from the 360-degree cover photo (see Figure 17-3). A detail from the office-exterior shot on Cover II could also have been repeated as a photographic theme. This would be particularly effective if a piece of distinctive sculpture were displayed on the lawn. The separate insert sheets, used to keep the total folder/brochure updated, carry the TU&I logo to identify and tie them to the other material. Susan suggested that two diagonal slits be die-cut in the folder flap to hold the business card of the TU&I representative handing out or sending the brochure. This was agreed to.

CAPTIONS

Another type of graphic theme carried through the brochure was the numbered-box caption identifications. Photographs were keyed to captions by reference to the box in the same position. Figure 17-4 shows a page of photographs identified by the numbered-box key.

Sometimes group photographs cannot be avoided. Figures 7-6 and 10-15 illustrated one method of identifying a fairly large group of individuals. A simple line drawing shows the position of each person with a number. Names are listed to the side of—or below—the outline drawing by number.

After getting general agreement from the three partners on the first layout in thumbnails, a full-size dummy was prepared. In this step the design was refined, type sizes generally established, and photograph and text-block dimensions finalized. The dummy, of paper stock the same as, or representative of, the final product, is to give printers the necessary information upon which to base their estimates. A paper company recently gave this explanation of a "dummy":

> A set of blank pages made up in advance to show the size, shape, form and general style of a printed piece. Constructed on the actual weight, finish, color and brand of paper specified.
>
> Some of the uses of a dummy: to suggest a particular paper and the effect it will produce prior to the actual reproduction; to reproduce preliminary drawings or layouts showing the position of illustrations and copy as they are to appear in final reproduction; and as a sales tool in the presentation of a proposed printed piece—to give the customer something to look at as well as feel.

TYPE SELECTION

The text type selected for the brochure was 12-point Bookface, leaded 1 (12/13). Galaxy or Univers 68 Demibold Italic in 18 point was selected for page headlines. Picture captions were to be set in 10-point Bookface, leaded 1 (10/11). Examples of Bookface and Galaxy Demibold Italic are shown in Figure 17-5.

LEGIBILITY is an outstanding characteristic of Bookface because of its openness, being almost entirely devoid of those eccentricities of letter-design in which this feature is sometimes overlooked in the designer's efforts to obtain beauty. The carefully balanced variation of weight between light and heavy lines in the letters is a feature highly important in composition intended for continuous reading whether they be printed letterpress, offset or rotogravure.

The openness of Bookface makes this type an excellent choice for printing on the roughest of antique stocks. The soft, simple line design, however, recommends it as well for coated papers where types of less balanced line values sometimes become too monotonous or too contrasting and "jumpy" for easy reading and eye comfort.

ABCDEFGHIJKLMNOPQRSTUVWXYZ&
abcdefghijklmnopqrstuvwxyz   fffiflffiffl
$1234567890   ,.-:;''?!
⅛ ¼ ⅜ ½ ⅝ ¾ ⅞ ⅓ ⅔

()*¢ ´` ^" ¯˜ ¸§%'@/#√[]†‡—....
+ × = ÷•−—()*¢■□

12 point—2 point leaded   2.13 characters to 1 pica

Simplicity is a very important feature in typography, because it produces the direct
ABCDEFGHIJKLMNOP $1234567890

Figure 17-5. Examples of Bookface and Galaxy Demibold Italic typefaces, as selected for the TU&I text and heads.

PRINTING ESTIMATES

Three estimates were requested from three reputable printing shops in the Columbus area. The printers were asked to supply figures on quantities of 1,000, 2,000, and 5,000 units. The partners had estimated that 1,000 brochures would meet office requirements for approximately two years (on an established average use of about ten brochures a week). Susan Andrews pointed out that just having a good promotion piece on hand would undoubtedly increase its use, so the two higher quantities were included in the printers' estimates.

(Note that so far we have been dealing with estimates rather than bids. An estimate, by definition, is not binding on the printer. The reason for requesting estimates first is to get a check on the designer's estimate and to be fairly certain that a gold-plated brochure has not resulted. If the trade estimates are uniformly high, some redesign will undoubtedly have to be done to bring costs into line with the budget.)

The estimates received were as follows:

Copies	Printer A	Printer B	Printer C
1,000	$2,850	$2,915	$2,775
2,000	3,700	3,755	3,810
5,000	6,275	6,390	6,310

Figure 17-6. If smell-and-print combinations interest you, send for the Micro-Scent Idea Kit. Perhaps such aromas as those of grass, milk, smoke, pizza, and new cars can be used with project photos of country clubs, dairies, fire stations, restaurants, and auto assembly plants.

The closeness of the three estimates was an indication that all printers were using the same basic specs—and showed that the consultant's estimate (and the firm's original budget) were in the ball park.

Armed with copies of the full-size dummy, the design team began a definitive review of the text, to refine, tighten, and generally edit it into final form. Assembly of the art work and photographs was going well, and as the schedule countdown reached week number 10 (see Figure 5-1), everything appeared to be under control.

The process of final photo selection, followed by sizing, cropping, and retouching where necessary, proceeded smoothly through schedule weeks 8 and 7. Picture captions were written and edited.

As soon as everything was delivered to the printer (an initial run of 2,000 copies was ordered), principals, associates, and everyone else in the office began working on a mailing list. The names of obvious recipients—past, present, and prospective clients, nearby schools of architecture, local media, suppliers, and professional consultants—were quickly collected. Each staff member was to be given five copies for personal distribution, including one copy for the home library. Eventually, copies were sent to the teachers of high school and vocational school drafting classes in the immediate five-county area. Copies were taken to local offices of senators and representatives. Other copies were left in Washington as the principals had occasion to travel there.

Best of all, the partners were no longer ashamed because they had to hand out an old, outdated brochure. The inherent flexibility of the new one, with the folder pocket, allowed for continuous updating by removing or adding supplemental loose project sheets.

Chapter 18

THE FOUR BASIC PRINTING PROCESSES

IN ORDER OF THEIR DOLLAR volume, the four basic processes used by most modern printers are offset, letterpress, gravure, and screen. The methods involved for each are the following:

Offset—planographic
Letterpress—relief
Gravure—intaglio
Screen—stencil or porous

OFFSET

Offset has had the most rapid growth of the four major printing processes. In dollar volume, it passed the previous most popular, letterpress, around 1966. In its simplest form the offset image is transferred from an inked plate to a rubber blanket and then (offset) onto the paper. Planographic printing is distinguished from other methods by the fact that both the printing and nonprinting areas are essentially in the same plane on the plate. There are two other distinguishing traits of offset: first, it is based on the physical fact that grease (the ink) and water (an aqueous solution) will not mix; and second, there is the offset method itself—the progression from plate to blanket to paper stock.

A variety of metal and paper plates are used in offset printing. Direct-image paper or paper-board plates can be made in the typewriter, by drawing directly on the plate, or by letterpress printing. Paper plates can also be made electrostatically, as by a Xerox machine. Metal plates are made of copper, zinc, aluminum, chromium, and stainless steel. Multi-metal plates, such as chromium on copper, have been known to print well over 2 million impressions.

Planographic printing has more variations than the other three methods—offset lithography, spirit duplicating, photogelatin process (collotype), and hectographic printing.

Offset has several advantages over letterpress. It is generally recognized as the best process for rapid, relatively inexpensive printing of illustrated work on sheets of small to large sizes, in one or in many colors. Offset paper may be coated or uncoated; the process does not require glossy paper for good halftone reproduction. It is definitely cheaper than letterpress when a large number of line drawings must be reproduced or when original material can be photographically copied. Process color and fake process work are normally less expensive when done offset. From a designer's standpoint, offset pasteup generally offers greater flexibility than letterpress makeup.

Offset printing can be recognized by its smoothness, a kind of softness in outlines, and a lack of any type impression in the paper. F. H. Wills commented on the process:

> With constant innovations in copying and printing techniques, with machines of improved design, with bimetal and trimetal plates that allow printing on coated papers, with printing also possible on papers with granular or uneven surfaces (as well as cloth, plastic, and acetate), offset is continually attracting new clients.
>
> The designer may prefer the sharpness of letterpress, but offset will often be chosen nevertheless, because of its greater economy. Offset and gravure—processes which until quite recently were still in their infancy—have made great conquests at the expense of letterpress printing. Photo-composition on film and other quite recent advances in methods of typesetting help offset more than letterpress, and innovations in color separation of polychrome illustrations apply equally to lithography. Designers will find that clients primarily attracted by low costs come back again and again to offset because it is more adaptable as well.[1]

LETTERPRESS

Letterpress is the oldest printing process—and some claim the most versatile. It is used for most newspapers, books, and magazines, as well as in job and commercial work. The term means that the raised surfaces of type, lines, and the dots of halftone plates are inked and then brought into contact with paper to make a print. Type characters and illustration plates for letterpress are always in reverse so that the printed image will read right.

Letterpress is capable of producing results ranging from excellent to mediocre, in very short to extremely long press runs. Books of the highest quality and daily newspapers are examples of the extremes in letterpress production.

For many centuries "letterpress" was synonymous with "printing." Other graphic arts reproduction processes—etching, engraving, lithography—could not handle bulk reproduction of text; they were used exclusively for pictures. Only when photography was mated with printing (letterpress), resulting in photoengraving and other photomechanical applications, was the traditional division between picture and text reproduction overcome.

The many different presses used for letterpress work may be classified as three basic types: platen, flatbed cylinder, and rotary.

Platen presses operate on the plane-to-plane principle, and generally are used for relatively small sheet sizes in short production runs. The type form and paper are carried on two opposing flat surfaces, known respectively as the bed and the platen. Following inking of the type form in an open press position, the two surfaces are brought together under pressures of up to 600 pounds per square inch. Production speed of a platen press is around 5,000 impressions an hour.

Smaller platen presses are used mostly for simple one-color work—job printing, as it is known in the trade. Circulars, invitations, stationery, business cards, tickets, small posters, and simple forms are examples of job printing and small-platen press work. Large platen presses may be used for stamping, die-cutting, scoring, embossing, creasing, hole punching, and other operations that usually require auxiliary machines.

The cylinder-to-plane principle of printing applies to work done on a flatbed cylinder press. The printing form is on a flat bed and the paper is applied to the horizontal form as it revolves around a cylindrical platen. The paper is sandwiched between the laterally moving bed and the rotating impression cylinder. The cylinder grips the paper and applies the necessary pressure for an impression. As the bed returns to its original position the impression cylinder is raised, the printed sheet released, and inking rollers reink the type form. The process is similar to an automobile tire leaving an impression of its tread on a wet roadway.

Most printing jobs can be produced on a flatbed cylinder press, including books, folders, brochures, catalogs, and printed forms, using a wide variety of paper stocks.

In another version of the cylinder press the bed is vertical. The form and cylinder move up and down in opposite directions with a reciprocating motion. Still another model of the cylinder-to-plane press is called a perfecting cylinder. A perfecting press prints both sides of the paper in one pass; it may be platen, cylinder, or rotary.

The drum cylinder, the simplest and least expensive of all cylinder presses, was a particular favorite of small-town weekly newspaper publishers who looked for reasonable speed and economical equipment. The single-revolution or drum-cylinder press has not been manufactured in the United States since the 1950s and rapidly is becoming obsolete in this country.

Rotary presses (cylinder-to-cylinder principle) consist of two cylinders turning in opposite directions and are the fastest and most efficient of the three types of letterpress machines. Rotaries are used primarily for long runs, such as newspapers and large-circulation magazines, because of their size, high makeready costs, and extremely fast running speeds. Modern rotary presses, at the rate of 35,000 revolutions per hour, theoretically can produce up to 140,000 newspapers an hour, although the actual average production rate is around half that amount.

Paper to be printed in a rotary press may come in sheets or from a roll (web). It is passed between two cylinders to receive the image. Due to the curved printing surface, forms must be made in one-piece curved plates, which adds to their expense. In recent years lighter-weight metal plates and photopolymer plates have been developed. These are known as direct printing plates.

Most rotary presses, unlike their platen and cylinder counterparts, are custom designed and built to the specifications of individual users. This is because of their size and complexity.

Multicolor web-fed rotaries, using special inks and driers, can be operated at speeds of 1,600 to 1,800 feet of paper per minute. The paper web is continuous, with automatic, on-the-run splicing of one roll to another. At the delivery end of the press the paper is either sheeted or folded into signatures (sections).

Letterpress printing produces good reproduction of photographs and other illustrations on *sheet-fed* machines, with two limitations: screening prevents the reproduction of pure white, and the use of more than four colors practically guarantees moire. *Web-fed* letterpress gives sharp reproduction of type, but only average-quality illustrations, at best. Color work on web-fed rotaries must be characterized as mediocre. For proof of this, study a few color photos in any large daily newspaper.

Letterpress printing can be recognized by its sharpness and crispness. With the aid of a magnifying glass a ring of ink around each letter can be seen, caused by pressure of the plate on the paper. If the press form has not been properly built up (makeready), a slight embossing may be detected on the back of the paper.

GRAVURE

In gravure printing, as in letterpress, contact is made directly from inked plate to paper. That is about the extent of the resemblance between the two processes, since gravure uses a depressed surface (intaglio) for ink transference, as opposed to the raised surface of letterpress and the flat surface of offset lithography. The printing design is etched into the flat or cylindrical copper gravure plate, forming tiny cup-shaped cavities below the plate's surface. When an etched cylinder is used, the process is called "rotogravure."

In gravure the entire image is screened—halftones, line art, and type. Gravure screens are comparable to the screens used in most offset work: 150 lines per inch. (Fine offset screens run to 300 or more lines per inch.) Gravure gives the highest-quality reproductions of continuous tone art, including photographs, even on newsprint. The relatively high costs of plate making ordinarily limits gravure work to long runs of 250,000 and up.

The screened type in gravure work is slightly fuzzy but completely legible unless it is too small (under 8 point) or has thin serifs, as in the Bodoni faces. Reverses in gravure can be disastrous. An 8-point Bodoni would be apt to close up almost completely in a gravure reverse.

In printing rotogravure the etched copper cylinder is inked by ink roll or spray. Before it comes into contact with the paper the excess ink is scraped from the surface by a sharp, flexible steel knife, called a "doctor blade." The ink remaining in the cavities of the plate is then transferred to the paper as it runs between the plate and impression cylinders.

In addition to fine photo reproduction work, gravure is used in printing specialty packaging jobs and mail-order catalogs. Other gravure specialties include wallpaper, vinyl floor coverings, postage stamps, and plastic laminates.

One-color duotones (see Chapter 10) will approximate by offset the effect and results of gravure printing.

SCREEN

For quantities of printed materials up to around 2,500, with no photographs or blocks of small type, silk-screening printing is usually the least-expensive process. Original work is reproduced on a variety of surfaces, including paper, by forcing thick ink through a narrow-meshed, porous screen of silk, nylon, or stainless steel and onto the material to be printed.

In its simplest form, screen printing requires a frame to hold the screen taut, viscous ink, and a rubber-bladed squeegee. A stencil is placed under the screen, where it is held by the thick ink. A sheet of paper is placed under the frame and the ink is squeegeed the length of the frame, forced through the mesh, and onto the paper—except for the nonprinting areas masked off by the stencil. The rate of production is controlled by the ink's drying time.

Rotary screen presses, aided by photomechanically produced stencils and improved drying methods, now allow continuous screen printing. Anything from glass bottles to draperies to electronic circuit boards are printed today by the versatile screen process.

REFERENCE

[1]F. H. Wills, *Fundamentals of Layout,* Dover Publications, Inc., New York, 1971, p. 119.

Chapter 19
SUPPLEMENTAL PUBLICATIONS

IN CHAPTER 16 WE DISCUSSED one type of supplemental publication—the proposal. Standard Forms 254 and 255, the successors to Standard Form 251, which pertain to establishing a firm's qualifications in government circles, were also covered in Chapter 16.

In this chapter we'll be concentrating on four other kinds of publications: newsletters (both internal and external), magazines (which almost always are external), booklets, and books. A few of the very large design firms use all these supplemental publications, but the average firm has neither the staff nor the bank account to include all four in its stable of promotion materials. A final section will cover the design and use of questionnaires.

NEWSLETTERS

Newsletter journalism dates from the sixteenth century. Early efforts served commercial, social, and political interests, and flourished for some time. Then, following many decades of decline, the medium came back full-flower in the early twentieth century to meet needs unserved by regular newspapers. Some of these newsletters are commercial and some are free. We will discuss the major differences below.

Commercial Newsletters. Commercial newsletters, published *for profit* by real or presumed experts in a certain field, and for a relatively limited group of subscribers, are one of the publishing phenomena of the post–World War II period in the United States. It is safe to say that there is a newsletter somewhere for practically every interest and field—with several dozen more in preparation on any given day. Perhaps the ultimate in this type of publication is the *Newsletter on Newsletters.*

The September 1974 meeting of the Deadline Club, New York City's organization of the working press, featured a panel of four newsletter journalists. The panel agreed that newsletters are successful when they fill in gaps left by the general press.

The panel members also pointed out that a commercial newsletter must help its readers make money—or at least hold out the promise thereof. Information in a newsletter must be "useful, fast or telegraphic in style, and without frills." According to Martin Edelston, publisher of the *Boardroom Reports* and *Business Hotline* newsletters, the basic formula for a profitable letter is to deliver information that fills in the information gaps left by business publications.

Another panelist, Leon Garry of the *Media Industry Newsletter*, pointed out that being first with the news is important, but so is having a different perspective. The cultivation of good sources is basic to any newsletter editor. As is apparent, these points apply to the general press as well.

Free Newsletters.   So far, we have been talking about for-profit news-letters, with annual subscription rates of from $25 up to several hundred dollars. I know of no design firm that has attempted to market a newsletter or a news magazine type of regular publication, although to my

Figure 19-1. Representative covers of the Dames & Moore magazine, *elements.*

knowledge there is no professional restriction against it. I am familiar with several such publications that could justify a subscription charge—they are that excellent.

One of the consistently excellent publications is *elements*, from Dames & Moore. In *Reader's Digest* format, its usual size is eighteen pages, plus cover. Featuring interesting covers, good layout and editing, well-written and not overly technical articles, and four-color photographs, *elements* is an effective extension of the firm to clients and friends. It is not cheap, but class seldom is. (See Figure 19-1.)

Newsletters and news magazines from design professionals do not have to be monthly publications. Since there is no consideration on the part of recipients, they do not have to have any regularity of issue at all. *elements* is published bimonthly. Another fine newsletter is the quarterly publication of Baldwin and Gregg, the Norfolk, Virginia, engineering firm. The center spread article in each issue features some kind of object that readers may remove for their own use. One newsletter contained three mint U.S. stamps honoring the design and planning professions, mounted as they would be in the most exacting collector's stamp book. Another issue, in an article on metrification, had an inch/centimeter rule tipped in. (See Figure 19-2.)

One could cite possibly another twenty-five or thirty equally outstanding publications issued by small to large firms. There are gimmicks in newsletters, of course. One large architectural-engineering-planning

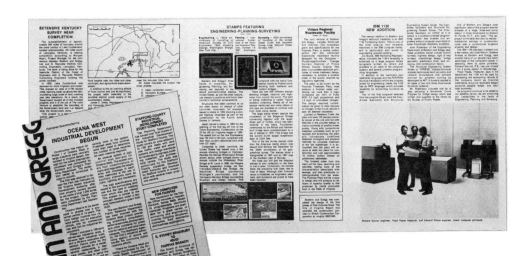

Figure 19-2. The excellent Baldwin and Gregg quarterly newsletter consistently comes up with unusual and interesting themes. The issue at the top of the figure featured United States stamps with design and planning motifs.

firm, with multiple offices, regularly issues several monthly and quarterly publications for its staff, clients, and friends. One of the newsletters
has CONFIDENTIAL printed across the top of the front page and is
routinely placed on reception room tables in its various offices. (No copies
are mailed.) The legend under CONFIDENTIAL implies that it is purely
an internal letter, for the firm's officers and upper-echelon staff members.
I have been told that the circulation of this newsletter exceeds several
hundred copies a month among consultants, suppliers, clients and
potential clients, and other office visitors who cannot resist the temptation
to pick up what appears to be real inside information. The material inside
is similar to that in most other newsletters—new-project descriptions, a
few technical and semitechnical staff-written pieces, new-employee photos and biographies—nothing remotely resembling proprietary information, of course. And the firm is saved the handling and postage costs of
mailing the newsletter out.

Where the newsletter is produced by professional editors and writers, it
is not unheard of to have articles picked up by the regular press. An
article in *Archives* (formerly published by the Vincent G. Kling Partner-

Figure 19-3. *Archives,* a monthly newsletter
of the Vincent G. Kling Partnership,
features excellent writing, layout,
and illustrations.

ship), titled "IBM Headquarters Gets Grass by the Gallon," received that kind of attention. (See Figure 19-3.)

How to Start a Newsletter.   Mention was made earlier of "internal" and "external" newsletters. Internal letters are written strictly for in-house staff, while external publications are for those outside the firm—other consultants, clients, potential clients, and so forth. Strictly speaking, there is no such thing as a purely internal newsletter, regardless of the intent of principals and editors. That is an important point to remember in deciding to whom a newsletter should appeal. Most newsletters end up as some combination of internal and external.

Some years ago a design firm headquartered in the Midwest decided to use its "internal" newsletter as an educational vehicle for staff designers and construction supervisors. Consequently, a series of articles was written about major problems of the firm's buildings that had been discovered during construction or after occupancy.

The first article was a very candid account of a wall collapse, explaining where and when goofs had been committed in the design and engineering and how the foulups had been compounded by poor supervision on the job. Altogether, an admirable idea for continuing education of the staff—right?

Wrong. At least two copies of the newsletter got into outside hands. The client was in the process of suing the design firm and the contractor, of course, and several of the plaintiff's attorneys suddenly found life much easier. The lawyers representing the design firm resigned in a huff, and the contractor left on an extended trip through Europe, Africa, and Asia.

Just as there is no such thing as a free lunch, there is no completely internal newsletter. This account is not given to scare anyone away from beginning a newsletter, but to emphasize the point that at least a minimum amount of judgment should be applied to its contents.

It is clear, therefore, that the best way to start a newsletter closely parallels the obligatory early steps in designing and producing a new general capabilities brochure. This is another area in which outside consultants can be helpful. Ideally, there will be someone on staff to serve as the nominal editor, who can be made responsible for content and for collecting information for each issue. A consultant can be retained on a continuing basis to handle the details of each issue.

As with the brochure, some thought should be given to whom a firm wants to reach with its newsletters (the publics) and what it wants to accomplish (objectives). As a rule, any mailing list for brochures and other publications can be used as the basis for a newsletter distribution list.

A full-size, finished art mockup of an issue is usually an early step. Several years ago we made up a dummy for a newsletter for Edward Durell Stone's office. The mockup, which somehow survived several moves and the ravages of time, is shown in Figure 19-4. It is complete with suggested masthead, logo, photostats of photographs to size, and articles as they would appear in the first issue. Occasionally, to increase

SUNY PLANETARIUM underground passageway from the planetarium basement. The accelerator facilities, which will be directed by Jagadish Garg, Albany State University Professor of Physics, are isolated to shield the 4 MeV high current dynamitron. This part of the complex is roofed with a two-foot-thick concrete slab and covered with five feet of earth.

The Albany accelerator is one of four currently being manufactured by Radiation Dynamics of Westbury, Long Island. The other three machines are for the Technical University of Stuttgart, Germany; University of Montreal, Canada and for the Goddard Space Flight Center, Greenbelt, Maryland.

According to Prof. Garg, the 4 MeV machine will be used primarily at Albany for research into neutron physics, charged particle spectroscopy and gamma-ray energy measurements, with particular emphasis on the study of neutron physics.

The underground accelerator and target rooms, occupying 3,900 square feet of space, will have provision for future expansion. An access panel in the ceiling of the accelerator room will allow large equipment to be moved in or out as necessary.

The planetarium basement includes photographic darkrooms, technical offices, storage, a library area and a complete laboratory workshop. Acoustical joints and wall and floor junctions will isolate noise from the basement shops and other activities from the projection chamber above.

The 17-foot high, 2 3/4-ton Zeiss planetarium machine consists of some 29,000 separate parts and is possibly the most complicated instructional machine ever made. It requires about 18 months to assemble and install. The typical full-size projector (actually a coordinated system of 153 separate projectors) can show the images of almost 9,000 stars on the reflective surface of the aluminum hemispherical dome. The Milky Way, star clusters, nebulae and other

bright star objects are also shown by the standard planetarium projector.

Supplementary projectors and special effects mechanisms, available as optional equipment, extend the range of demonstrations possible with a planetarium. These include a solar system projector, giving viewers the illusion of a journey into space, and projectors to show artificial satellites, shooting stars, constellation figures and sun and moon eclipses.

A Zeiss planetarium in use

The planetarium is able to compress the 25,800 years of the precession of the equinoxes in nature into four minutes of viewing time. In the polar altitude variation, the machine simulates a journey around the earth through North and South Poles in six-and-a-half minutes.

The main planetarium chamber at Albany will seat 300 spectators in special chairs with adjustable reclining backs to make overhead viewing more comfortable.

Parking for 176 cars will be provided just west of the planetarium chamber.

-4-

VOLUME I - NUMBER I

No April Fool joke this - as the headline indicates, you are reading the first issue of what is planned to be a regularly published newsletter of, by and for the employees of Edward Durell Stone & Associates and Edward Durell Stone, Inc.

- - - - EDS - - - -

GOOD GRAPHICS WORTH $50

The masthead of this initial newsletter is a "working head" only. One of the first orders of business in connection with this fledgling mini-newspaper is a competition to select a permanent masthead (title) design. The competition is open to all employees of the firm, with the exception of members of the selection jury. The winning entry will be worth $50.00 (no second, third or consolation prizes).

The awards jury is composed of William S. Smith, John Rainey and Gerre Jones.

Rules are few and simple:
1. Entries should be in "finished art" form.
2. The design may be for black and white reproduction - or black plus one color.
3. The design should be capable of being scaled down to 1 3/4-inches in height by 8 1/4-inches long.
4. Competition closes May 15, 1968. Winner will be announced by May 31, 1968.

Refer any questions about the masthead design competition to Gerre Jones or Salli Olowecki in the Public Relations office.

- - - - EDS - - - -

"All these buildings should possess strength, utility and beauty."
Marcus Vitruvius Pollio

LETTER TO GM EMPLOYEES --
"A NEW VISTA ON FIFTH AVENUE"

The General Motors Corporation recently began distribution of a series of information bulletins for its New York employees (above). Some excerpts from the first bulletin follow.

"Sheathed in white Georgia marble and rising 50 stories into the Manhattan skyline, the new General Motors building at 767 Fifth Avenue will be a place about which you will be able to say proudly: 'That's where I work'.

"The exterior marble will soon be completed, making the building's dignified design and serene simplicity more evident to all who are watching it take shape as truly 'A New Vista on Fifth Avenue'."

(continued on page 2)

"A NEW VISTA ON FIFTH AVENUE"

"The 'vista' will not only be on Fifth Avenue. Viewed from any side of the 84,000-square-foot block -- Madison Avenue, 58th or 59th St. -- the GM building will be an urbane compliment to its famed setting.

"But enough of the really unnecessary sales talk! We all know that famed architects Edward Durell Stone and Emery Roth & Sons have designed a fine building -- but just how big will it be?

"The building will be the 12th tallest in New York City with the 50 stories extending 705 feet. For comparison, the Empire State Building's 102 stories and TV tower go up to 1,472 feet. The closest comparison with its fellow tall sentinels on the New York City skyline are the 707-foot, 52-story Union Carbide building on Park Avenue at 47th St. and the 50-story Metropolitan Life Insurance building which rises 700 feet from Madison Avenue between 23rd and 25th Streets.

"The first two floors of the General Motors Building will contain a total of 84,000 square feet. The 48 tower floors will each have about 31,600 square feet -- enough room to park about 270 Chevrolets.

"The tower floors will be 296 feet long east to west, 100 feet wide at

the Fifth Avenue and Madison Avenue ends and 120 feet wide through the center.

"All of this, together with two below street level floors, will add up to more than 1-3/4 million square feet, or over 40 acres of space. If this space were stretched flat, it would be big enough to lay out about 30 football fields, including end zones.

* * * * * *

"Destined to become a popular place with the pedestrian sightseer, the visitor and the shopper, as well as with GM employees and other tenants, will be the sunken courtyard on Fifth Avenue. It will be surrounded by tree-lined promenades on the street level. Small speciality shops will be in the arcade around the courtyard below street level. This area will cover the 200-foot Fifth Avenue front and go back 100 feet to the building entrance. A smaller plaza will front the Madison Avenue side of the building.

"If all of these statistics still don't give you a picture of our new home, why not stroll over to Fifth Avenue and look for yourself. As you stand gawking skyward or peeking through the fence, you will be able to say proudly: 'That's where I'm going to work'."

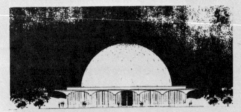

-2-

ALBANY STATE UNIVERSITY TO BUILD
PLANETARIUM-LINEAR ACCELERATOR

(This material about the SUNY planetarium and nuclear accelerator was originally prepared for the use of the New York State Construction Fund)

ALBANY--A combination planetarium chamber and underground linear accelerator laboratory will be one of the major additions to get underway in 1968 on the 364-acre campus of the New York State University at Albany.

The planetarium building was designed by Edward Durell Stone & Associates of New York City, architects for the entire Albany campus. The school, which moved to its new location in 1967, has a current capacity of some 10,000 students.

Completion of the new State University astronomical and nuclear particle research complex is expected in 1969 - which is coincidentally the fiftieth anniversary of the invention of the planetarium machine by the late Prof. Walther Bauersfeld of the Carl Zeiss Company in Germany. The massive projector, properly known as the planetarium, will be supplied to the State University by the Zeiss Company, Oberkochen, West Germany.

Site preparation for the planetarium building and linear accelerator laboratory is now nearing completion. A construction contract for a Spring, 1968 start is expected to be awarded soon, with building time now estimated to take approximately 18 months.

The planetarium will be a 100-foot square building, located in the southeast corner of the campus. The one-story structure is capped by a double dome, with the outer hemisphere measuring 75 feet in diameter. This exterior shell is of pneumatically--

(Left) Rendering of the exterior of the planetarium-nuclear accelerator building for New York State University at Albany.

-3-

applied reinforced concrete. A multiple ring pattern will decorate the dome's outer surface, which ranges in thickness from eight inches at the base to six inches at the highest point. The perforated aluminum inner, or projection, dome is 65 feet in diameter. A pivot-hung aluminum ladder is suspended between domes to enable technicians to service the sound and special effects equipment installed in the dead space between the two shells.

The ground floor section of the building will have poured-in-place arched columns, in keeping with the architecture of other campus buildings. Walls between the columns will be ribbed precast panels, also reflecting completed university structures. A pierced roof overhang projects out 12 feet from the exterior walls.

The sub-basement will have provisions for a planetarium labor-

Star Gazing in Comfort

atory; a 24-foot diameter version of the larger public projection room above. The laboratory, to be equipped with a smaller Spitz projector, will be used for instructional and research purposes. According to Dr. Harry E. Crull, director of the new planetarium and professor of astronomy, the University plans to establish a program for the training of planetarium technicians and lecturers. There is now no formal educational program for planetarium personnel anywhere.

The linear accelerator laboratory and target rooms are located below grade and are reached by an

(continued on page 4)

Figure 19-4. Finished art mockup of a newsletter for Edward Durell Stone's (EDS) office. Such internal/external publications can be a good continuing public relations tool to maintain contact with past, present, and lost clients.

staff interest, the new publication will announce an in-house competition for a title and/or a masthead design. The first article in the "EDS Newsletter" announces a competition to select a permanent masthead design. The winning entry was worth $50 to its originator. The competition rules were the following:

1.   Entries should be in finished art form.
2.   The design may be for black-and white reproduction—or black plus one color.
3.   The design should be capable of being scaled down to 1¾ inches in height by 8¼ inches in length.
4.   Competition will close May 15, 1968; winners to be announced by May 31, 1968.

The other articles in the mockup issue dealt with a series of employee information bulletins being issued by General Motors about its new Fifth Avenue headquarters building and a planetarium for the New York State University at Albany.

When making up the newsletter distribution list, don't overlook employees' homes. It is fine to make copies available in the office, but many spouses become loyal, interested readers when copies are also mailed to home addresses.

Finally, on this subject, many design firms with small offset-printing equipment have found that their newsletters can be produced in-house, giving greater flexibility in production and scheduling.

MAGAZINES

For some firms the publication of a magazine has been the logical next step up from a newsletter. Dames & Moore's *elements* (see Figure 19-1) is certainly in the small-magazine class. Daniel, Mann, Johnson & Mendenhall (DMJM) has several excellent magazine-type publications, as do a number of other design offices.

A magazine—even a small one—presumably projects a more solid image to its readers than does a newsletter. While I know of no definition of a magazine that includes a minimum number of pages, for our purpose here we'll assume that anything less than eight pages would be a newsletter, and more than eight pages would be a magazine.

A full-fledged, illustrated magazine naturally is more expensive than a newsletter. It probably will require more input from outside consultants and certainly is more demanding of staff time. The advantages of a magazine, other than promulgating a more solid image, as mentioned above, include better photo reproduction because better paper stocks usually are used; additional interest from libraries, schools of architecture and engineering, and even professional societies; and a more impressive promotion tool for use with most prospective clients.

BOOKLETS

Perhaps more accurately called minibrochures, booklets usually are

Figure 19-5. *(a)* The cover of the ISD booklet opens up to 14 inches in width. *(b)* The EDG pocket-sized booklet can be handed to prospective clients almost as easily as a business card.

small enough to fit into a number 10 (business) envelope or an inside coat pocket. The booklet contains basic information about a firm, perhaps photographs, and should be keyed graphically to other promotional materials, including regular brochures. One might think that the last point would seem extraordinarily obvious to design-oriented professionals, but it apparently does not. Far too many firms neglect to organize their public faces—letterheads, envelopes, business cards, brochures, newsletters, proposal covers, and so on—into a graphically related family.

Some firms use their booklets as leave-behind items when meeting with prospective clients at other than formal presentations. The regular capabilities brochure is then used as a follow-up to the meeting. By delaying the turnover of the full-size brochure until later, a business-development representative has the opportunity to effect some customization of it. In the meantime the prospective client has the booklet, as a kind of "teaser."

Other firms find it productive to prepare and leave a regular brochure with the client during the first meeting, and use the booklet as an enclosure in the follow-up letter. Either way, the booklet plays a definite role in the marketing process.

Two examples of booklets are shown in Figure 19-5—that of the Environmental Design Group (EDG), Inc., in Winter Park, Florida, and one used by ISD, Inc., with offices in Chicago, New York, Boston, and Houston.

Aside from the cover photo, EDG's booklet is all text. A center spread chart explains the several organizations that make up the Environmental Design Group. ISD's booklet, conversely, consists only of illustrations on inside pages. Scope of services is outlined on the inside front cover and a "Partial List of Clients" is given on the inside back cover. A fold-out cover treatment, plus the heavy silver-colored stock used, gives a feeling of richness and solidity to even this minibrochure.

BOOKS

The sponsorship of hardbound books traditionally has been reserved to only the largest of design firms. Cost is a definite factor, of course, but it does not have to exclude even smaller offices from the book publishing field.

Most of us have seen typical project catalogs, often disguised as coffee-table books. Edward Stone, among others, has proved that project catalogs can also be very attractive books, to be kept by clients in office and home libraries. Two of the Stone organization's hardbound publications are shown in Figure 19-6.

On many occasions I have watched Ed Stone bring out one of his books with a flourish, ask the prospective client how he would like it signed, write an appropriate inscription on the first page, and then present it to an awed and grateful corporate officer with the same pomp reserved for gifting someone with an original Gutenberg.

Stone's books were handled by a New York City publisher, who also distributed them to book stores for regular sale and sent review copies to

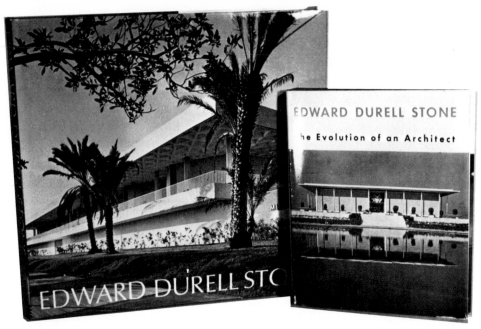

Figure 19-6. Two of the hard-cover books produced by Edward Durell Stone. Possibly the ultimate in brochures, these books make a definite impression on prospective clients.

the usual list of reviewers. Few sales, and fewer reviews, resulted, but the books were never really intended to be sold through commercial channels. Incidentally, as the sponsor, or subsidizer, of such a book you can have any price you want shown on the book, since it's mostly for show. Clients and potential clients seemingly are more appreciative of being given a book that is clearly priced at $45 than one priced at $9.50, regardless of what it cost to produce.

Another approach, again, unfortunately, open only to the largest of firms, is to interest an author and a publisher in doing a book about your firm. The late Welton Becket followed this method with author William Dudley Hunt, Jr., and the McGraw-Hill Book Company in the publication of *Total Design: Architecture of Welton Becket and Associates.*

A few design principals who are also accomplished writers manage to turn out books on various subjects, but these usually are not histories of their firms. Books by the principals of Skidmore Owings & Merrill and Caudill, Rowlett & Scott come to mind. Since the author's firm is always mentioned on the dust jacket, and in most reviews, the public relations advantages still pertain.

An interesting book publishing effort was undertaken a few years ago by the firm of August Perez & Associates, of New Orleans. Using the

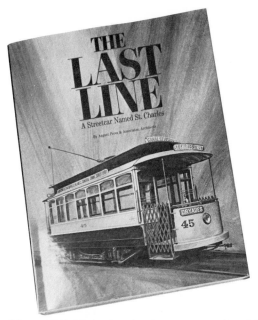

Figure 19-7. These two hard-cover promotional books by the firm of August Perez & Associates illustrate yet another approach. Not about design per se, the well-researched, well-written, copiously illustrated books have proved to be an excellent public relations tool for the New Orleans–based firm.

considerable talents of the office's public relations consultant, Myron Tassin, a book was prepared on the importance of preserving the last of New Orleans' streetcar lines. The book, *The Last Line: A Streetcar Named St. Charles*, was given a large share of the credit for saving the St. Charles line. This book was followed by *The Delta Queen: Last of the Paddlewheel Palaces*. New safety regulations for ocean-going vessels threatened to put the *Delta Queen* into early retirement. Again, the Perez-sponsored book played a significant role in the public campaign to save her. (See Figure 19-7.)

The publisher was pleasantly surprised to find the books enjoying a brisk popular sale through bookstores, and the Perez office donates all royalties to a student scholarship fund.

Therefore, not only did the sponsor gain from a public relations standpoint, but the books played an identifiable part in a public service effort and continue to make a civic contribution by providing scholarship funds for design students.

The point here is that an alert firm, no matter what its size or importance, may come up with an idea for a book. When it happens, pursue the idea with a writer and a publisher. The benefits can be extremely worthwhile.

QUESTIONNAIRES

The use of questionnaires is occasionally indicated in the collection of research data for a firm's marketing efforts. The four basic types of questionnaires are mail, telephone, one-to-one personal interviews, and group interviews.

The mail form of questionnaire is probably the most used and usually is built around closed-end, direct questions. Professionals in this specialized information-gathering field break down closed-end questions into six types of questions:

1. Preference
   If you were selecting an A-E firm tomorrow, which one of the following would you prefer?
   ( ) S.O.M.
   ( ) DMJM
   ( ) H.O.K.
   ( ) Ellerbe
2. Ranking
   How would you rank these firms as to their design abilities?

	Rank
S.O.M.	( )
DMJM	( )
H.O.K.	( )
Ellerbe	( )

3. Multiple choice
   If you were buying a car today, which of the following manufacturers would you consider?
   ( ) General Motors
   ( ) Ford Motor Company
   ( ) American Motors
   ( ) Chrysler
   ( ) Other
4. Dichotomous
   A. Are you responsible for design in your firm?
      ( ) Yes   ( ) No
   B. Smaller firms do better design.
      ( ) True   ( ) False
5. Closed response
   A. What brand of drawing ink do you usually buy?
   B. List all brands of drawing ink about which you have heard.
6. Rating scales
   How would you rate the quality of most brochures you have seen?
   ( ) Excellent
   ( ) Good
   ( ) Fair
   ( ) Bad
   ( ) Very bad
   ( ) Don't know

Another form of questionnaire rating scale is the 1 to 10 scale illustrated in Chapter 3. The 1 to 10 answers often are more difficult to interpret than are those in the above example.

Expert questionnaire constructors give the following DOs and DON'Ts:

- Do keep questions to twenty words or less.
- Do use simple questions.
- Do use language respondents will understand and relate to.
- Do pretest questionnaires.
- Do start with simple but interesting questions.
- Do make it easy to answer, by use of checkmarks, cross-throughs, and the like.
- Do enclose a self-addressed, postage-paid envelope for replies to mail questionnaires.
- Do plan a follow-up questionnaire to those who do not respond to the original one.
- Do not compound two questions into one.
- Do not use ambiguous words.
- Do not ramble.
- Do not attempt to lead or bias responses to questions.
- Do not mix up general and specific questions; move from one into the other.
- Do not ask respondents to rank more than five items in order of their importance.
- Do not include too many questions in a mail questionnaire.

Mail questionnaires should be transmitted to respondents with a brief covering letter explaining the importance of the survey and assuring confidentiality of all answers. The questionnaire's appearance must convince recipients that it is simple to answer, interesting to do, and important to complete and return. A generous use of white space is important in the design of mail questionnaires.

Chapter 20

GLOSSARY

THE TERMS LISTED IN THIS glossary were selected because of their widespread use in editing and publishing. The glossary generally is based on one developed at the Lackland Air Force Base, Texas, Air Training Command, and used by the Air Force Extension Course Institute in its study program for information officers.

The *Graphic Arts Encyclopedia*, by George Stevenson, is an excellent, detailed, A-to-Z reference on copy preparation and reproduction terminology. We can also recommend the "Glossary of Technical Terms," in the University of Chicago's *A Manual of Style*. See the bibliography for complete citations.

absorbency A paper's ability to take up or absorb liquids, such as ink.
align (verb) To place type and cuts in a straight line.
antique finish The natural rough finish of the surface of book and cover papers.
art Any illustrative material used in a publication.
ascender The part of a lowercase letter that projects above the average level of the other letters (examples: the tops of "b," "d," "h," etc.).
author's alterations Changes made by the customer in his or her manuscript on proof copy. Printers normally charge for such changes after type has been set.

backup Printed impression that is run off on the backs of sheets already printed on one side.

bank (1) Stand or racks in composing room on which type rests before printers make up page forms; (2) a section or deck of a headline, consisting of one or more lines of the same kind of type, set off from the rest of the head by dashes or white spaces.

banner Headline in large type running the full width of page.

basis weight Paper is cut to standard sizes for given grades, i.e., cover papers are cut to 20 x 26 inches; book papers to 25 x 38 inches, etc. The basis weight (also known as "substance") of a specific grade of paper is the weight in pounds of one ream (500 sheets) cut to that grade's standard size. For example, 500 sheets 25 x 38 inches of 60-pound coated book paper weighs 60 pounds. Basis weights for book-grade papers range from 30 to 120 pounds.

benday (1) A manual method (named after its inventor) of producing a shaded, stippled, or mottled background on a line cut; (2) a general term to describe toned effects introduced into line art by any method.

blackface See BOLDFACE.

black letter A class of type with angular and often ornate characters; sometimes known as "text," "Old English," or "Gothic."

blanket Rubber blanket surrounding cylinder on photo-offset printing press.

bleed Printed matter or art so placed that it extends to trim edge of page.

blind stamp The bas relief effect obtained by stamping a logotype or other design into a paper without ink, gold leaf, or other form of color. A form of embossing.

blow up (verb) (1) To enlarge art in reproduction; (2) to play up significance of story.

body matter Body type when set up.

body type Small type used for body of a story as compared to larger headline and display types.

boldface Type with a black, heavy appearance, as distinguished from lightface.

box A section of type enclosed in rules (i.e., ruled lines).

brownprint A brown photograph or silverprint for proofing, made on special photographic paper.

bullets A series of large dots.

calendering In the manufacturing of paper, the process of running the paper between polished metal rolls to impart smoothness and gloss to its surface.

camera-ready copy Any material ready to be photographed for reproduction without further changes. May include halftone photographs, type proofs, artwork, etc.

caption Specifically, headline above an illustration; loosely used to refer to any descriptive material appearing above or below an illustration (strictly speaking, material below an illustration is a cutline in a newspaper, a legend in commercial usage).

card out (verb) To space out a column of type by inserting thin pieces of cardboard between slugs. See LEAD OUT.

caret A character used to indicate where corrections are to be inserted in copy.

cast (1) (verb) To mold, as for stereotyping; (2) (noun) the piece of metal thus molded; (3) (verb) to calculate space manuscript copy will occupy in type (called "casting copy").

cast coated High-gloss, enamel-finished coated paper, dried under pressure against a polished cylinder.

centered dot A heavy dot, often called a bullet, used as a margin ornament to set off words, sentences, or paragraphs.

character count Number of type characters that will fit into one line of a given measure.

chase Rectangular steel or iron frame into which pages or columns of type are assembled and locked for printing.

clean proof Printer's proof pulled after printer's own corrections have been made.

clean type Type after corrections have been made; type assumed to have no errors.

coated paper Expensive paper with a high-gloss finish, for use in halftone printing and for reproduction proofs.

cold type Type set (and usually justified) on typewriter composing machines or by the direct impression method, for offset printing.

collate (verb) To examine the folded sheets of a publication to see that forms or signatures are in proper order; colloquially, one term for gathering folded or flat sheets for binding.

column inch Type 1 inch deep by 1 column wide.

column rule Dividing line between two columns of type.

combination (cut) Cut in which both halftone and line art are used.

composing room Part of printing plant in which type is set and made up.

composing stick Small metal hand tray etched with graduation marks in picas, in which type is assembled and justified in the process of handsetting.

composition The setting and arrangement of type.

condensed type Typeface designed narrower than standard width to permit a greater number of characters to the line.

continuous tone Unscreened photographic image, containing gradient tones from black to white.

copy The original, either written stories or art, of any material that is being prepared for reproduction.

count See CHARACTER COUNT, COLUMN INCH.

cover Normally top and back sheet of any publication except a newspaper.

credit line Single line under art, crediting source.

crop (verb) To eliminate irrelevant or poorly composed portions of a picture intended for reproduction.

crop marks Marks on a picture to show which portion is to be reproduced.

crosshatch A toned effect put into a drawing by use of crisscross lines.

cursive Class of type, usually graceful sweeping letters; an italic face.

cut (1) Metal plate upon which an illustration has been etched for reproduction in letterpress printing; (2) loosely, any piece of art when intended for makeup in publication.

deadline A set time by which a particular phase of publication operation must be completed (e.g., "copy deadline" means time at which all copy is due at printer's).

densitometer An optical device for measuring density (darkness or lightness); usually of negatives.

descender The part of a lowercase letter that descends below main or "waist" line (e.g., the tail of the "g" or "y").

die-cut A cutout shape from paper, as in a brochure, or from light board, as for a cover with fold-in pockets. Where the die-cut appears *within* a page, it normally is to allow type, an illustration, or a color spot to show through from the page beneath. Die-cuts can be made during the printing process or during a separate operation.

display type Large type (used for heads) as contrasted to body type.

distribute (verb) To return type to its cases for reuse after coming off press.

dot Individual element of a halftone.

double truck Center spread of a saddle-stitched publication; the same sheet going all the way across. (Cuts used across gutter are not broken in two.) Also any two-page spread.

dropout Halftone cut on which highlight dots have been etched or routed away to create highlight white space in printed impression.

dummy (1) Sheet pasted up by editor from galley proofs to show printer position in which type and cuts should be placed (see LAYOUT); (2) blank paper book showing page-by-page plan for contents of book or magazine (see also MOCKUP).

duotone A two-color halftone reproduction made from a black-and-white photograph.

electrotype Hard metal reproduction plates.

elite type Small-size typewriter type, 12 characters to an inch.

em Horizontal space measurement equal to depth (in points) of the type being used.

embossing Printing in which certain areas are raised above other areas of the surface; a relief effect. Usually done intentionally for decoration.

em indention Moving in of type the same number of points as the type size, as at the beginning of a paragraph.

em quad Square piece of metal the size of the type with which it is used to fill in space in makeup.

en One-half em.

engineering See LINE CUT

engraving Plate that will print a design or illustration; also called a cut. See ETCHING.

en quad Piece of metal one-half the width of an em quad.

etching For publication purposes, an engraving; sometimes distinguished from engraving as being a line cut, whereas engraving is a halftone. See ENGRAVING.

expanded type Extrawide type, opposite to condensed.

extra-bold type Extremely heavy black type.

extra-condensed type Extremely narrow type.

face (1) The part of a type character that makes the printed impression; (2) abbreviated form for typeface, meaning a particular kind of type having definite characteristics.

family Typefaces that have similar characteristics making them a related group. See also TYPE FAMILY.

fillers (1) Short items used to fill space where needed; (2) any items, regardless of length, used primarily to fill space.

flat (1) A negative of one or more pages from which an offset printing plate is made; (2) in photoengraving, a combination of negatives processed together.

flatbed press Kind of letterpress on which type form rests flat on the bed of the press.

flush Even with left type margin (the absence of indentation).

folio (1) Number identifying page of copy; (2) page number in a book or magazine. Right-hand pages always have odd numbers.

font Assortment of type of one size and style, including supplies of all letters, numerals, and punctuation to be used. See WRONG FONT.

form Type and cuts arranged in one or more pages and locked in a chase.

format All the individual elements of a publication, including size, shape, binding, typography, illustrations, headlines, and subheads; the general style of makeup of the product.

foundry In printing, place where electrotype plates are made.

foundry type Permanent, individual-letter type for hand-setting, as distinct from Monotype or Linotype.

fullface Type with no shoulder, so that face is larger than faces requiring allowances for descenders.

furniture Wood or metal strips less than type-high used to fill blank spaces in chase where type or cuts will not be used.

galley Flat metal tray that holds type when composed.

galley proof Proof of a galley of type, not made up into page form and usually without leading.

ganging up Process whereby various pieces of not necessarily related art copy for reproduction are combined so that the engraver will shoot it all on one negative, thus reducing expense.

gathering In binding, process of collecting one copy of each signature to make a complete book or magazine in sewed or sidewired books.

gothic Class of type, usually a businesslike sans serif; also loosely used to mean black letter or text type.

grain (1) In photo-offset, the roughened surface of a press plate; (2) the direction of fiber in paper stock. Since paper resists folding against the grain, the grain should run vertically to assure both neat folds and that the brochure lies flat when opened.

graphic arts Overall class of arts, including printing and engraving, which pertain to expression by means of lines, marks, or characters impressed on a surface.

gravure An intaglio printing process involving photography.

grippers (1) On most presses, the short curved "fingers" that grip the sheet of paper and carry it through the presses; (2) on job presses, the "fingers" that remove the paper from the form.

gutter White space at edge of page that runs into the binding. Sometimes called "back margins."

hairline In printing, a thin rule.

halftone A screened engraving for letterpress reproduction of a photograph or drawing, having continuous gray tones or graduations from white to black.

halftone screen Glass plate with crossed lines forming a screen, used in making photographic halftones to capture tonal variations from white to black. See SCREEN.

hand set (verb) To assemble individual letters of type together by hand to form words and lines of type. See TYPESETTING.

image Area or material that prints or reproduces.

imposition The process of laying out made-up pages in a press form so that the pages will be in the proper order after the printed sheet is folded.

impression The printed matter as reproduced on the sheet.

initial Large letter beginning a paragraph.

insert New material placed in the body of a story already written; in binding, the collecting and placing of signatures into one another, in saddle-stitched books.

inset Line or halftone art which, through the engraving process, is made to appear as though it were actually set into another piece of line or halftone art.

intaglio   (1) In printing, type of printing in which the plates used have the image impressed below the surface (e.g., rotogravure); (2) any design which is impressed below the surface of the material it is on.

intertype   Typesetting machine similar to linotype.

italic   Class of type, with slanted letters.

job press   Small press for short-run letterpress reproduction of material to be printed on small sheets.

job work   Commercial or outside printing jobs, as distinguished from a newspaper plant printing its own paper.

jump-over   Cut running over the binding edges of two facing pages, as distinguished from double truck.

justify (verb)   To space a line, column, or page of type so that it is exactly the intended length and width.

keyline   Reproduction proofs of type pasted up in position for a lithographic plate camera.

kill   (1) Delete from copy; (2) destroy type involved.

layout   (1) Drawn up scale plan for a printed page; (2) various pieces of related art work fitted together in pattern, usually sent to engraver as unit. See DUMMY.

layout sheet   Ruled sheet of paper upon which layout is drawn or dummy copy pasted.

lead (pronounced "led")   Thin strip (1- or 2-point) of metal which the printer may place between two lines of type to obtain more white space between lines on the printed page.

leaded   Type that has been leaded out.

leader   Dots in a row, as in an index.

lead out (verb)   To lengthen a column of type by inserting leads between slugs. See CARD OUT.

lettering guides   Grooved transparent plastic sheets in which display letters are cut to simplify tracing with a stylus onto a mimeograph stencil.

letterpress   A relief process of printing, done directly from the inked surfaces of type and cuts (or from their plates), as distinguished from photo-offset, gravure, and mimeographing.

letterspace (verb)   To put space between letters.

libel   Defamation of character or unwarranted invasion of an individual's privacy by published material. ("Slander" is spoken defamation.)

lift (verb)   To have the ability to be lifted. Type that lifts will not fall out when form is lifted from stone.

ligature   Two or three characters combined on a single type body (e.g., "ff," "œ," etc.).

lightface   Type that makes a light printed impression, as distinguished from standard or boldface.

line copy   Art composed of lines or dots suitable for reproduction by a line cut.

line cut or engineering   Engraving that prints only black and white, without photoengraving screen, as distinguished from a halftone engraving.

line drawing   Drawing in black-and-white with no tone graduations requiring a screen.

line gauge   Ruler graduated in picas, used by printer to measure type; has an extended side at one end to catch against the type.

Linotype   Trade name for a type-composing machine that sets a line of type in one piece or slug.

lithography   Generally used interchangeably with planography to indicate printing from a flat surface, as distinguished from relief and intaglio. See PHOTO-OFFSET, PLANOGRAPHY.

live type   Printing matter still in use or to be used.

lockup   Process by which made-up pages are properly positioned and securely wedged into chase after page forms are made up so they will lift. See QUOIN.

logotype (or logo)   (1) Similar to ligature, except that it contains one or more words; (2) an identifying type layout or piece of art representing in effect the trademark of the product (such as a flag or any miniature of it); in advertising a logo is called a "sig" for "signature cut."

lower case   Small letters, as distinguished from caps; abbreviated "lc."

Ludlow   Trade name for slug-casting machine for which the matrices are set by hand.

makeover   Generally, any change in a page already locked up.

makeready   Preparation of type, press, and plate forms to obtain uniform impression.

makeup   Arrangement of type and cuts into columns and pages by the printer.

mask (verb)   (1) In photography, to block out portion of negative that is not to be printed; (2) in offset reproduction, to cover with black ink or paper the areas on the master offset copy where halftones will be used, resulting in windows in the negative into which halftone negatives will be stripped.

master copy   Pasted-up copy for photo-offset reproduction.

matrix (or mat)   (1) In stereotyping, a paper composition sheet on which type or engraving form is pressed and from which a stereotype cast is then made; (2) in typesetting for Linotype, Ludlow, etc., brass plate having an intaglio of a character it is to cast or produce in relief.

measure　Width, designated in picas, in which type is to be set, or length in which it is to be made up.

mechanical　Completed, camera-ready copy. All elements of the job to be printed and pasted up into a single unit.

medium face　Type halfway in printing tone between lightface and boldface.

Mimeoscope　Trade name of an illuminated glass easel on which stencils are placed for tracing art, etc.

mockup　A "rough" layout for visualizing purposes, showing in some detail how a page or book will look in finished form; sometimes involves pasted-up proofs, but is to be distinguished from a dummy, which is specifically for the guidance of the printer in makeup. See DUMMY.

modern　Class of type with flat serifs, such as Bodoni.

Monotype　Trade name of a type-composing machine that sets separate letters in columnar or tabular form.

montage　An illustration made by exposure of more than one negative on the same sheet of photographic paper, usually for symbolic or stylist effect; distinguished from layout or gang-up.

morgue　Place where pictures and background information (usually about persons) are filed.

mortise　Cutaway part of an engraving, base and all, so that type or another engraving can be fitted in.

Multigraph　Trade name of a duplicating machine that will reproduce from individual letters set in by hand on a rotary-type plate.

Multilith　Trade name of a small offset press.

negative　In photography, and in photoengraving or similar processes, the film, paper, or glass that bears the image or picture in reverse of the way the final or positive picture is to be produced (i.e., the white parts are black and the black parts are white).

newsprint　Cheap machine-finished paper made chiefly from ground-up pulp and used mostly for newspapers.

nonpareil　(1) Used interchangeably with "slug" to mean a 6-point slug; (2) 6-point type.

offset　(1) Shortened form of photo-offset reproduction, a form of printing; (2) smudgy transfer from the wet, inked surface of one sheet to the back of another sheet when they are stacked together.

offset reproduction　See PHOTO-OFFSET.

Oldstyle　Class of type having thick-and-thin stroked letters with curved or wedge-shaped serifs. Examples are Garamond and Caslon. Also known as Transitional.

opaquing   Process of covering a photographic negative with a coating through which light cannot pass, concealing all blemishes for the purpose of getting a clean print plate.

optical center   The center of balance of a page as the eye sees it; slightly above the mathematical center.

overage   More copies of the printed job than ordered.

overlay   Transparent paper placed over art copy on which tracing or specifications for the engraver are shown.

page proof   Proof of type matter that has been made up into page form.

paper stock   Supply of paper for a printing job.

photocomposition   Type for reproduction assembled by keyboard action on clear film or photographic paper. No metal type is involved.

photoengraving   Etching of pictures and drawings on metal to bring the printing surface into relief.

photolithography   Lithography in which copy is transferred photographically to the plate; lithography is used as the short term.

photo-offset   A photolithographic printing process in which the impression is first received by a rubber-blanketed cylinder from which it transfers to the sheet. See LITHOGRAPHY.

photostat   Photographic image recorded by camera which photographs, develops, and fixes the copy directly on paper in negative values without reversal (i.e., type is not backwards); positive images can in turn be made from the photostatic negative.

pi   Type matter that has been disordered or scrambled.

pica   Printer's linear measure equaling 12 points (approximately ⅙ inch).

pica type   Typewriter type that is approximately 1 pica high; larger than elite type, it has 10 characters to the inch. See ELITE TYPE.

planography   Printing which uses the principle that oil and water do not mix and which produces from a flat plane, as distinguished from relief or intaglio. See LITHOGRAPHY.

plate   (1) In letterpress, a duplicate in one piece of metal of a form or page, the printing being done from the plate instead of the original; (2) in offset, the grained zinc or aluminum sheet carrying the image to make an impression on the offset blanket; (3) an engraving.

point   Printer's measure approximating ¹⁄₇₂ inch (actually 0.013837 inch). Twelve points equal one pica—approximately ⅙ inch.

positive   (1) Exact image of original object or copy as distinguished from reverse image or negative; (2) image made by exposure of negative to sensitized plate or paper under light.

positive negative   Negative which has reversed tone values, resulting in printing of white letters on black background. See REVERSE OR REVERSE PLATES.

press run   (1) The running off of a publication on presses on duplicating equipment; (2) the number of copies to be printed on a press run.

printing   (1) Process of obtaining impressions from plates or type; (2) reproduction of positives from negatives in photography.

printing plate   See PLATE.

printing surface   Actual area of type of cuts that will make a printed impression on the page in letterpress.

proof   Trial printing impression for correction purposes made by laying a sheet of paper over inked type or cuts and applying pressure.

proofing press   Machine built expressly for making proofs.

proofreader   One who reads printer's proofs to catch errors and mark corrections.

proofreading symbols   Marks used by proofreader to indicate corrections.

prove up   Strictly, "proof up," meaning to pull a proof.

pull   Make a proof.

quad   Metal blank less than type-high used as spacing in type.

quire   Quantity of paper, 24 uniform sheets to a set.

quoin   Locking device for wedging type and cuts firmly into chase. See LOCKUP.

rag pulp   Used in the manufacture of high-grade bond and other "fine" printing papers; made from disintegrated cotton and linen rags after the fibers are cleaned and bleached.

ream   Quantity of paper, 500 uniform sheets to a set.

recto   A right-hand page. See also VERSO.

register   Correct relative position of two or more colors in the process of printing from color plates.

relief printing   Method of printing in which printing surfaces are raised (e.g., letterpress).

reproduction proof   Type proofed very carefully for purposes of incorporating it photographically into a plate.

reset (verb)   To set type over again, usually in a different size or style.

retouch (verb)   To rework, by artwork, a photograph or drawing to improve harmony of tone and to remove blemishes or objectionable details.

reverse or reverse plates   (1) (noun) Plates or portions of plates which are negative in tone values to copy; e.g., letters printing white on a black background (see POSITIVE NEGATIVE); (2) (verb) to turn negative over to make a portrait; for instance, face the other way.

river   A band of white space running down through text. Caused by inept typesetting.

roman   Vertical type, as distinguished from italic.

rotary press   Press having curved printing plates.

rotogravure A mass-production gravure printing process using a rotary press.

rout (verb) To finish an engraving, a cast, or type, by grinding off unwanted areas.

rule (1) Strip of metal for printing a line; (2) impression made by metal rule.

run See PRESS RUN.

run around (1) (verb) To run type that is not full measure alongside a narrow cut to fill a column; (2) (noun) type so set.

running head Title of a publication that appears on every page, usually at the top of the page.

saddle stitch (verb) To bind a publication, wiring it through the middle. (Folded leaves are fitted together and placed on the machine saddle-like, and wire-stapled.)

sans serif (1) Term applied to all typefaces having no serifs; (2) name of a particular typeface.

scale Plan for proportionate reduction or enlargement of art to fit a given space.

screen (1) Term used to denote particular coarseness or fineness of ruled screen to be used in halftone reproduction (see HALFTONE SCREEN); (2) refers to benday or other pattern effects in art.

script Class of type that looks like writing.

serifs Fine-line cross-strokes at top and bottom of letters.

set (verb) To compose or arrange type.

set solid Type that is not leaded.

shading sheet Transparent sheet with printed-pattern surface that can be cut out and applied to drawings to give a toned or patterned effect for line cut or photo-offset reproduction.

sheet A sheet of paper stock.

shoulder (on type) Space below printing of typeface.

side stitch Stitch used in binding when folded sections of book or magazine are placed one on top of the other and stitched together from top to bottom, rather than on the edge, as in saddle stitch.

signature Multiple-page sheet printed with forms on both sides.

silhouette halftone Any halftone that is irregular in shape. See SQUARE HALFTONE.

slant Mark used to separate words or figures (e.g., and/or). Also called virgule.

slipcase A protective holder for a book or set of volumes. Some brochure systems fit into a slipcase for shipping and filing.

slipsheeting Alternating printed sheets with blank sheets or cards to prevent the wet ink on the surface of one sheet from offsetting onto the back of the next.

slug (1) (noun) Line of type cast in one piece on a type-composing machine; (2) (noun) 6-point piece of metal used for spacing; (3) (verb) to put on a guideline; (4) (noun) the guideline in type.

solid matter   Lines of type not leaded.

space   (1) Blanks less than type-high used to separate words in type matter; (2) same as white space. See WHITE SPACE.

spread   A layout.

square halftone   Halftone with squared sides, as distinguished from silhouette or vignette. See SILHOUETTE HALFTONE.

standard   Type of normal weight, as distinguished from boldface, etc.

stereotype   Printing plate made by taking a mold or matrix of a type form or engraving and making from this a cast in type metal.

stet   Proofreading and copyreading term ("let it stand") used to cancel a correction or change already made on a proof. The stetted matter usually is "underlined" with a series of dots.

stick   See COMPOSING STICK.

stitching   Operation of stapling a publication together with wire.

stock   See PAPER STOCK.

stone   In composing room, the surface on which lockup is done. Publications are made up on stones.

straight matter   Plain composition, as compared to display material, usually set in standard size and width.

strike-through   Impression on sheet which has come through from heavy printing on the back.

strip-in (verb)   To put a negative into place as part of a larger negative for making a cut or offset plate.

style book or style sheet   Collected rules on spelling, punctuation, and grammar used in a particular publication.

tabular matter   Matter presented in a table or statistical form.

tack   In printing, a measure of an ink's stickiness, or the resistance of ink to splitting between two surfaces—as between rollers or blanket and paper.

text   (1) Body matter of a story or advertisement; (2) a class of type, meaning black letter.

thumbnail sketch   Rough version of a layout, usually at reduced scale.

tight writing   Condensed writing with no excess wordage.

toning sheet   See SHADING SHEET.

transparency   A positive copy on transparent film.

trim size   (1) Size of publication after being finally trimmed in bindery; (2) marks on dummy or paste-up sheet for master copy to indicate the actual border of the page after it has been trimmed.

two-page spread   Layout for two pages.

type   A block of metal or wood with its face so shaped and raised as to produce, in printing, a letter, figure, or character.

typeface   (1) The printing surface of a type with reference to its shape, form, model, or character; (2) the proper name of a type.

type family   Typefaces of a related design. See also FAMILY.

type gauge See LINE GAUGE.

type-high Standard height of type (0.9186 of an inch).

type series The range in point sizes of one kind of type.

typesetting Arranging of type characters into lines, or composition. See HAND SET.

typography The arrangement, appearance, style, and characteristics of matter printed from type.

upper case Capital letters.

vandyke proof Proof made from photographic negatives.

Vari-Typer Trade name for a machine that operates like an electric typewriter and makes printed copy that looks like commercial type.

Velox Black-and-white print of a halftone (screened) image. A Velox print eliminates the need for a composite negative (stripping halftone art into line art) because it is prescreened and included with other line art.

verso A left-hand page. See also RECTO.

vignette Type of halftone which has softened, "feathered" outlines in contrast to severe lines of silhouette halftone.

virgule The slant (/).

wash drawing Drawing in watercolor with a range of tones, usually in shades of gray and black.

web The uncut roll of paper which is threaded through a large rotary press.

weight (of type) The tone of the type in printing, from lightface to extra bold.

wetting agent A substance for lowering surface tension of water and other solutions to increase their wetting power.

white space (1) The blank sheet on which the printed matter goes; (2) specifically, white space showing from behind the printed impression and considered as a factor in typography and layout.

widow A short line of type at the end of a paragraph, usually one or two words.

wrong font Type which is by error a different kind or size from the body of type matter of which it is a part. *See font.*

zinc (or zinc etching) An engraving made on a zinc plate; usually refers to a line cut only.

BIBLIOGRAPHY

This bibliography is listed in six sections, in the following order: general, illustrations, layout, printing production, typography, and writing and copy preparation.

General

Bahr, Leonard F.: *ATA Advertising Production Handbook*, 4th ed., Advertising Typographers Association of America, Inc., New York, 1969.

Craig, James: *Production for the Graphic Designer*, Watson-Guptill Publications, New York, 1974.

Croy, Peter: *Graphic Design & Reproduction Techniques*, Hastings House Publishers, Inc., New York, 1972.

Garland, Ken: *Graphics Handbook*, D. Van Nostrand Company, New York, 1966.

Guide to Reference Books, American Library Association, Chicago, 1967.

Pocket Pal, 11th ed., International Paper Company, New York, 1974.

Stevenson, George A.: *Graphic Arts Encyclopedia*, McGraw-Hill Book Company, New York, 1968.

Style Manual, U.S. Government Printing Office, Washington, D.C., 1959.

Illustrations (Including Photography)

Biggs, Dorsey, and K. W. Beattie: *How to Print and Publish Photomechanically*, North American Publishing Company, Philadelphia, 1967.

Burnham, W. R., R. M. Hanes, and James Bartleson: *Color: A Guide to Basic Facts and Concepts*, John Wiley & Sons, Inc., New York, 1967.

Carraher, Ronald G., and Jacqueline B. Thurston: *Optical Illusions and the Visual Arts*, Reinhold Publishing Corporation, New York, 1966.

Evans, Ralph M.: *Eye, Film and Camera in Color Photography*, John Wiley & Sons, Inc., New York, 1948.

Gernsheim, Helmut, and Alison Gernsheim: *A Concise History of Photography*, Grosset and Dunlap, Inc., New York, 1965.

Hicks, Wilson: *Words and Pictures*, Harper & Brothers, New York, 1952.

Hurley, Gerald D., and Angus McDougall: *Visual Impact in Print*, Visual Impact, Inc., Chicago, 1971.

Jaffe, Erwin: *Halftone Photography*, Graphic Arts Technical Foundation, Inc., Pittsburgh, 1960.

——, Edward Brody, Frank Preucil, and Jack W. White: *Color Separation Photography*, Graphic Arts Technical Foundation, Inc., Pittsburgh, 1959.

Kalish, Stanley, and Clifton C. Edom: *Picture Editing*, Rinehart & Company, Inc., New York, 1951.

Kemp, Weston, D.: *Photography for Visual Communications*, Prentice-Hall, Inc., Englewood Cliffs, N.J., 1973.

Luckiesh, Matthew: *Visual Illusions*, D. Van Nostrand Company, Inc., New York, 1922.

Neblette, C. B.: *Photography: Its Materials and Processes*, 6th ed., D. Van Nostrand & Company, Inc., Princeton, N.J., 1962.

Spear, Mary Eleanor: *Practical Charting Techniques*, McGraw-Hill Book Company, New York, 1974.

Stone, Bernard, and Arthur Eckstein, *Preparing Art for Printing*, Reinhold Publishing Corporation, New York, 1965.

Weld, Walter E.: *How to Chart*, Codex Book Company, Norwood, Mass., 1959.

Layout

Ballinger, Raymond A.: *Layout and Graphic Design*, Van Nostrand-Reinhold, New York, 1970.

Felten, Charles J.: *Layout*, 3d ed., Appleton-Century-Crofts, Inc., New York, 1954.

Maurello, Ralph S.: *How To Do Paste-ups and Mechanicals*, Tudor Publishing Company, New York, 1960.

Smith, Cortland Gray: *Magazine Layout: Principles, Patterns & Practices*, published by the author, Plandome, N.Y., 1973.

Turnbull, Arthur T., and Russell N. Baird, *The Graphics of Communication*, Holt, Rinehart and Winston, Inc., New York, 1964.

White, Jan V.: *Editing by Design*, R. R. Bowker Company, New York, 1974.

Willis, F. H.: *Fundamentals of Layout*, Sterling Publishing Company, Inc., New York, 1965.

Printing Production

Arnold, Edmond C.: *Ink on Paper*, Harper & Row, New York, 1963.

Cabibi, John F. J.: *Elementary Printing*, The Delgado Press, Delgado Junior College, New Orleans, 1964.

Cogoli, John E.: *Photo-Offset Fundamentals*, 2d ed., McKnight & McKnight Publishing Company, Bloomington, Ill., 1967.

Hymes, David: *Production in Advertising and the Graphic Arts*, Holt, Rinehart and Winston, Inc., New York, 1958.

Lee, Marshall: *Bookmaking: The Illustrated Guide to Design and Production*, R. R. Bowker Company, New York, 1965.

Reed, Robert F.: *What the Printer Should Know About Paper*, Graphic Arts Technical Foundation, Inc., Pittsburgh, 1970.

Shapiro, Charles: *The Lithographers Manual*, Graphic Arts Technical Foundation, Inc., Pittsburgh, 1966.

Silver, Gerald A.: *Printing Estimating*, American Technical Society, Chicago, 1970.

Strauss, Victor: *The Printing Industry*, Printing Industries of America, Inc., Washington, D.C., 1967.

Typography

Biggs, John R.: *Basic Typography*, Watson-Guptill Publications, New York, 1968.

Burns, Aaron: *Typography*, Reinhold Publishing Corporation, New York, 1961.

Craig, James: *Designing with Type*, Watson-Guptill Publications, New York, 1971.

Karch, R. Randolph: *How to Recognize Type Faces*, Taplinger Publishing Company, Inc., New York, 1958.

Mathematics in Type, William Byrd Press, Richmond, Va., 1954.

Morison, Stanley: *Typographic Arts*, Harvard University Press, Cambridge, Mass., 1950.

Ruder, Emil: *Typography: A Manual of Design*, Hastings House Publishers, Inc., New York, 1967.

Swann, Cal: *Techniques of Typography*, Watson-Guptill Publications, New York, 1969.

Tinker, Miles A.: *Bases of Effective Reading*, University of Minnesota Press, Minneapolis, 1965.

————: *Legibility of Print*, The Iowa State University Press, Ames, Iowa, 1963.

Typography and Design, U.S. Government Printing Office Training Series, Washington, D.C., 1963.

Updike, Daniel B.: *Printing Types: Their History, Forms and Uses*, 3d ed., Harvard University Press, Cambridge, Mass., 1962.

Writing and Copy Preparation

Barnett, Lincoln: *The Treasure of Our Tongue*, Alfred A. Knopf, Inc., New York, 1964.

Bartlett, John: *Familiar Quotations*, 14th ed., ed. by Emily Morison Beck, Little, Brown and Company, Boston, 1968.

Bernstein, Theodore M.: *The Careful Writer: A Modern Guide to English Usage*, Atheneum Publishers, New York, 1965.

Burack, A. S. (ed.): *The Writer's Handbook*, The Writer, Inc., Boston, 1970.

Cabibi, John F. J.: *Copy Preparation for Printing*, McGraw-Hill Book Company, New York, 1973.

Flesch, Rudolf: *The Art of Plain Talk*, Harper & Brothers, New York, 1946.

————: *The Way to Write*, Harper & Brothers, New York, 1946.

————: *The Art of Readable Writing*, Harper & Brothers, New York, 1949.

————: *How to Test Readability*, Harper & Brothers, New York, 1951.

Fowler, H. W.: *A Dictionary of Modern English Usage*, 2d ed., Clarendon Press, Oxford, 1965.

Lasday, Stanley B.: *Handbook for Graphic Communications*, Graphic Arts Technical Foundation, Inc., Pittsburgh, 1972.

Lasky, Joseph: *Proofreading and Copy-Preparation*, Mentor Books, New York, 1954.

The McGraw-Hill Author's Book, McGraw-Hill Book Company, New York, 1968.

A Manual of Style, 12th ed., The University of Chicago Press, Chicago, 1969.

New York Times, *Style Book for Writers and Editors*, McGraw-Hill Book Company, New York, 1962.

Perrin, Porter G.: *Writer's Guide and Index to English*, 4th ed., Scott, Foresman and Company, Glenview, Ill., 1968.

Strunk, W., Jr., and E. B. White: *The Elements of Style*, The Macmillan Company, New York, 1959.

Webster's Third New International Dictionary of the English Language, Unabridged, G. & C. Merriam Company, Springfield, Mass., 1964.

INDEX